Human Relationship Skills

# Human Relationship Skills

Training and Self-help

RICHARD NELSON-JONES

CASSELL

Cassell Educational Ltd: 1 St Anne's Road,
Eastbourne, East Sussex BN21 3UN

**British Library Cataloguing in Publication Data**

Nelson-Jones, Richard
    Human relationship skills: training
    and self-help.
    1. Interpersonal relations
    I. Title
    158'.2        HM132

ISBN: 0-304-31381-5

Typeset by Paston Press, Norwich
Printed and bound in Great Britain by
Biddles Ltd, Guildford and King's Lynn

Last digit is print no: 9 8 7 6 5 4 3 2

# Contents

# Preface

I am keen that this book helps you gain more happiness and fulfilment in your relationships. Relationship skills are viewed as series of choices which may be either well or poorly made. The goal of this book is to help you make better choices. There are three subgoals. First, imparting an *attitude* that you are personally responsible for making the choices that maximise your happiness and fulfilment. The buck ultimately stops with you. Second, helping you gain *knowledge* regarding relationship skills, for example, identifying the skills and expanding your repertoire of relevant terms. Third, developing your *skills* by converting knowing into doing by means of eighty-five exercises.

The subtitle of this book is training and self-help. This indicates the two main ways in which the book may be used. However, training and self-help overlap in that effective training in relationship skills is basically aiding people in acquiring a set of self-help skills that they can apply in their daily lives. In particular I hope this book, in both its training and self-help uses, is a contribution to strengthening marital, parental and family relationships. There are far too many walking wounded around. Unfortunately those who have been psychologically damaged can also then damage themselves and others.

This book is a text around which human relationship skills training courses can be built. Such courses may be run in schools and colleges, thus highlighting the need for preventive work. Additional training settings include: the health and social services, the public service, religious settings, industry and commerce, and voluntary agencies, for instance marriage guidance councils. Training courses require skilled trainers. Consequently another use of this book is in the training of counsellors, psychologists, social workers and others in the helping professions.

There are a number of ways in which the book may be used for self-help. You may read it on your own and work through the exercises. Alternatively, partners may work together with the book in an attempt to improve their relationship. Relationship skills, once acquired, need to be maintained and developed. Those who have been on human relationship skills training courses may wish to use the book for revision. A further self-help use of the book is in conjunction with individual and group counselling and psychotherapy. Clients may find it valuable to gain greater insight into the processes and skills entailed in their relationships.

This book has a number of distinctive features. It is based in the theoretical position outlined in my earlier book *Personal Responsibility Counselling and Therapy: An Integrative Approach.* It is comprehensive in its coverage of relationship skills. It is written in simple and clear language. In fact, during the course of writing the book, I conducted some research with school and college students on which relationship skills terms they preferred. Numerous exercises are integrated with the text so that you are encouraged to participate actively in your own learning. Almost all of the exercises can be performed on your own, in pairs or as part of a training group. Additionally, the book uses inner speech, the use of the first person singular, to summarise the salient points in each chapter.

I encourage you to tailor your approach to using this book to meet your own needs or those of the group of trainees with whom you work. For instance, stay with any one exercise only as long as you find it useful. Also, if working with a group of trainees, you might consider consulting with them and starting with the skills that they most want to learn. I also encourage you to be diligent about practising the skills in your daily life. This includes both learning from mistakes and also persisting despite setbacks.

I thank the following people who have contributed to the writing and publishing of this book. David Dyer, Headmaster, and Stephen Lee, Student Counsellor, at Camberwell Grammar School for Boys in Melbourne for allowing me to try out much of the material in a year-long human relationship skills course I taught there. Also, many thanks to the boys themselves. The learning certainly went both ways. Juliet Wight-Boycott and her colleagues at Holt-Saunders in Britain for editing and preparing the manuscript. Also, Ian Swallow and Saul Kammerman of Holt Saunders, Australia for their interest and support in co-publishing the book. Last, my thanks go to my employers, the Royal Melbourne Institute of Technology, for allowing me sufficient time to write and redraft it.

I have found that writing this book has helped me. It brings together many threads in my background. These include being: a counsellor trainer, a practising counselling psychologist, a human relationship skills trainer both with secondary school and mature-aged trainees, a researcher into how people talk about themselves, and last but not least a person with the daily struggle to make good rather than poor choices. I like to think that I have improved my relationship skills through writing this book. Also, that you will do likewise through reading and working with it. I wish you inner strength and good skills in the opportunities and challenges that lie ahead in your relationships.

Melbourne

Australia

*Richard Nelson-Jones*

August 1985

# List of Exercises

**Chapter 5. Starting and developing relationships**

**Chapter 6. Defining and asserting yourself**

**Chapter 7. Becoming a good listener**

## Chapter 11. Maintaining and developing your relationship skills

# 1 You Can Relate More Effectively

Relationships are a central part of most people's everyday lives. We frequently make comments about the ways in which we and others relate. Such comments include:

> 'I thoroughly enjoyed meeting her. She is a terrific person.'
> 'I would like to get closer to him, but he is a hard person to get to know.'
> 'When my parents don't listen to me I find myself drying up and wanting to be somewhere else.'
> 'Once I start getting angry, oh boy, people had better watch out.'
> 'When things go wrong, she at least makes an effort to understand my viewpoint.'
> 'You don't need to shout.'
> 'He has shifty eyes.'

Just as our conversations are liberally sprinkled with relationship statements, so the success and failure of relationships provides novelists and playwrights with much of their material. Through their characters authors not only depict relationships, but also have them as mouthpieces for observations about relationships. Here are a couple of quotations that illustrate the theme that relationships are perhaps the major source of human pleasure and pain. On the one hand the novelist E.M. Forster has a character say:

> 'Only connect! That was the whole of her sermon. Only connect the prose and the passion, and both will be exalted, and human love will be seen at its highest.'[1]

On the other hand in a Sartre play a character observes:

> 'So that's what Hell is. I'd never have believed it. . . . Do you remember, brimstone, the stake, the gridiron? . . . What a joke! No need of a gridiron, (when it comes to) Hell, it's other people.'[2]

On a rather more mundane note, one wag has quipped: 'Make love, not war. I'm married, I do both!'

People in the helping professions are also interested in relationships. Doctors, psychologists, social workers, counsellors and priests are in frequent contact with the painful consequences of disturbed relationships. Indeed most of so-called 'mental illness' can be viewed in terms of difficulties of communication, both past and current. However mental pain is not restricted to psychiatric patients. For example, in the United States, one in five children are step-children, one in two marriages ends in divorce, and a high proportion of remarriages fail. It has been projected that, by 1990, more families will be one-parent or step-families than families headed by both natural parents.[3]

Though in Britain approximately one in three marriages ends in divorce, Britain tends to follow where the United States leads. Like the United States, the impact of divorce is on children as well as marital partners, with the vast majority of children being under sixteen at the time of divorce.[4] Furthermore, many marriages, without going so far as divorce, contain a huge amount of hostility. Australia is also affected by the same pattern of family and marital disruption and distress as are the United States and Britain. McDonald estimates that the overall Australian divorce rate is probably between 30 and 35 per cent.[5] Additionally, in all three countries many single people suffer much loneliness from their failure to make or to sustain relationships.

## WHY ARE RELATIONSHIPS IMPORTANT?

Let's pause for a moment and consider why relationships are so important both for the human species and for its individual members. Some of the reasons why relationships are important for the human species include the following:

- *Reproduction of the species.* Despite scientific advances it generally takes two to make babies.
- *Avoiding the pain of isolation.* Humans are biologically programmed to need contact with other humans and, without this, they suffer psychological pain.
- *Nurturance when young.* Physically and mentally the human maturation process is slow. Consequently people need the help of others when growing up.
- *Help in old age, when sick etc.* There are times in people's lives when their own physical and/or mental resources may be insufficient for them to cope on their own.
- *Specialisation of occupation.* There are great economies of time and effort due to people relating to one another as specialists – for instance, as miners, farmers and doctors.

- *Cooperation to achieve tasks.* Many tasks are more pleasant if done jointly and for other tasks, for instance building a big edifice, cooperation is essential.
- *Learning new ways of doing things.* The human race can advance more quickly when inventions can be shared than, as earlier in history, when people were much more isolated.
- *Defence against aggression.* Cooperation may be necessary for defence against others. Also, for coping with what is sometimes a hostile natural environment.

The above set of reasons is not exhaustive. Neither does it take into account that, for the human species as well as for individuals, relationships can be for better or worse. Wars and the potential for a nuclear holocaust illustrate the latter.

The major thrust of this book is not on global concepts such as the human species, but on how you as an individual can relate more effectively. Below is a list of reasons why relationships are important for most individuals, though some of the reasons may not apply to all of you.

- *Identity.* One of the main ways in which you create and define yourself is through your relationships with others. You need other people to be able to create and sustain an identity, a sense of continuity and sameness about who you are. You are likely to use words like 'I', 'Me' or 'Myself' to describe your identity or your picture of yourself.
- *Intimacy.* Intimacy in relationships has connotations of depth, privacy, closeness and familiarity. Intimacy does not necessarily entail sexual intimacy and sexual intimacy does not necessarily involve the ability to communicate intimately in other areas. Here intimacy in a relationship is defined as sharing and being attuned to each other's thoughts and feelings, including those likely to be threatening to reveal in other contexts. This entails revealing both vulnerabilities and strengths. Ideally intimacy represents the interdependence of two separate, equal and developing persons. Put simply, you have a need to know and be known at least by one other at a deep level.
- *Effective family life.* Families are for better or worse as the earlier section on divorce indicated. Family relationships are of vital importance to virtually everyone be they children, parents, grandparents or playing other roles. Not only are these relationships important to you as an individual, but your success or

failure in them affects those with whom you relate inside and outside your immediate family.

● *Friendship.* People require a circle of friends beyond a core intimate relationship and their families. These friendships provide a network in which you can feel affirmed and supported. Additionally, with your friends you can express different parts of yourself and gain a wide variety of stimulation, more so than by just relating to either a single partner or inside a family. Also friendships provide the soil out of which more intimate relationships grow.

● *Work satisfaction and effectiveness.* For many one of the main sources of satisfaction in work is the opportunity for rewarding relationships. Conversely, low morale at work is frequently associated with poor relationships either with peers or a boss. Additionally, many jobs require you to relate well to consumers, be they labelled customers, patients or clients. Also, when you are selected for a job there are often three sets of relationship criteria applied: how you are likely to relate to superiors, colleagues and consumers.

● *Enjoyment of leisure.* For many there is a trend toward a shorter working week. Others through retirement or unemployment find that they have considerable spare time. Even those who have busy work lives still require maximum fulfilment and enjoyment from free time. Many leisure pursuits involve other people, for instance almost all sports. Consequently another reason why relationships are important is that they open the door to and provide companionship for all sorts of leisure activities.

● *Helping others.* Though occupational psychologists have found that people differ in their need to help others,[6] for many people relationships are important because they offer a means of fulfilling this need. In the 'helping professions' the relationship with clients is often a central part of the job ideally meeting the needs of both parties. Others, for instance those in business or industry, may also engage in helping contacts with people, such as subordinates, as part of their jobs.

● *Physical health.* There are many reasons why relationships are important for physical health. They are a major reason why people consider that life is worth living. People with relationship problems are subject not only to loneliness, but also may suffer from stress and anxiety. Attempts to anaesthetise the pain of relationship difficulties include excessive use of tranquillisers, alcohol, cigarettes and of non-prescribed drugs. These habits may be fatal.

## WHAT ARE RELATIONSHIP SKILLS?

If you are serious about improving the way you relate, it is important that you adopt the concept of relationship skills. This enables you to know what skills are required. Also, to pinpoint your strengths and weaknesses so that you know where you need to improve.

### Defining relationship skills

One way of viewing *relationships* is that you are connected in some way with other people. Though these connections usually involve face-to-face contact, this need not necessarily be the case. However, just being connected is a threadbare way of defining a relationship. Relationships are ongoing processes. What brings them to life is the quantity and quality of communication that exists in them. Communication involves the sending and receiving of messages or information. These messages can be conveyed by words, by tone of voice and by body movements. People can also communicate visually in writing or in pictures, and even by absence of communication. Other considerations in relationships are: the contexts in which they take place, for example home or office; the nature of the other or others, for example parent or boss; their length, for example well-established or recent; and their intimacy level, for example deep or shallow.

The meanings of the word *skill* include proficiency, competence and expertness in some activity. However the essential element of a skill is the ability to make and implement an effective sequence of choices so as to achieve a desired objective. For instance, if people are to be good listeners they have to make and implement the choices entailed in being good listeners. The fact that all skills involve choices does not mean that the activities have to be carried out in a mechanistic way. Rather a skills approach to relationships may free the participants to be more spontaneous.

The concept of skill is best viewed not as an either/or matter in which you either possess or do not possess a skill. Rather it is preferable to think of yourself as possessing skills *resources* and *deficits* or a mixture of the two. If you make good choices in a skills area, for instance either in listening or in talking about yourself, this is a skills resource. If you make poor choices in a skills area, this is a skills deficit. In all relationship skills areas you are likely to possess both resources and deficits in varying degrees. For example in the skills area of listening, you may be good at understanding talkers but poor at showing them that you actually have understood. The object of training in relationship skills is, in one or more skills areas, to help you to shift the balance of your resources and deficits more in the direction of resources. Put another way, it is to help you to become a better chooser.

In your various relationships you need to possess a *repertoire* of skills. Some of you may not have a specific skill in your repertoire: for instance the ability to say no to an unreasonable request. Others of you may wish a skill already in your repertoire to be strengthened: for instance, carrying on the previous example, by being able to say no less aggressively. Sometimes a skill may require improvement by altering the thoughts and feelings interfering with its appropriate execution. For instance, your fear of what other people are thinking of you may cause you to feel anxious. Your anxiety may contribute to your behaving in a shy way which in turn makes it hard for others to get to know you.

Though not wishing to get too academic, below is the definition of *relationship skills* which is used in this book.

> Relationship skills are sequences of choices which enable you to communicate effectively with those with whom you relate or wish to relate. These sequences of choices involve thoughts, feelings and actions. Your repertoire of relationship skills comprises your resources and deficits in each skills area.

### Identifying relationship skills

At this stage of the book it is only possible to identify relationship skills in an introductory way. Further elaboration must be left to the remaining chapters. Rather than just list the skills, Exercise 1.1 below asks you to rate yourself on a number of different skills in ten broad skills areas. Remember that you are viewed as having good skills if you make good choices and as having poor skills if you make poor choices.

Even though the meaning of some of the skills may not be altogether clear to you so early in the book, the identification and listing of skills has been made into an exercise to encourage you to participate actively in thinking about what are the skills. Also, it is hoped that by making this exercise about *you*, you will gain in appreciation of the importance to you of possessing effective relationship skills. Hopefully, this will then further motivate you to work and practise at remedying the deficiencies you have identified.

**Exercise 1.1   Initial assessment of relationship skills**

This exercise may be done in a number of ways.

A  *On your own*
   The questionnaire below lists a number of relationship skills in ten broad areas. Rate how satisfied you are with your skills in each of the ten areas using the rating scale below:
   3  *Much* need for improvement
   2  *Moderate* need for improvement
   1  *Slight* need for improvement
   0  *No* need for improvement
   Put a question mark (?) rather than a rating by any skill whose meaning is not clear to you at this stage of the book.

*Your rating   Skills*

**1.   Awareness and understanding of yourself**
_____  Listening to your feelings
_____  Identifying and labelling your feelings accurately
_____  Possessing a reasonably clear and stable view of yourself
_____  Understanding the influence of your background
_____  Assuming responsibility for choosing to use your relationship skills
_____  Awareness of your current relationship skills resources and deficits

**2.   Talking about yourself**
_____  Communicating well with your voice
_____  Communicating well with your body
_____  Ability to speak for yourself and to 'own' your thoughts and feelings
_____  Sharing personal information
_____  Expressing feelings appropriately

**3.   Starting relationships**
_____  Making opportunities for meeting people
_____  Initiating conversations
_____  Taking risks and initiating further contact
_____  Appropriately revealing yourself to relative strangers
_____  Coping with shyness

**4.   Developing relationships**
_____  Progressively matching and deepening the level of intimacy of your disclosures
_____  Revealing strengths and weaknesses
_____  Giving feedback

*Your rating*    Skills
_____    Receiving feedback
_____    Identifying and overcoming barriers to trust
_____    Ability to use touch and to be touched
_____    Assessing and discussing your relationship constructively
               **5.   Defining and asserting yourself**
_____    Awareness of how assertive you currently are
_____    Ability to overcome your mental barriers to assertion
_____    Expressing wants and wishes
_____    Being able to take initiatives regardless of your gender
_____    Expressing liking and being likeable
_____    Coping with others' behaviour you perceive as negative
_____    Not letting others define you on their terms
_____    Coping with others' defensiveness and resistances
               **6.   Good listening**
_____    Awareness of your barriers to listening
_____    Being a safe person to talk to
_____    Ability to step into another person's world
_____    Demonstrating interest and attentiveness
_____    Disciplined listening: hearing the words accurately
_____    Disciplined listening: observing and understanding bodily communication
_____    Disciplined listening: tuning into feelings
_____    Disciplined listening: understanding verbal, vocal and bodily communication
               **7.   Helpful responding**
_____    Awareness of how you currently respond
_____    Communicating accurate understanding of words
_____    Communicating accurate understanding of feelings
_____    Communicating accurate understanding of words and feelings
_____    Ability to help another clarify a problem
_____    Helping another generate and evaluate alternative courses of action
               **8.   Managing anger**
_____    Awareness of when you feel angry and how much
_____    Expressing your anger constructively
_____    Where appropriate, regulating your angry feelings
_____    Handling criticism constructively
               **9.   Managing conflict**
_____    Possessing a problem-solving orientation
_____    Being collaborative
_____    Assuming responsibility for managing conflict

*Your rating*    *Skills*
_____    Where necessary, confronting conflicts
_____    Understanding the other's position
_____    Ability to state your own position clearly
_____    Defining problems constructively with another
_____    Searching for and evaluating alternative solutions
              with another
_____    Agreeing upon and making a clear 'contract' to
              implement the best solution
_____    Maintaining your morale when conflicts persist
              10. **Maintaining and developing your relationship
              skills**
_____    Monitoring and maintaining your relationship skills
_____    Improving and developing your relationship skills

Conclude the exercise by writing out a summary statement of the
areas in which you consider you could develop your relationship
skills. Where possible, be specific about the skills you think require
development.

B    *In pairs*
Independently complete the questionnaire. Discuss with your
partner your respective strengths and weaknesses in each area
before moving on to the next area. Then independently write out a
summary statement of the areas in which you wish to develop your
relationship skills. Be specific about which skills need further
development. Discuss your summary statements.

C    *In a training group*
The trainer can facilitate a discussion in which group members
assess and explore their current level of relationship skills. Preferably the trainer allows group members to write out their self-
assessments as singles or pairs prior to conducting a plenary
sharing and discussion section. The trainer needs to be sensitive to
the level of trust in the group, including being aware that some may
find it hard to admit their difficulties in public. The trainer may
encourage members to observe the processes of the training group
– for instance, fears about disclosure and the development of trust –
as a way of developing their insight into using relationship skills
outside the training group. Where appropriate, the trainer may also
encourage members to provide specific examples illustrating how
they perform in a skills area. Also, if appropriate, the trainer may
encourage group members to give each other feedback about how
their relationship skills are perceived.

THE RELATIONSHIP SKILLS DEBATE

This book strongly advocates viewing relationships in skills terms. However, a number of both helping service professionals and lay people have reservations about this approach. Below some of the arguments for and against are presented and assessed.

### Reasons for viewing relationships in skills terms

Below are some reasons for the approach adopted in this book.

- *Relationships are too important to be left to chance.* Earlier it was pointed out that relationships are perhaps the major source of human pleasure and pain. Also, reasons were presented why relationships are so important to humans both as a species and as individuals. Paradoxically, despite their importance, most often little systematic attempt is made to train you in relationship skills.[7] Instead you are expected to acquire them by informal learning and by chance in your homes, schools, workplaces and communities. What tends to happen is that skills deficits are acquired along with skills resources, thus diminishing your effectiveness. Given the critical importance of your being able to relate well throughout your life, it seems equally critical that systematic attempts are made to train you in the skills that are so central to your being able to meet your own and others' needs.
- *Specification of skills.* A systematic attempt to train people in relationship skills means that these skills need to be identified and clearly stated. A major advantage of viewing relationships in skills terms is that it encourages such specificity. For instance, it is one thing to talk in generalities about the beauty of love and another to develop and practise the skills of being a loving person. Though this may be less poetic and more prosaic, in the long run it is likely to lead to more stable and realistic relationships.
- *Amenability to training.* When relationship skills are clearly stated a number of important consequences follow. Some attempt can be made to assess the degree to which you possess or are deficient in the skills. Such assessments can be made by either yourself or others. Furthermore, the notion of skills implies that you have learned your skills resources and deficits. As such you can be trained to learn different and better ways of relating. In a

very simplified version of training, specification of skills enables assessment which encourages awareness of deficits, which in turn can be improved by training.

● *Amenability to self-help.* The notion of relationship skills allows you to monitor and work on your relationship difficulties. Instead of just describing a situation, for instance 'I don't get on with Bill', you can now examine the skills that you use in relating to Bill and, if appropriate, alter them. Additionally, once you acquire skills you need to maintain them. This is much easier to do if you are clear in the first place what the relevant skills are.

**Reservations about a relationship skills approach**

There are a number of fairly common reservations about taking a skills approach to relationships. On closer inspection some of these are more concerned with doing it poorly rather than doing it at all. Though their wording may differ from person to person, below are some of the main reservations about a skills approach.

● *It is unnatural.* Here the assumption is that people are born with styles of relating and that reducing these to skills goes against nature. At a more sophisticated level there is the issue of the degree to which a skills approach is insufficiently sensitive to individual differences and may be encouraging unnecessary conformity. The idea that, as people physically mature, their ability to relate unfolds is scarcely tenable given the widespread evidence of relationship difficulties amongst people of all ages. The charge that a relationship skills approach may level out desirable individual differences in style appears more important for alerting trainers and others to a danger in the approach rather than as an indication that it should not be done at all. One reason why some of you may feel that a relationship skills approach is unnatural is that you find it hard to accept how much of your behaviour is learned habit. This represents a challenge to your sense of free will and autonomy.

● *It is superficial.* There are many strands to the superficiality argument. One strand is that people may need longer term counselling because their relationship skill difficulties are the result of considerable past deprivations in their emotional lives. This appears more an argument for ensuring that those who need counselling receive it rather than an argument against skills training. Another strand is that just focusing on people's observable behaviour is unlikely to lead to long term changes. Partly in response to this criticism, there has been an increasing emphasis on viewing skills training as incorporating a focus on people's thoughts and feelings as well as on their observable actions. Still a further strand is that skills training is mechanistic. For instance, one writer has observed that he has known a number of ineffective people who have possessed many of the mechanistic skills of being an effective person.[8] This may be more an argument for not doing relationship skills training in a superficial way than saying that it is in itself superficial.

- *It is manipulative.* The argument here is that it is not so much the training as the outcomes of the training that lead to manipulative rather than to genuine relationships. Again this is an argument that signals a potential danger of relationship skills training – that it will be used for the opposite purposes than those for which it was intended – than one for not doing it at all. Furthermore it is naive to think that people are not already being highly manipulative in their everyday relationships. Thus it is conceivable that relationship skills training may help people give up some of their manipulative game playing rather than increase it. This is partly a matter of how well the training is conducted.

- *It usurps the role of the family.* Despite considerable evidence that there seems to be a *relationship lag* in the Western world, that our technological advances have far outstripped people's ability to relate to one another, there is still the notion that traditional approaches to acquiring relationship skills through the family should be maintained. This is despite the statistical evidence that so many parents are themselves experiencing serious difficulties in their marital relationships. Clearly parents have a fundamental role to play in helping their children acquire and sustain the self-esteem and skills for effective relating. However the basic role of the family needs to be supplemented by more systematic attempts to teach young people relationship skills to prevent them repeating many of the mistakes of their elders. Allied to this there is room for training parents in relationship skills, both in relation to their children and to each other.

CONCLUDING INNER SPEECH

This and subsequent chapters will end with a segment of 'inner speech' that you can tell yourself to remind you of the main points in this chapter.

> Much of my happiness in life will be derived from my relationships. However, if they do not go well, I may experience considerable psychological pain. Also, I am likely to be less successful in my work. Already there is ample evidence that many people have distressed rather than fulfilled relationships.

> To relate well I need to develop a repertoire of effective relationship skills. Each skill represents a series of choices made in an area: for example, listening. If I make good choices I exhibit skills resources. If I make poor choices, I exhibit skills deficits. Relationship skills are too important to be left to chance. I need to assess my skills resources and deficits and to identify those skills areas on which I need to work. Focusing on improving my relationship skills is an exciting challenge. It will benefit both me and those with whom I come into contact. I CAN RELATE MORE EFFECTIVELY!

REFERENCES

1. Forster, E.M. (1910) *Howards End*. Harmondsworth: Penguin.
2. Sartre, J.P. (1962) *Huis Clos*. Englewood Cliffs, NJ: Prentice-Hall.
3. Jenkins, H. (1983) Families and family therapy: future directions. Keynote address, British Psychological Society Counselling Psychology Section Conference on Counselling Psychology and the Family, London, June 10.
4. Working Party on Marriage Guidance (1979) *Marriage Matters*. London: H.M.S.O.
5. McDonald, P. (1985) Report on divorce in the Melbourne *Age*, December 21. Dr McDonald is Deputy Director of the Institute of Family Studies.
6. Holland, J.L. (1973) *Making Vocational Choices*. Englewood Cliffs, NJ: Prentice-Hall.
7. Nelson-Jones, R. (1985) Research in progress with Australian college and secondary school students on variables pertinent to human relationship skills training.
8. Arbuckle, D.S. (1976) Comment on A.E. Ivey's paper 'The counselor as teacher', *Personnel and Guidance Journal*, **54**, 434.

# 2   How You Learned to Relate

From the moment of birth you are bombarded with messages about what sort of person you are. If you are born in China, Britain, the United States or Australia you receive messages that help you acquire Chinese, British, American or Australian relationship skills, respectively. Furthermore, within each nationality there are numerous subgroupings differing in the nature of their relationship skills depending on such factors as social class, economic circumstances, region and minority group membership.

Numerous people give you messages that influence your relationship skills. Some of these messages help you to relate more effectively whereas others weaken your ability to do this. Sometimes these messages are consistent and at other times they may be contradictory, not just to the extent of different messages from different people but also from the same person. Children especially are influenced in acquiring good and bad relationship skills. They are physically and emotionally dependent on others and also intellectually immature.

Let us now look at the kinds of people who may have influenced and may still influence the choices you make in your relationships. Such people include:

- *Parents*. These include step-parents and other substitute parents.
- *Brothers and sisters*. They may be influential especially if older, but not too old to be out of frequent contact.
- *Grandparents*. Your grandparents brought up your parents and consequently their influence lives on through others as well as through themselves, if alive.
- *Aunts and uncles*. Like grandparents, aunts and uncles may be important. However, greater geographic mobility than previously within families may sometimes lessen their importance.
- *Older friends*. Friends of the family who visit fairly frequently.
- *Community leaders*. People in church, medical, sporting and other visible positions.
- *Peer groups*. People of roughly your own age, outside your immediate family, with whom you play and study.
- *Teachers*. Contact with teachers may be either in class or in extracurricular activities, for instance games, music.

● *Famous people.* Such people may be well known sports or entertainment personalities. Some may be historical and religious leaders.
● *Fictional people.* Characters portrayed in books, on T.V. and in movies.
● *Advertising.* People behaving in specific ways with the purpose of influencing purchasing decisions.

Each of you has different people who are or have been influential in helping you to acquire relationship skills. A distinction can be made between people who relate to you in terms of *roles* and those relating as *persons.* When people relate to you in terms of roles they require you to complete their definitions of themselves. For example, parents require children and teachers require pupils. Thus in role relationships people relate to each other in terms of categories. In person relationships, the emphasis is on person-to-person contact rather than on roles. Here both parents and children reveal to each other what they really think and feel rather than feel heavily constrained by role expectations. Though role and person relationships contain much overlap, intimate relationships require people to relate as persons. Those who have been unlucky enough to have missed this quality of relationship in their pasts may have received insufficient opportunity to learn the skills necessary for future close personal relationships.

A further useful distinction is that between *acquiring* relationship skills and *maintaining* them. In a sense each one of you has at least two learning histories for every skill: acquiring the skill in the first place, which is the traditional definition of learning, and then improving, diminishing or maintaining your initial level of skill. It is an important distinction because changing or improving a skill entails changing what is *maintaining* the skill at a lower level than desirable in the present and future. It is impossible to go back and change how a skills deficit was first *acquired.*

For example, Jill initially learned to be shy because her parents had a 'children should be seen and not heard' policy or rule. She maintained her shyness throughout her childhood and adolescence since her parents continued not to encourage her to talk about herself. At this stage we cannot change how she became shy. Also, it is uncertain whether her parents' behaviour, which plays an important part in maintaining her shyness, can be changed. However, we can offer Jill skills training. Also, if necessary, counselling designed to provide her with learning experiences enabling her to become less shy. Thus, we provide a third learning history that enables people to make new choices and to overcome skills deficits that have previously been both acquired and maintained. A further reason why a distinction between acquisition and maintenance is desirable is that, even when you have acquired good relationship skills, you still have to work to maintain them.

## LEARNING FROM OBSERVATION

'Monkey see, monkey do' is one way of viewing learning from observation. A mother smiles at her infant and the infant smiles back. Learning from observation starts at a very early age. Psychologists call learning from observation learning from modelling. You learn from people who demonstrate behaviour, including relationship skills. The other main way of learning, namely learning from the consequences of your behaviour, gets discussed in the next section. In reality, learning from consequences and from observation are related. Albert Bandura is a psychologist who has conducted much research into modelling. He states that the observer is more likely to adopt the modelled behaviour if it: (a) brings external rewards; (b) is internally positively valued; and (c) has been observed to bring rewards to the model.[1]

Modelling involves both an observer and a model. The behaviours that can be modelled include feelings and thoughts as well as actions. For example, an angry parent may model that it is all right to express anger, that he or she has 'legitimate' reasons for being angry, and that expressing anger is achieved by thumping on the table and calling other people names. Three further points are implicit in the above example: modelling may be unintentional as well as intentional; it may involve lack of as well as presence of good relationship skills; and the observers may remain unaware that they are learning through observation. Sometimes observers may consciously think about whether adopting modelled behaviour will have the desired consequences for them, for example a way of 'chatting up' women. In families, it is all too easy for children to absorb some of their parents' patterns of relating without conscious choice. A consequence of this is that each of you may not only have absorbed some poor relationship skill habits, but also have acquired the added barrier of remaining unaware that you have done so.

As mentioned earlier, you acquire and maintain your relationship skills through messages received from many categories of people. The most influential category is usually your parents. You were exposed to them first, in a very intense way, when you were dependent on them and at an age when your critical powers were still in process of development. Exercise 2.1 is designed to put you in the observer's role to explore the relationship behaviours (feelings, thoughts, actions) that were being modelled and may still be being modelled by your parents. These include both strengths and weaknesses.

---

**Exercise 2.1   What relationship skills messages have you received from your parents? Part 1: from observing their example\***

This exercise may be done on your own, in pairs or as part of a training group.

A   *On your own*
  1.  Write down the example set by your parents in the following skills areas.

| *Sender skills* | *Your mother* | *Your father* |
|---|---|---|
| Talking about their experiences | | |
| Showing their feelings | | |
| Standing up for themselves | | |

| *Receiver skills* | *Your mother* | *Your father* |
|---|---|---|
| Being prepared to listen | | |
| Understanding what others say | | |
| Responding helpfully to others | | |

---

\*   In most instances 'parents' refers to your natural parents. Where this is not the case, answer the questions as appropriately as you can.

| Managing conflict skills | Your mother | Your father |
|---|---|---|
| Avoiding blaming others | | |
| Managing their anger | | |
| Working for rational solutions | | |

2. Write down what you consider the effect of your parents' example has been on your relationship skills in the following areas:

    – sending information
    – receiving information
    – managing conflict

B   *In pairs*
*Either* each write out your responses to all nine of the above areas, then discuss with your partner.
*Or* each write out your responses to the above questions by section (sending information, receiving information, managing conflict), then together discuss your responses before moving on to the next section.
*Or* for each section, listen to your partner as he/she verbally gives his/her responses, reverse roles, then discuss.

C   *In a training group*
The trainer discusses how an important way in which we learn relationship skills is by observing the behaviour of others (modelling). The trainer may illustrate the concept of learning from others' example by demonstrating how he/she might answer one of the questions above. The trainer divides the group into pairs and gets members to write down and/or discuss their responses to the questions. Alternatively the questions can be set as a homework assignment. The trainer then conducts a plenary session in which group members share and discuss their responses. He/she avoids bringing pressure on members reluctant to discuss their parents' behaviour with the group. The trainer encourages the group to explore the possible effects of their parents' example on their relationship skills.

## LEARNING FROM CONSEQUENCES

When a child is perceived as naughty, a parent may well say 'bad boy' or 'bad girl'. When the child behaves well, the parent is more likely to say 'good boy' or 'good girl'. In each instance the parent is either granting or withholding a reward, namely parental approval, as a consequence of the child's behaviour. Children not only learn from the consequences of their behaviour provided by other people but from the consequences or feedback they receive from their feelings. If teasing a friend is pleasurable, this is likely to increase the probability of subsequent teasing of that friend – and perhaps others as well. For children, possibly the main set of external consequences revolves around whether their behaviour is perceived as good or bad. This is especially likely to be so in relating to adults, but also applies with their peers. The main set of internal consequences concerns whether their behaviour provides them with pleasure or pain.

Sometimes a conflict occurs in that behaviour that has pleasurable consequences for the child receives parental disapproval. Some parents are poor at acknowledging and not feeling threatened by the feelings of their children. Some children are very vulnerable. The combination of threatened parents and vulnerable children may lead to children burying their true feelings. Instead, they may think, feel and act in ways more likely to generate parental approval. All children do this to some extent. Consequently, for the sake of short-term reward, children may suffer much more serious long-term psychological damage by becoming alienated from their feelings. Thus they experience difficulty in assessing whether consequences are pleasurable for *them* rather than for other people. People tend to talk about themselves as though they have access to their own feelings without distortion. Frequently, however, they behave on the basis of rewards internalised from significant others such as parents rather in accord with their underlying feelings.

Behaviour may not only be *acquired* on account of its consequences, but also *maintained* by them. Such maintaining consequences can be both external and internal. An external consequence example is that of a girl who increases the probability of a boy's 'taking an interest in her' behaviour by indicating that she likes him. Once his interest is aroused this behaviour is more likely to be maintained if she continues indicating that she likes his attention. The boy's 'taking an interest in her' behaviour is likely to fall off and even be extinguished if she stops giving him positive messages. Basically encouragement is providing the consequences leading to the acquisition and maintenance of his behaviour while discouragement provides the consequences leading to its falling off and possible end. An example of an internal consequence maintaining behaviour is that of a young man who feels pride if he gives up his seat to a lady and guilt if he does not. He may not have true freedom of choice as to whether he wants to do it or not.

In relationships, another way in which people provide or fail to provide rewarding consequences is by labelling themselves and others. If I label myself as a 'good father' and my children provide feedback that fits my self-image, I am likely to provide rewarding consequences for them. However, if they challenge my self-image, the consequences I provide for them may not be so rewarding. Along the same lines, a parent may label a child as a 'trouble-maker' or 'difficult' and then fail to reward any of the child's behaviour that does not fit into this image. Conceivably the child may then become more rewarded for behaviours that are unrewarding to the parent than for those that are not. The psychiatrist Eric Berne called such transactions psychological games.[2]

Many people provided consequences for your relationship behaviour as you were or are growing up. However, as with modelling, the main people providing consequences for your behaviour were likely to be your parents. Exercise 2.2 is designed to help you further understand how you came to learn your current relationship skills behaviour. This exercise looks at the consequences provided for you by your parents. It assumes that many other people may have provided significant consequences for your behaviour. Also, that your behaviour once acquired and maintained is capable of being unlearned by the provision of new consequences and/or modelling.

---

**Exercise 2.2   What relationship skills messages have you received from your parents? Part 2: from the consequences they provided for your behaviour\***

This exercise may be done on your own, in pairs or as part of a training group.

---

\*   In most instances 'parents' refers to your natural parents. Where this is not the case, answer the questions as appropriately as you can.

A *On your own*

1. Write down how your parents react/have reacted to your behaving in each of the following ways.

| *Sending information* | *Your mother* | *Your father* |
|---|---|---|
| Expressing positive feelings (e.g. affection) toward her/him | | |
| Expressing negative feelings (e.g. anger) toward her/him | | |
| Expressing your opinions on current affairs to her/him | | |
| Expressing negative feelings (e.g. depression) about yourself to her/him | | |
| Expressing positive feelings (e.g. happiness) about yourself to her/him | | |
| Indicating that you do not wish to be involved in parental disagreements | | |

| *Receiving information* | *Your mother* | *Your father* |
|---|---|---|
| Being prepared to listen to her/him | | |
| Interrupting and otherwise not listening to her/him | | |

| | | |
|---|---|---|
| Showing understanding of what she/he says | | |
| Failing to show understanding of what she/he says | | |
| Trying to respond helpfully to her/him | | |
| Deliberately responding unhelpfully to her/him | | |

| *Managing conflict* | *Your mother* | *Your father* |
|---|---|---|
| Requesting participation in decisions involving you | | |
| Blaming her/him for causing a conflict | | |
| Having a serious disagreement with her/him | | |
| Competing rather than cooperating to solve a problem with her/him | | |
| Placating and giving in to her/him | | |
| Working for a rational solution to a conflict with her/him | | |

2. Give examples of other people who have influenced your current relationship skills by providing significant conse- quences for your behaviour. Such people might include brothers and sisters, grandparents, aunts and uncles, friends and teachers, amongst others.

3. To what degree was and/or is the example of your parents consistent with the ways in which they reacted and/or react to your relationship behaviour? Do they have double standards?

B *In pairs*

*Either* each write out your responses to all the above questions, then discuss with your partner.

*Or* each write out your responses to the above questions by section (sending information, receiving information, managing conflict), then together discuss your responses before moving on to the next section.

*Or* for each section, listen to your partner as he/she verbally gives his/her responses, reverse roles, then discuss.

C *In a training group*

The trainer discusses the importance of the consequences other people provide for your behaviour to the way you learn relationship skills (learning by presence or absence of reward). The trainer models how he/she might answer one of the questions above. The trainer divides the group into pairs and gets members to write down and/or discuss their responses to the questions. Alternatively the questions can be set as a homework assignment. The trainer then conducts a plenary session in which group members share and discuss their responses.

## LEARNING FROM FAMILY RULES

Much learning from observation and consequences can be viewed in relation to family rules. These rules establish the nature and limits of permissible behaviour. Some of these rules have strongly influenced your relationship behaviour. Many family rules concern obvious topics such as getting the family maintenance chores done. Even here there are issues of power concerning who makes the rules, what happens if people break them and whether there is right of appeal. Thus an obvious rule, 'If mother prepares the meal, children are responsible for clearing it away', may contain some implicit rules: for example, 'Father does not have to do anything in the kitchen' and 'Once we parents agree on a rule, it is up to you children to obey'. Rules that have been openly discussed and agreed upon by family members are like legal contracts. Members acknowledge their rights and responsibilities, the consequences of breaking rules, and the need to renegotiate any changes.

Two important considerations in relation to family rules are whether your family represents an *open* or *closed* communication system and the degree to which many important rules may be more implicit than explicit. In an open family communication system you can reveal your thoughts and feelings about yourselves, each other and about what you see going on in the family. Though family members may have different roles, each is related to as a person of worth. Feelings like anger and affection can be expressed and do not always have to be inhibited. Where possible decisions are made on the basis of discussion between interested parties. The rules in an open family system emphasise 'Thou shalts': for example, 'Thou shalt be free to express feelings' and 'Thou shalt participate in decisions affecting you'. Conversely, the rules of a closed family communication system emphasise 'Thou shalt nots': for example, 'Thou shalt not ask parents (or children for that matter) to justify their behaviour', 'Thou shalt not be too open in showing affection' and 'Thou shalt not question the rules that have been made in your best interests'. Whereas open family systems encourage discussion and cooperation, closed family systems are much more based on power and coercion.

Family rules are often implicit. Writing of rules regarding the acceptance of sexuality in families, family therapist Virginia Satir observes that most families employ the rules 'Don't enjoy sex – yours or anyone else's – in any form' and 'Keep your genitals clean and out of sight and touch. Use them only when necessary and sparingly at that.'[3] Implicit family rules often entail what is *not* rather than what is talked about. You refrain from talking openly about sex, masturbation, your fears, your achievements and your hopes when there are implicit rules that such disclosure is unwelcome. Implicit rules can also apply to what feedback it is appropriate to give to others: for instance, if a grandparent is boring you, you may have learned that no one in the family directly conveys this message. However, they may indirectly convey the message by not inviting them around too often. Families have implicit rules about dealing with conflict. These may include: 'Avoid it at all costs', 'Conflict is part of family life, so let's try to resolve it as best as possible' and 'Might is right'.

Exercise 2.3 gives you a chance to explore your own family's rules and the impact they may have had on your current relationship behaviour. Other settings in which you relate, for instance schools or workplaces, also have implicit and explicit rules setting expectancies for appropriate behaviour. Exercise 2.3 could be extended to cover such settings.

---

**Exercise 2.3   Understanding your family's rules**

This exercise may be done on your own, in pairs or as part of a training group.

A   *On your own*
  1.  What are or were the main 'do's' and 'don'ts' involved in the way your parental family either relates or related to each other. List five 'do's' and five 'don'ts' as though they were biblical commandments starting with 'Thou shalt . . .' for the do's and 'Thou shalt not . . .' for the don'ts.
  2.  To what degree are or were the family rules consistent?
  3.  To what extent does/did your family represent an open or closed communication system? State reasons for your answer.
  4.  How is your relationship behaviour *currently* being influenced by the do's and don'ts of your family rules regarding communication?

B   *In pairs*
  *Either* each write out your responses to the above questions, then discuss with your partner.
  *Or* for each question, listen to your partner as he/she verbally gives his/her responses, reverse roles, then discuss.

C   *In a training group*
  The trainer discusses how the modelling and consequences involved in family rules influences the way we learn relationship skills and sustain relationship skill resources and deficits. The trainer divides the group into pairs and gets members to write down and/or discuss their responses to the questions. Alternatively the questions can be set as a homework assignment. The trainer then conducts a plenary session in which group members share and discuss their responses.

---

## LEARNING A GENDER ROLE

The nursery rhyme goes:

> What are little girls made of, made of?
> What are little girls made of?
> Sugar and spice and everything nice.
> That's what little girls are made of.

> What are little boys made of, made of?
> What are little boys made of?
> Shells and snails and puppy dog tails.
> That's what little boys are made of.

Blue for a boy and pink for a girl. From birth boys and girls are given messages about what is appropriate behaviour for their gender. Girls play with dolls, boys with trains. Girls can show hurt feelings, boys should be brave. Girls get asked out, boys ask out. Women bring up children, men are breadwinners. Thus there are many implicit and explicit rules surrounding how each gender can think, feel and act.

Increasingly stereotyped gender roles are being challenged. There has always been cultural variation. This indicates that the way gender roles currently exist in Western societies need not always be the case. A contemporary example is that there is a much higher proportion of women doctors in Russia than in the West. Many women and men wish to feel and become freer in how they relate and in which occupations they pursue. There is no biological difference in ability that means that a higher proportion of women than now cannot fill senior administrative and professional positions. Additionally, there is no reason based on biological differences why women should not ask men out and be prepared to foot their share of the entertainment expenses. The gay movement and the increasing recognition of the amount of homosexuality and bisexuality that exists[4,5] also challenges traditional gender roles.

Men and women tend to be brought up with different relationship skill and resources and deficits. As such, they may have different requirements for relationship skills training, sometimes called social skills training or SST. Reviewing new developments in social skills training, leading British social psychologist Michael Argyle writes:

> We have seen a number of areas in which women are usually more socially competent than men – they are better at sending and receiving NVC* and are more rewarding and polite. They disclose more and form closer friendships, and are better at reducing the loneliness of others. However it is mostly women who seek assertiveness training, and their problems are more general than this.[6]

Argyle goes on to say that many research studies have shown how women like to form close friendships with equals. However, they appear to have more difficulty than men in coping with hierarchical,

---

* NVC means non-verbal communication.

structured groups engaged in joint tasks. Furthermore they rarely emerge as the leaders of such groups.[7]

Exercise 2.4 encourages you to explore the degree and ways in which you have learned a role 'appropriate' to your gender. It also encourages you to examine whether or not the way you currently feel, think and act is being restricted by your prior gender-related learning. Such learning may have come from observation, consequences or from explicit and implicit family rules. The word script implies that you may unquestioningly be acting out a story that has been written for you by others. Your gender-related behaviour may also be maintained by *present* rather than *past* observation, consequences and family rules.

---

### Exercise 2.4  Exploring your gender script

This exercise may be done on your own, in pairs or as part of a training group.

A  *On your own*
The following are characteristics associated more with one gender rather than the other*

| Masculine | Feminine |
| --- | --- |
| acts as leader | affectionate |
| aggressive | cheerful |
| ambitious | childlike |
| analytical | compassionate |
| assertive | does not use harsh language |
| athletic | eager to soothe hurt feelings |
| competitive | feminine |
| defends own beliefs | flatterable |
| dominant | gentle |
| forceful | gullible |
| has leadership abilities | loves children |
| independent | loyal |
| individualistic | sensitive to the needs of others |
| makes decisions easily | shy |
| masculine | soft spoken |
| self-reliant | sympathetic |
| self-sufficient | tender |
| strong personality | understanding |
| willing to take a stand | warm |
| willing to take risks | yielding |

---

\*   These lists are taken from the Bem Sex-Role Inventory[8]

Write down

1. to what extent you consider you were brought up, by being rewarded and by observing others, to exhibit the characteristics mainly associated with your gender
2. specific examples of the ways in which you were brought up to exhibit the characteristics more associated with your gender
3. specific examples of the ways in which you were brought up to exhibit the characteristics more associated with the other gender
4. how you would really like to be in relation to being able to exhibit the characteristics listed above for either gender

B   *In pairs*
*Either* each write out your responses to all the above questions, then discuss with your partner.
*Or* for each question, listen to your partner as he/she verbally gives his/her response, reverse roles, then discuss.

C   *In a training group*
The trainer introduces the idea of gender conditioning and how this can influence the ways in which you behave in relationships. The trainer then divides the group into pairs and gets members to write down and/or discuss their responses to the questions. Alternatively the questions can be set as a homework assignment. The trainer then conducts a plenary session in which group members share and discuss their responses.

---

## LEARNING TO FEEL WORTHWHILE

American psychologist Robert Carkhuff categorises families into two broad groupings, facilitative and retarding. He writes: 'The members of the facilitative family are in the process of becoming persons. The members of the retarding family are becoming non-persons.'[9] In facilitative families parents are likely to have a secure sense of their own self-worth which is transmitted to their offspring. In retarding families either or both parents feel insecure. Lacking a true sense of their own worth, they send messages that undermine the sense of worth of their children.

Intentionally or unintentionally when people communicate they send two broad categories of messages. One set is specific, having to do with the ostensible purpose of the communication. The other set of messages may be much less intentional and specific. These give the receivers messages pertaining to their worth as persons as well as also revealing how high or low the senders value themselves. Virginia Satir writes: 'Every word, facial expression, gesture, or action on the part of the parent gives the child some message about his worth. It is sad that so many parents don't realise the effect these messages have on the child, and often don't even realise what messages they are sending.[10] Furthermore, children may pick up the habits of their parents and relate back to them and other family members in ways that undermine their confidence. Eric Berne has labelled the position where people feel good about themselves and others the 'I'm OK – You're OK position'.[11] All too often people learn to feel that they are 'Not OK' and then it is a short step to feeling that other people are 'Not OK' as well.

Let us now look at some of the behaviours whereby parents are likely to help their children feel worthwhile. For each, behaving in the opposite way is likely to diminish their children's self-esteem.

- *Showing commitment.* Children need to feel that their parents are dependable in their commitment to them. They need a secure base from which to explore and learn.
- *Expressing affection.* Warmth and prizing needs to be clearly demonstrated. This includes using physical contact, for instance hugging.
- *Understanding feelings.* Children need to feel that someone is accessible enough to understand their feelings. To be so understood is an affirming experience.
- *Listening to content.* This involves taking the time and trouble to listen accurately to what the child is saying.
- *Acknowledging separateness.* Parents need to be secure enough in their own identities to acknowledge and value the separateness of their children, including not just treating them as extensions of themselves.
- *Direct communication.* The sending of messages needs to be as clear as possible with an absence of 'hidden agendas'.
- *Openness.* Parents reveal themselves as three-dimensional human beings with thoughts and feelings as well as actions. There is a minimum of unnecessary editing of self-disclosure so that parents present a reasonably full rather than a highly selective picture of themselves to their children.
- *Working through problems.* Being prepared to work through problems in the family as they arise on the basis of mutual respect.
- *Providing suitable learning opportunities.* Helping children feel and become more competent by providing them with learning opportunities geared to their stage of development. This includes provision of relevant information.

● *Encouragement.* Encouraging children rather than discouraging them as they learn skills and competencies.
● *Assertiveness.* Being prepared to set realistic limits for children. This often entails offering explanations for the limits.
● *Modelling personal responsibility.* Helping children learn from observation that ultimately each person is responsible for making the choices that create their unique happiness and fulfilment.

Exercise 2.5 aims to help you explore how you learned to feel worthwhile or worthless as a person. More colloquially this can be expressed as how you learned to feel good or bad about yourself. In fact you probably had a range of experiences, some helpful and some harmful. You are asked to identify experiences that developed your confidence and those that were 'put-downs'. You are further asked to explore ways in which your level of confidence affects the degree of skill that you exhibit in your current relationships.

---

**Exercise 2.5   Developing the confidence you bring to relationships: helpful and harmful experiences**

This exercise can be done on your own, in pairs or as part of a training group.

A *On your own*
Think back over what you saw and experienced in your growing up that influences the amount of confidence that you bring to your current relationships. Some of these experiences were helpful and constructive whereas others were harmful and destructive. Write down
   1.  five experiences that you consider were helpful in developing your confidence in relationships and that you would like to repeat with your children
   2.  five experiences that you consider were destructive in undermining your confidence in relationships and that you would like to avoid with your children
   3.  the ways in which your level of confidence affects how you relate to others.

B *In pairs*
Each partner writes out his/her responses to the above questions and then the partners share and discuss them together.

C *In a training group*
The trainer discusses the concept of confidence in relationships. He/she divides the group into singles, pairs or larger groups and gets

members to write down and/or discuss their responses to the questions. Alternatively the questions can be set as a homework assignment. The trainer then conducts a plenary session in which members share and discuss their responses. The trainer encourages members to become aware of the ways in which their level of confidence affects their relationship skills.

## PUTTING IT ALL TOGETHER

This chapter has focused on how you learned your relationship skills. Five areas, which inevitably overlap, were identified: learning from observation, learning from consequences, learning from family rules, learning a gender role and learning to feel worthwhile. Exercise 2.6 encourages you to summarise your learnings about yourself when working through this chapter.

### Exercise 2.6   How you learned your relationship skills

This exercise can be done on your own, in pairs or as part of a training group.

A  *On your own*
   Write a summary statement of how you learned your relationship skills. What were the key influences in relation to particular skills?
B  *In pairs*
   *Either* write out your summary statement independently, then discuss together.
   *Or* while your partner listens, take 5 to 10 minutes to summarise verbally how you learned your relationship skills, then reverse roles.
C  *In a training group*
   The trainer discusses the importance of viewing relationship skills in learning terms. He/she encourages members to complete their summary statements either as a singles or pairs exercise. Alternatively, members are encouraged to complete their summaries as a homework assignment. This has much to recommend it since the statements can involve a considerable amount of reflection and pulling together of diverse threads. Afterwards the trainer conducts a plenary sharing and discussion session.

**Learning better relationship skills**

This chapter has attempted to increase your awareness of how you learned many of your relationship skills resources and deficits. Also, a distinction has been made between the initial learning of a skills resource or deficit and then maintaining it. Thus, right now both you and your environment may be maintaining deficits that make your life less happy and fulfilled. You have the choice of whether to learn better relationship skills. Sometimes this entails discarding bad habits altogether. Sometimes it involves learning completely new skills. On other occasions it involves altering the balance in a skills area more in the direction of resources than deficits.

The fact that you have learned your relationship skills should act as an encouragement rather than as a deterrent to improve them. If poor relationship skills can be learned, good ones can too. You need not stay stuck in repetitive and unproductive patterns of behaviour. You can respond to the exciting challenge to make life better for yourself and for others.


CONCLUDING INNER SPEECH

Below is a segment of inner speech that summarises some of the main points in this chapter.

> To a large extent I have learned my relationship skills resources and deficits. A useful distinction is that between initial learning of skills and maintaining them afterwards. Just because I have learned skills deficits in the first place is no reason why I should blight my life by maintaining them. I can work to learn new and better ways of relating.

> Two of the main processes through which I learned my relationship skills were learning from seeing the examples set by others and learning from consequences or from the rewards provided for my behaviour. The implicit and explicit rules concerning appropriate behaviour in my family influenced me. I also received many messages about the appropriate ways for girls and boys to think, feel and act. Though some learnings helped me to feel worthwhile as a person and to bring confidence into my relationships, others undermined my sense of worth and confidence.


REFERENCES

1.   Bandura, A. (1977) *Social Learning Theory*. Englewood Cliffs, NJ: Prentice-Hall.

2. Berne, E. (1964) *Games People Play*. New York: Grove Press.
3. Satir, V. (1972) *Peoplemaking*. Palo Alto, California: Science and Behavior Books.
4. Kinsey, A.C., Pomeroy, W.B. & Martin, C.E. (1948) *Sexual Behavior in the Human Male*. Philadelphia: W.B. Saunders.
5. Kinsey, A.C., Pomeroy, W.B., Martin, C.E. & Gebhard, P.H. (1953) *Sexual Behavior in the Human Female*. Philadelphia: W.B. Saunders.
6. Argyle, M. (1984) Some new developments in social skills training. *Bulletin of the British Psychological Society*, **37** (December issue), 405–410.
7. Shaver, P. & Buhrmeister, D. (1983) Loneliness, sex-role orientation and group life: a social needs perspective. In P.B. Paulus (ed.), *Basic Group Processes*. New York: Springer-Verlag.
8. Bem, S.L. (1974) The measurement of psychological androgyny. *Journal of Consulting and Clinical Psychology*, **44**, 155–162.
9. Carkhuff, R.R. (1983) *The Art of Helping V*. Amherst, Massachusetts: Human Resource Development Press.
10. Satir, V. (1972) *Peoplemaking*. Palo Alto, California: Science and Behavior Books.
11. Berne, E. (1972) *What Do You Say After You Say Hello?* London: Corgi Books.

# 3 Personal Responsibility and Feelings

In the preceding chapters we have looked at why it is important to view relationships in skills terms and at some of the ways in which you learned your relationship skills. This chapter develops two themes that are fundamental to the skills approach adopted in this book. The first is that of assuming personal responsibility for the way you relate. The second is that of being in touch with your feelings and your biological functioning as a human animal.

## PERSONAL RESPONSIBILITY FOR RELATIONSHIP SKILLS

A basic premise of this book is that ultimately each of you is personally responsible for your survival and unique fulfilment.[1] More bluntly stated, ultimately the buck for your life stops with you. Now what does this stark existential truth really mean? Here are some considerations.

### Defining personal responsibility

When you are being personally responsible you are in the process of making the choices that maximise your happiness and fulfilment. Personal responsibility is a positive concept whereby you are responsible *for* your well-being and making your *own* choices. It contrasts with a common meaning of responsibility, namely that of responsibility *to* others, including living up to their standards. Though the process of personal responsibility can be far from easy, adopting it as a basic attitude toward living liberates you to concentrate on how you can be most effective. It entails neither focusing on other people's faults nor feeling that you need to say 'my fault' all the time. There is an apt statement by the ancient philosopher Epictetus on this matter:

> It is the act of an ill-instructed man to blame others for his own bad condition; it is the act of one who has begun to be instructed, to lay the blame on himself; and of one whose instruction has been completed, neither to blame another, nor himself.

This book aims to help you assume a fundamental attitude of personal responsibility for your life. There is no intention to saddle you with a 'guilt trip'. The focus is on your present and future behaviour. Instead of emphasising what has been done wrong in the past, the book aims to confront you continuously with your existential choices. These choices define for yourself and for others the kind of person that you are in this far from perfect world.

The word choice keeps reappearing in this attempt to clarify what personal responsibility means. During your waking hours you are in a continual process of choosing. The American psychologist Abraham Maslow saw life as a series of two-sided choices. One side represented safety and being afraid: the other moving forward and growth. He wrote: 'To make the growth choice instead of the fear choice a dozen times a day is to move a dozen times a day towards self-actualisation.'[2] Thus he acknowledged that your fears can act as barriers to your making the choices that serve you best. The Viennese psychiatrist Viktor Frankl emphasises that, despite your fears and external difficulties, at no point in your life can you escape 'the mandate to choose among possibilities'.[3] Added weight is put to Frankl's observation in light of his own harrowing experiences as a Jewish doctor in Nazi concentration camps.[4]

**Limitations on personal responsibility**

Are you always responsible for your choices? The answer is 'yes', but with qualifications. The first qualification is that there is a maturational lag in that children's capacity for reasoning develops later than their need to make some of the choices that help them live most effectively. Consequently, one way in which you develop skills deficits is through not having the early reasoning power to make good choices. Also, bad initial choices can then develop into bad relationship habits.

A second qualification, albeit related to the first, is that an attitude of personal responsibility and the ability to make effective choices are learned. If your learning from observing models and others' behaviour has been deficient, that may well have diminished your effectiveness. Additionally, if your environment continues to be deficient in providing corrective learning opportunities this may further contribute to maintaining your skills deficits.

Third, many social factors may work against your assuming personal responsibility. Adverse conditions like poor housing, unemployment, poverty, racial discrimination, and poor educational facilities and content each may make it difficult for you both to learn to make and keep making the choices that serve you best despite such adversities. However, remove these adverse social conditions and problems of personal responsibility are still likely to be rife, if less physically uncomfortable. There are many poor little rich people around, especially when the Western world's affluence is compared to the level of existence of the third world. Some find the lack of structure of affluence much harder to face than the straightjacket of poverty. They are confronted with the need to create their own meaning in their lives.

### Personal responsibility and relationship skills

In the first chapter a definition of relationship skills was offered, namely that 'Relationship skills are sequences of choices which enable you to communicate effectively with those with whom you relate or wish to relate'. There are a number of aspects relevant to your assuming responsibility for your relationship skills.

There is no need to blame yourself or others if your relationship skills are not what you would like them to be. The important thing is to become aware of present strengths and deficits and to work to shift the balance more in the direction of better skills for the future.

All the skills mentioned in Exercise 1.1 in Chapter 1, for instance, listening, talking about and defining yourself, and managing conflicts involve choices for which you probably need to learn to assume more effective responsibility. Change in the direction of developing your relationship skills is more likely to occur if you learn to take responsibility for the ways in which you are maintaining your skills deficits. As this book progresses, hopefully you will gain a greater awareness of your present pattern of relating. If you do this, you are also likely to become more aware of the range of relationship skills options available to you. It then becomes a matter of whether you wish to make the change choice rather than the 'stick-in-the-mud' choice. In short, whether you wish to assume or to avoid making the choices conducive to your happiness and fulfilment.

Relationship skills involve feeling, thinking and acting. Taking responsibility for these skills also involves this triple focus. For example, responsibility for feelings can involve both the capacity to be in touch with your feelings and to regulate them where appropriate. Responsibility for thinking encompasses making the choices that diminish your engaging in self-defeating thinking: for instance, thinking contributing to anxiety, depression, anger and blaming. Responsibility for acting entails developing the skills so that you actually communicate to others what you really intend.

It is probably easier for you to develop your practical relationship skills if you work as part of a training group led by a skilled trainer. You can learn both from the trainer and from the other group members. You can receive feedback on how you relate as well as practise your skills. Furthermore, you can be supported by the group as and when you try your new skills in real life. Being personally responsible does not mean that you have to do it all on your own. If you have access to a suitable relationship skills training group, by all means consider joining it. Failing that, if you can work with a congenial partner, that may make it easier for you to develop your *practical* skills than working on your own, though you may still learn a lot on your own.

Before introducing a couple of exercises, below is a sample of inner speech that may help your understanding of this section.

> I am personally responsible for the way I feel, think and act in my relationships. I can always make choices as to how I behave. Though other people and my circumstances may be difficult, nobody can remove the necessity for choice from me. Consequently I need to develop my skills of being a good chooser in my relationships.

> The way I learned my relationship skills in the past may have diminished my effectiveness as a chooser. Nevertheless, for the sake of my own happiness and fulfilment in the present and future, I am responsible for developing my capacity for effective choosing. I have a lot to gain from working hard to develop good relationship skills.

Exercises 3.1 and 3.2 are designed to get you further exploring the idea of personal responsibility for relationship skills. Exercise 3.1 is more focused on analysing how others behave while Exercise 3.2 gets you looking at your own behaviour.

---

**Exercise 3.1   Exploring personal responsibility for relationship skills in others' lives**

This exercise may be done on your own, in pairs or as part of a training group.

A   *On your own*
   For each of the following excerpts write down
   1.   the specific ways in which the main character or characters are behaving ineffectively

2. whether or not you consider they have a *choice* in regard to behaving differently

3. what relationship skills they require to behave more effectively

*Excerpts*

(a) Rob is a 17 year old who is shy with girls. He never makes the first move, but expects a girl to demonstrate clearly her interest in him before he would consider asking her out.

(b) Tina is a 15 year old who says of herself 'I am very bad-tempered'. She is moody and sulky much of the time and has frequent rows with her parents and others with whom she comes in contact.

(c) Beryl and David have two sons, Tom aged 16 and Geoff aged 13. Both parents have strict ideas about how they want their sons to grow up. When either Tom or Geoff verbally challenges one of their cherished standards Beryl's way of handling it is to withdraw affection by 'freezing' while David tends to get angry and sometimes loses his temper. When, in turn, the boys withdraw either physically or emotionally from their parents, they are told how ungrateful they are since they are lucky to have such a good home.

(d) Joan, aged 36, is a married woman with two children aged 13 and 15. She has always tried to live up to her ideal of the good wife and mother who puts other people's needs before her own. She is nurturing, affectionate and has a Hoover-like ability to go around sweeping up after other people's untidiness. However, recently Joan has started to wonder whether she is allowing too many of the household chores to come her way. Also, whether she should start sharing more of her own opinions rather than mainly encouraging others to express theirs.

(e) John has been having a steady relationship with Diana for the past twelve months. They have had a lot of good times together, enjoy each other's company, and share many of the same interests. John has thought of asking Diana to marry him, but has not brought himself to do this yet. The major stumbling block seems to be that every now and then Diana spends some time with another male friend. To date, John has not been able to share his feelings and anxieties about this other relationship. Instead he thinks Diana should be able to see that she is creating a problem for him.

(f) Jim is a 44 year old factory manager who lives on his nerve-ends and exudes tension. He is a high energy and demanding perfectionist who is extremely hard on himself as well as on others. His work relationships are characterised by constant criticism of those around him for not living up to his expectations.

(g) Jane and Brian are both aged 17 and in their last year at school. Though they enjoy each other's company, they also have frequent arguments. Brian can be inconsiderate and aggressive, yet in the arguments he is skilled at defining himself as the victim and Jane as the aggressor. Brian, who is quick with words, always takes as his starting point what Jane is doing to him rather than exploring his own negative behaviours which contributed to Jane's reactions. Jane is getting increasingly depressed at the way things are going and blames herself much of the time.

B *In pairs*
*Either* each write out your responses to the above excerpts one at a time, then together discuss your responses before moving on to the next excerpt.
*Or* for each excerpt, listen to your partner as he/she verbally gives his/her responses, reverse roles then discuss before moving on to the next excerpt.

C *In a training group*
The trainer discusses the concept of personal responsibility for relationship skills and the importance of developing the skills of identifying choices that people can make. The trainer divides the group into pairs or other sub-groups and gets members to write down and/or discuss their responses to the questions. Alternatively the questions can be set as a homework assignment. The trainer then conducts a plenary session in which members share and discuss their responses. The trainer highlights the choices the characters in the excerpts are making to behave the way they do now and what other choices are available to them in these relationships.

---

**Exercise 3.2   Exploring personal responsibility for relationship skills in your own life**

This exercise can be done on your own, in pairs or as part of a training group.

A *On your own*
Take a relationship or a situation in a relationship in your life that is not going as well as you would like. Write down
1. the specific ways in which *you* may be behaving ineffectively
2. whether or not you consider that you have a *choice* in regard to behaving differently
3. the relationship skills *you* require to behave more effectively
4. what actions you intend taking to improve the relationship in future

B *In pairs*
*Either* write out your response to the above exercise, then discuss with your partner.
*Or* listen to your partner as he/she verbally gives his/her response, then give any feedback you consider appropriate, then reverse roles.

C *In a training group*
The trainer gives the group time either as singles or as pairs to explore taking responsibility for their skills in a relationship or situation in a relationship in their lives that is not going as well as they would like. The trainer then conducts a plenary sharing and discussion session and facilitates members' exploration of their *own* behaviour in their relationships. The trainer is sensitive to possible resistances on the part of members. His/her role is more to highlight the importance of personal responsibility in relationships rather than to attempt to alter anyone's behaviour. In short, the role of the trainer is to help members see their choices.

---

**Playing the percentages**

The following analogy may help further your understanding of what is meant by a personal responsibility approach to relationships. Imagine that you are a top sportsperson. You are about to compete in the final of a major tournament, be it in tennis, golf, soccer, baseball or some other sport of your choosing. You have much natural talent. However that is insufficient. You have been fortunate enough to have good coaches to point out your skills resources and deficits and to help you remedy them. Additionally, you have had to show commitment by practising long and hard to reach a really high standard. In the final of the tournament you are under considerable pressure both from your fears and anxieties as well as from your opponent's play. Thus you have to discipline your temperament as well as demonstrate your skills. Throughout the final you have a series of choices to make involving your feelings, thoughts and actions. If you make good choices you are more likely to win. If you make poor choices you are more likely to lose. In the last analysis no one else can make your choices or play your game for you. You are out there on your own.

Your approach to relationships should not be much different. Your success depends on your taking responsibility for identifying, learning, practising and implementing the required skills. You discipline your temperament and 'play the percentages' in how you behave in relationships to maximise your own and others' happiness and fulfilment. However, unlike in sports, no one has to be the loser. You can each be winners. However, also unlike in sports, you can each be losers. In the last analysis no one can make your choices or live your relationships for you. Like the top sportsperson, you are out there on your own.

## UNDERSTANDING YOUR FEELINGS

A two person relationship can be viewed as involving at least three relationships, each partner's relationship with himself or herself and the joint relationship. All three of these relationships involve feelings, thoughts and actions. Much of the emphasis in relationship skills is on how to relate to others. However here the focus is more on your relationship to yourself, especially to your feelings.

**What are feelings?**

Dictionary definitions of feelings tend to use words like 'physical sensation', 'emotions' and 'awareness'. All three of these words illustrate a dimension of feelings. Inasmuch as feelings are physical sensations they represent your underlying animal nature. People are animals first and persons second. As such you need to learn to value and live with your underlying biological nature. Also, to get it working for rather than against you. The word emotions implies movement. Feelings are processes. All people are subject to a continuous flow of biological experiencing. An important meaning of awareness is that you are capable of being conscious of your feelings. However, you may remain unaware of or deny some feelings like anger and sensuality. Furthermore you may have learned some unexamined standards with their related feelings from your parents. Thus what you may call your feelings could be based more on *their* standards rather than on *your own* valuing processes. Elsewhere the word *responsiveness* has been used to illustrate that acknowledging feelings entails the capacity to be in tune with and respond to your underlying animal nature.[5]

**Why are feelings important?**

There are many reasons why it is important for you to be responsive to the flow of your feelings when starting, maintaining and, if necessary, ending your relationships. These include:

● *Acknowledging liking and attraction.* Here liking is used as a less strong term than attraction. Whereas liking implies congeniality and pleasure in another's company, attraction has the connotation of sexual interest. In any event, whether it be either to initiate a friendship or a love affair, at least one of you has in the first instance to be responsive to your feelings about the other. Then if the relationship is to persist, it is desirable that both of you acknowledge your positive feelings for each other.

● *Spontaneity.* If you are in touch with your feelings you are free to respond in fresh and creative ways in your relationships. You can exhibit a range of emotions appropriate to the situations in which you find yourself. Relationships without spontaneity are like two tape-recorders playing back the same information to each other – in other words, dull and uninspiring.

● *Sensuality.* At one level sensuality means touch. Affectionate use of physical contact between family and friends can be affirming and need not have a sexual goal. However, sensuality can also involve sexuality. This entails the capacity to experience your own and relate to another's sexual feelings.

● *Rationality.* It may seem surprising to list rationality among a list of reasons why feelings are important. However, when you are truly in touch with what *you* feel about situations, you are less likely to be reacting to the prohibitions and inhibitions you have unthinkingly learned from others. This being responsive to your own valuing process can cut through much of the self-defeating thinking that makes for irrational feelings and behaviour.

● *Existential awareness.* Being fully in touch with your feelings entails acknowledging the reality of your finitude. This is likely to lend a sense of urgency to making the most of your relationships. Awareness of a sense of personal responsibility is a feeling helped rather than hindered by a realistic awareness of mortality. Ageing and dying are part of everyone's lives. To deny and repress feelings concerning them can impoverish your relationships both with yourself and others.

● *Finding meaning.* People are meaning seeking beings. Happiness and fulfilment entails finding meaning in life. The opposite of having meaning in your life is a feeling of meaninglessness.

Meaninglessness has connotations of emptiness, apathy, bore-dom, despair and nonbeing. Most people's main avenues for finding meaning in their lives are their relationships and the other activities, both work and leisure, with which they occupy their time. Your feelings provide a fundamental source of knowledge about the people and activities that have meaning for you. Furthermore, relationships in which you can find meaning in pursuing at least some significant activities together possess a valuable source of stability and cohesion.

● *Identity*. Relationships are most satisfactory when both of you have a secure sense of your own identity as separate individuals as well as of the identity you possess in relation to each other. Identity means that you are centred in your unique capacity for responding to life with your own feelings. You are secure in your sense of continuity and sameness. Nevertheless, you are capable of joining your identity with that of another to achieve cooperative goals, for instance a stable and committed relation-ship. Also, you can flexibly take into account the realities of emerging situations. People who think and feel 'I don't really know who I am' or 'I know who I am and I'm not going to change under any circumstances' both exhibit their underlying feelings of insecurity regarding their identity.

**Listening to your feelings**

For the reasons suggested above, one of the main skills entailed in relating to others is the capacity to relate well to yourself. Central to this inner relationship is the ability to be attuned sensitively to your own bodily reactions and feelings: in short, to be attuned to your animal self. This does not mean that you are being encouraged to express all your feelings. Later in the book there is a focus on some skills involved in regulating feelings. However, listening to your bodily reactions and feelings means that it is important to be aware of all significant ones. Though not wishing to go so far as the founder of gestalt therapy, Fritz Perls, in denying the role of your mind, there is nevertheless much truth in his aphorism 'Lose your mind and come to your senses'.[6] Perls was intensely aware of your need not to block your animal capacity for responsiveness with unnecessary intervening thoughts. Here we echo his focus on becoming aware of the flow of your bodily sensations. Now complete Exercise 3.3 which is designed to help you become aware of how you are grounded in your bodily feelings.

**Exercise 3.3   Listening to your body**

This exercise may be done on your own, in pairs or as part of a training group.

A  *On your own*
   1. Sit in a quiet place, close your eyes for about five minutes and try to tune into your bodily sensations. Focus on the flow of what your body is feeling rather than on what you are thinking. In other words focus on physical sensations.
   2. Sitting in a quiet place with your eyes closed, focus on the physical sensations in the following parts of your body for about a minute each
      your arms
      your head
      the trunk of your body
      your legs
   3. Sit in a quiet place with your eyes closed and for the next three to five minutes focus on the sensations of your breathing.
   4. Write down the bodily sensations attached to your experiencing the following emotions
      anger
      grief
      joy
      fear

B  *In pairs*
   Do the exercises described above on your own. After each one discuss your reactions with your partner.

C  *In a training group*
   The trainer discusses the ideas of how we are grounded in our bodies and the importance of listening to our feelings. The trainer then takes the group through the exercises described above, either stopping for a discussion after each one or else leaving the discussion until the end.

Listening to your feelings entails not just being aware of bodily sensations, but the capacity to identify and label your feelings accurately. For instance, Alan asks Lois out for a date and she politely but firmly refuses. There are a range of possible feelings that Alan might have. These include hurt, anger, humiliation, inferiority, anxiety, tension, relief, resolution, confidence, cheerfulness and optimism. Alan has some choice in which feelings he experiences depending on how he chooses to interpret Lois's refusal. For instance he could choose to think either 'It's the worst thing that has ever happened to me', or 'That's her problem, the stupid bitch', or 'She is perfectly entitled to her position, its unrealistic to expect to succeed all the time with women and I can try elsewhere'. The first choice may contribute to feelings of anxiety and depression, the second to anger and the third to confidence and to trying again elsewhere.

At this stage, all that you are being asked to do is to try and identify and label what you actually feel. In relating both to yourself and to others, it is useful if you build up a repertoire of words to describe and catch the nuances of your own and their feelings. Learning to become a good counsellor or psychotherapist involves building up a repertoire of feelings words so that you can help clients to feel accurately understood. In a sense you need to learn to become a good counsellor to yourself so that you can accurately understand your own feelings. This inner empathy, or being sensitively attuned to your feelings, is a relationship skill well worth developing.

Table 3.1 provides a list of words to help you identify and label feelings. There are undoubtedly many others, some of which you may consider are more appropriate for describing *your* feelings in

**Table 3.1**  *List of feelings words*

| | | | |
|---|---|---|---|
| accepted | dependent | involved | supported |
| adventurous | depressed | irresponsible | suspicious |
| affectionate | discontented | jealous | tense |
| aggressive | embarrassed | joyful | tired |
| ambitious | energetic | lonely | trusting |
| angry | envious | loved | unambitious |
| anxious | excitable | loving | unappreciated |
| apathetic | fit | optimistic | unassertive |
| appreciated | free | outgoing | unattractive |
| assertive | friendly | pessimistic | underconfident |
| attractive | frightened | powerful | uneasy |
| bored | grieving | powerless | unfit |
| carefree | guilt-free | rejected | unfree |
| cautious | guilty | relaxed | unfriendly |
| cheerful | happy | resentful | unloved |
| competitive | humiliated | responsible | unsupported |
| confident | hurt | sad | unwanted |
| confused | indecisive | secure | uptight |
| contented | independent | shy | vulnerable |
| cooperative | inferior | stressed | wanted |
| daring | insecure | strong | weak |
| decisive | interested | superior | worried |

particular situations. Your own feelings words may have more meaning and impact for you. Exercise 3.4 is designed to give you practice at listening to, identifying and labelling your feelings. In completing the exercise remember to focus on your *feelings*. For instance, if you answer that 'When someone ignores me I feel that they are rude', this is really focusing more on your thoughts than on your feelings. If you answer, 'When someone ignores me I feel angry', this is more focused on your feelings. The thinking contributing to your feelings may be your perception that they are rude and should not be so, but that is not the point of this particular exercise.

---

**Exercise 3.4   Identifying and labelling your feelings**

This exercise may be done on your own, in pairs or as part of a training group.

A   *On your own*
Complete the following sentences regarding your feelings in relationships. Focus on how you actually feel rather than on your thoughts about the other person. Complete each of the sentences below by writing down two alternative words or phrases that describe your feelings accurately.
1.   When someone ignores me I feel _____
2.   When someone cries I feel _____
3.   When someone praises me I feel _____
4.   When someone talks about themselves all the time I feel _____
5.   When someone gets mad at me I feel _____
6.   When someone attracts me I feel _____
7.   When someone really cares for me I feel _____
8.   When someone acts superior to me I feel _____
9.   When someone breaks a confidence I feel _____
10.   When someone is very late for an appointment I feel _____
11.   When I am in a group of strangers I feel _____
12.   When someone really listens to and understands me I feel ____
In which, if any, of the above situations do you have conflicting feelings?

B   *In pairs*
*Either* independently write out your answers to the above exercise, then you and your partner share and discuss.
*Or* go through each of the above sentences, be quiet for a moment while each of you listens to yourself and identifies and labels your feelings, then you and your partner discuss.

C *In a training group*
The trainer discusses the importance of listening to yourself and being able to identify and label your feelings. The exercise may be done either singly, in pairs or as a homework assignment. Then the trainer conducts a plenary sharing and discussion session. Alternatively, the trainer may take the whole group through the exercise one sentence at a time.

---

Another way of looking at your feelings is to explore those that are most characteristic of your current life. Note that the term 'most characteristic of you' was not used. This is to avoid implying that the kinds of feelings that currently predominate in your life are givens. For instance, at the moment, you may experience feelings of sadness, depression and pessimism. There could be many contributing factors to such feelings: for instance, your prior learning history, your current environment, the standards by which you judge your behaviour, the degree to which you fail to engage in rewarding activities, and whether you have learned an attitude of personal responsibility, to mention but some. However, this does not mean that sadness, depression and pessimism are inherently characteristic of you as a person. Hopefully, in time you will either have a more benign environment or develop the skills of making better choices in your life or both. Similarly those of you who list yourselves as happy and cheerful need to continue having the kinds of environments and/ or making the kinds of choices that are conducive to maintaining such feelings.

Exercise 3.5 asks you to describe the kinds of feelings that seem to predominate in your life at the moment. The way you answer this exercise will give you some insight into your picture or concept of yourself. List the feelings that you think are most important and that best describe the feelings dimension, as contrasted with the thinking and action dimensions, of your current existence. The exercise asks you to further explore whether your view of your main feelings, and hence very likely of yourself, is a positive or negative one. Thus it seeks to discover both what you feel about yourself and how you evaluate what you feel. Finally Exercise 3.5 gets you to draw together your positive and negative evaluations of your feelings into a statement about how confident you feel as a person. Your level of confidence can be critical in the success or failure of your relationships. For instance, if somebody criticises an underconfident person, this may generate anger or withdrawal or other negative emotions and actions. On the other hand, if somebody criticises a confident person he or she is less likely to feel threatened by it and more inclined, if necessary, to take a problem-solving approach to handling any valid criticism.

Some other points are relevant here. First, you may feel differently about yourself at different times with the same or different people. This may reflect partly the behaviour of the other or others, partly the changing process of any relationship, and possibly also that you have yet to achieve a reasonably stable sense of your own identity. Second, you may have conflicting or ambivalent feelings both about yourself and others. Third, how you see your predominant feelings may not be the same as the way others assess your feelings. For example, you may feel sad and yet they may perceive you as cheerful. This could be due to their lack of skills at reading feelings, but you may also not be communicating your feelings loud and clear. At this stage our interest is only in how you describe yourself in feelings terms. Later there is a focus on how accurately you send messages about yourself to others. If you have not done so already, now complete Exercise 3.5.

---

**Exercise 3.5   Describing yourself in feelings terms**

This exercise may be done on your own, in pairs, or as part of a training group.

A   *On your own*
Look at Table 3.1 and make a list of the ten feelings words that best describe you. You may include feelings words not listed in Table 3.1. Write 'positive' after those feelings you like in yourself and 'negative' after those feelings you dislike. Use the following format

*Feeling*                                          *Positive or negative*
I feel _____          _____

I feel _____          _____

Assess how confident you feel as a person.

B   *In pairs*
*Either* each write out your responses to the above exercise, then discuss with your partner.
*Or* listen to your partner as he/she verbally discusses the feelings that best describe him/her, including whether he/she views them positively or negatively, then reverse roles.

C  *In a training group*
   The trainer discusses the idea of how each of you may have similarities and differences in terms of your predominant feelings. The trainer divides the group into pairs and gets members to write down and/or discuss their responses to the questions. Alternatively the questions can be set as a homework assignment. The trainer then conducts a plenary session in which group members share and discuss their responses. The trainer also encourages members to assess their level of confidence.

---

In your relationships you are consistently required to listen to your own feelings. This does not mean that you ignore the other person's feelings. Being really sensitively attuned to your own feelings gives you an excellent basis for tuning into others' feelings. Listening to your feelings ideally means that these feelings are appropriate to the present or 'here-and-now' situation and not residues from your childhood or other relationships. This second sort of listening to feelings, namely transferring feelings derived from past situations and treating them 'as if' they are relevant to the present, indicates lack of full access to your own valuing process. Listening to past feelings in a present context lessens the relevant information available for you to meet your needs now. Indeed, the chances are that it contributes to your being too focused on your own needs and insufficiently focused on being able to understand the other person. Since you neither understand yourself nor them properly this is an excellent recipe for a poor relationship.

As you were reading the above paragraph you may have thought: 'What . . . me . . . it surely applies only to others that, often without knowing it, they drag their past feelings inappropriately into the present.' If so, the news for you is that it applies to you as well, if in varying degrees. One of the illusions that many of you may carry around is that you act rationally and autonomously most of the time without distracting interference from residues of childhood and other learning experiences. The purpose of a personal responsibility approach to relationship skills is to increase your degree of choice rather than to sustain your illusions.

One of the main barriers that impedes you using your feelings to best effect is the notion that other people *make* you feel this way or that. The clear implication of the use of the word 'make' is that you have no choice in how you feel in such instances, rather your feelings are determined and controlled by others. Though others may influence how you feel, nobody can *make* you feel anything. Earlier in this chapter it was stated that personal responsibility for relationship skills incorporates feelings, thoughts and actions. Also, that responsibility for feelings involves both the capacity to be in touch with your feelings and also to regulate them where appropriate.

Exercise 3.6 is designed to give you some time and psychological space to listen to your feelings concerning a current relationship. Frankly, an exercise like this can only go so far. Most of us are like onions with layer upon layer of psychological skins that may need peeling off as we delve deeper into our true feelings. Often such listening and exploration is best done with the facilitation or 'making it easier' of a skilled other. Consequently, for some of you, Exercise 3.6 may only offer a glimpse toward a deeper understanding of your feelings in a relationship. Also, you may gain some insight into whether and how you consider the other person is *making* you feel the way you do.

---

**Exercise 3.6   Listening to your feelings in a relationship**

This exercise can be done on your own, in pairs or as part of a training group.

A   *On your own*
   1.   Take a significant relationship in your life, for instance with a close friend, parent or a partner. Sit down in a quiet place, close your eyes and for about five minutes listen to and explore your feelings in the relationship – about yourself, about the other person and about the relationship. Afterwards write down your main feelings.
   2.   To what degree have you felt able to share the above feelings with the other person?
B   *In pairs*
   *Either* each answer the above questions separately, then discuss with a partner.
   *Or* listen to your partner as he/she verbally explores his/her feelings in a relationship, then reverse roles.
C   *In a training group*
   The trainer introduces the topic of the importance of being able to listen to your own feelings in relationships. The trainer divides the group into pairs and gets members to write down and/or discuss their responses to the questions. Alternatively the questions can be

set as a homework assignment. The trainer then conducts a plenary session in which group members share and discuss their responses to the extent that they feel able at this stage.

---

## CONCLUDING INNER SPEECH

Below is some sample inner speech or self-talk that summarises some of the main teachings of the latter part of this chapter.

> I am a human animal. As such I need to develop my skills of listening to and understanding my physical sensations and feelings. I will have more vitality and more choice as to how I behave if I do this. Also, I will develop a more secure sense of my identity. It is important that I identify and label my feelings accurately. Also, that in my relationships, I respond with fresh feelings relevant to present or 'here-and-now' situations rather than with old feelings from my past.

> Being accurately in touch with my own feelings forms the basis for being able to listen to others' feelings in relationships. Also, it is a vital part of my assuming personal responsibility for my feelings rather than having them derived from people in past relationships or 'made' or determined by people in current relationships. Listening to my own feelings is not always easy. I may have to work really hard at getting access to my deeper feelings.

## REFERENCES

1. Nelson-Jones, R. (1984) *Personal Responsibility Counselling and Therapy*. London and Sydney: Harper & Row.
2. Maslow, A.H. (1971) *The Farther Reaches of Human Nature*. Harmondsworth: Penguin Books.
3. Frankl, V.E. (1969) *The Doctor and the Soul*. Harmondsworth: Penguin Books.
4. Frankl, V.E. (1959) *Man's Search for Meaning*. New York: Pocket Books.
5. Nelson-Jones, R. (1984) *Personal Responsibility Counselling and Therapy*. London and Sydney: Harper & Row.
6. Perls, F.S. (1973) *The Gestalt Approach and Eyewitness to Therapy*. New York: Bantam Books.

# 4 Talking About Yourself

The next three chapters focus more on sender than on receiver skills in relationships. Though the chapter is called 'Talking about yourself', an important assumption of both chapter and book is that your 'self' is not something which is fixed and only needs to be uncovered. Rather your 'self' is a process which it is your personal responsibility to create and define so that you can best meet your needs in relationships. Thus not only do you *have* a self in your relationships but you *make* a self as well.

Talking about yourself is best achieved in the context of a democratic relationship. Not only will you be talking about and sharing yourself, but the people with whom you relate have equal opportunity to do likewise. Here talking about yourself is not being dominating, overwhelming or boring. Rather it represents the gift of sharing yourself as a person and enabling others to do the same. The following is a more poetic statement of the kind of relationship being advocated in this book, be it in friendship, marriage, family, work or leisure. Though the request is being made of another, you too have the potential to use your relationship skills to provide the quality of human contact that is being sought.

> Don't walk ahead of me
> I may not follow
> Don't walk behind me
> I may not lead
> Just walk beside me
> And be my friend[1]

## REASONS FOR TALKING ABOUT YOURSELF

Though obviously it can be overdone, there are many positive reasons for talking about yourself in your relationships. Psychologists refer to this as self-disclosure. A leading advocate of self-disclosure in relationships was the late Sydney Jourard. In his book *The Transparent Self* he paraphrased the 'Know Thyself' advice of the

Delphic Oracle by stating 'Make Thyself Known, and then Thou Wilt Know Thyself.'[2]

In this chapter, talking about yourself and self-disclosing, tends to be viewed in three ways, albeit overlapping. First, that of revealing personal information, often related to your previous life. Second, that of expressing feelings. This may have much more of a 'here-and-now' quality about it than disclosing personal information, though often disclosure of intimate personal information can be accompanied by considerable expression of feeling. Third, that of self-definition in which your disclosures are not only revealing an existing self, but may also be making or creating a new self.

Below are some reasons why developing good skills at talking about yourself is a vital part of relating effectively to others.

● *Defining yourself.* The way you talk about yourself is a fundamental way in which you create and define, for yourself and others, the sort of person you choose to be. You may fail to realise the choices you have in how you can create yourself, which means that you live less fully than you might. Furthermore, if you do not define yourself to others, they may define you anyway in ways that meet their own rather than your needs.

● *Knowing yourself.* It can be very hard to know what you really think and feel if you keep it bottled up. Talking about yourself contains elements of exploration in which, by verbalising thoughts and feelings, you identify those which may be most appropriate for you. For instance, counselling and psychotherapy is sometimes known as the 'talking cure'. There, in talking about themselves, clients obtain deeper insights and understandings about the kinds of people they are. Relationships are also processes of self-discovery whereby in talking about yourselves, you may not only communicate to others but acquire greater insight about yourselves.

● *Making contact.* Talking about yourself, and letting others talk about themselves, is essential in starting relationships. If, for example, you were to keep letting others talk about themselves, not only might you become very bored but they also might become very bored with you. A reason for this is that you have not been matching or reciprocating their disclosures. Consequently, you may be seen as not sharing anything of yourself, thus creating an imbalance in your relationship. Additionally, you have not given them information with which to develop links with you.

- *Developing intimacy.* In Chapter 1 intimacy was defined as sharing and being attuned to each other's thoughts and feelings, including those likely to be threatening to reveal in other contexts. A sharing of yourself is at the heart of intimacy.[3] Often this is likely to entail risk. You may be rejected or misunderstood as you embark on a deeper or more expressive level of disclosure. However, talking about yourself can have many positive consequences for the relationship. For instance, trust may be enhanced, misunderstandings may be cleared up, and the other may in turn find openness easier. In short, greater honesty in the relationship means that you are more able to encounter to each other as you are as contrasted with relating to incomplete personifications of each other.

- *Asserting yourself.* There will be instances in your relationships and in everyday life in which you have to stand up for yourself, say what you want, think or feel, and possibly set limits on others' behaviour. This may involve the courage to talk about yourself in adverse circumstances. Asserting yourself is a form of defining yourself to others, including the limits you may wish to place either on their or on your own behaviour.

- *Listening to others.* The more you develop your skills in talking about yourself, the more likely it is that you will improve your listening skills. You will have more energy and attention to focus on others if you are relaxed about revealing yourself. Constant preoccupation with what you are going to say and with others' reactions acts as a barrier to good listening. Also, the more you are able to disclose and express yourself, the easier it is for others to disclose and express themselves. Consequently, by talking about yourself you may be creating an emotional climate in which you can be a good listener.

## BARRIERS TO TALKING ABOUT YOURSELF

There are many reasons why you may find it difficult to talk about yourself in a relationship. Some reasons may have to do with your environment: for example, difficulty finding a suitable place to talk without noise and interference. You are more likely to talk about yourself if other people reward your talking about yourself behaviour than if they do not. If they either do not have the time or are too preoccupied with their own stresses and fatigue, they are less likely to listen to you. Also, if they are emotionally involved in a situation with you, you may find the strength of their feelings interfering with their listening. Furthermore, there are numerous ways in which people 'put-down' others when they talk about themselves and thus contribute to their feeling that it is unsafe to do so. Later in the book we review possible barriers to your being a good listener. The same barriers are relevant to people who do not listen to you properly.

Another set of barriers to talking about yourself resides in you rather than in the listening skills deficits of others. Shyness is an everyday term used to describe those of you who have difficulty in talking about yourselves.[4] Other words and phrases that describe shyness are 'timid', 'bashful' and 'uneasy in company'. Here we are concerned with whether there are times when you feel shy and how it affects your behaviour. Exercise 4.1 encourages you to look at how shy you are. The exercise explores shyness in relation to the following components:

● your own assessment of your shyness;
● whether and how you consider any shyness you possess to be a problem;
● your feelings and physical reactions related to shyness;
● thoughts about yourself and others related to shyness;
● how you actually behave when you feel shy;
● and people and situations associated with your feelings of shyness.

Later on in the chapter there is a focus on specific areas of personal information that you may have difficulty revealing. Difficulty disclosing specific personal information in appropriate circumstances represents another facet of shyness.

---

**Exercise 4.1   How shy are you?**

This exercise is designed to explore how difficult you find it to talk about yourself with other people. The exercise may be done on your own, in pairs or as part of a training group

A   *On your own*
Complete the following questionnaire.
1.   Do you consider yourself to be a shy person? Using the rating scale below, circle the number that best applies to you.

0   Not at all shy
1   Slightly shy
2   Moderately shy
3   Very shy
4   Extremely shy

Those giving a 0 rating are encouraged to complete the questionnaire, partly to check out the validity of their rating and partly to understand others better.

2. Do you consider that shyness is a problem for you? Please tick your answer. Yes _____ No _____ Maybe _____ If you have ticked Yes or Maybe please give reasons why shyness is/may be a problem for you. _____
_____
_____
_____

3. What are some of the other *feelings* that go to make up your feeling of shyness? Place a tick by those of the following feelings that apply to you.

| | | | |
|---|---|---|---|
| angry | _____ | lonely | _____ |
| anxious | _____ | powerless | _____ |
| confused | _____ | stressed | _____ |
| depressed | _____ | tense | _____ |
| embarrassed | _____ | uneasy | _____ |
| frightened | _____ | uptight | _____ |
| humiliated | _____ | vulnerable | _____ |
| insecure | _____ | weak | _____ |

List any other feelings here. _____
_____

4. What *physical reactions* do you get when you feel shy? Place a tick by those of the following physical reactions that apply to you.

| | | | |
|---|---|---|---|
| blushing | _____ | feeling faint | _____ |
| nausea | _____ | perspiring | _____ |
| pounding heart | _____ | knotted stomach | _____ |
| shallow breathing | _____ | shaking | _____ |
| mind going blank | _____ | mouth going dry | _____ |
| stammering | _____ | | |

Others (please specify) _____
_____

5. What *thoughts* are associated with any feelings of shyness that you may have? Place a tick by those of the following thoughts that apply to you.

*Thoughts about yourself*

| | |
|---|---|
| It is O.K. to be shy | _____ |
| I am a solitary person | _____ |
| I am uninteresting | _____ |
| I am weak | _____ |
| I lack self-confidence | _____ |

I am not as good as others     _____
I might get hurt or rejected     _____
I lack social skills     _____
Others (please specify) _____

---

*Thoughts about others' thoughts*
Others accept my shyness     _____
Others notice my physical symptoms     _____
Others may reject me     _____
Others may think I'm incompetent     _____
Others may consider me uninteresting     _____
Others are very aware of my behaviour     _____
Others are shy too and understand     _____
Others get uncomfortable with me     _____
Others (please specify) _____

---

6. What *behaviours* are associated with any feelings of shyness that you may have? Place a tick by those of the following behaviours that apply to you.

Avoiding situations associated with shyness     _____
Avoiding people associated with shyness     _____
Keeping silent     _____
Talking as little as possible     _____
Disclosing very little about myself     _____
Averting my gaze     _____
Smiling a lot     _____
Tight body posture     _____
Being too ready to agree with others     _____
Speaking quietly     _____
Escaping from the situation     _____
Others (please specify) _____

---

7. What *people* are associated with any feelings of shyness that you may have? Please tick those people relevant to your shyness.

| | | | |
|---|---|---|---|
| Mother | _____ | Same sex | _____ |
| Father | _____ | Opposite sex | _____ |
| Aunts | _____ | Children | _____ |
| Uncles | _____ | Friends | _____ |
| Grandparents | _____ | Neighbours | _____ |
| Boyfriend/ | | Authorities by virtue | |
| Girlfriend | _____ | of knowledge | _____ |
| Marital partner | _____ | Authorities by virtue | |
| | | of role | _____ |

| | | | |
|---|---|---|---|
| Unmarried partner | ———— | People of higher status | ———— |
| Strangers | ———— | People of lower status | ———— |
| Mother-in-law | ———— | Father-in-law | ———— |

8. What *situations* are associated with any feelings of shyness you may have? Please tick those situations relevant to your shyness.

| | |
|---|---|
| Meeting people for the first time | ———— |
| Asking someone out for a date | ———— |
| Giving a talk in front of a group of people | ———— |
| Participating in a discussion group | ———— |
| Asking for help (e.g. when ill) | ———— |
| Going to a party | ———— |
| Situations requiring assertiveness (e.g. returning a record to a shop) | ———— |
| Situations involving evaluation (e.g. an interview) | ———— |
| Having a conversation with a person of the opposite sex | ———— |
| Having a conversation with a person of the same sex | ———— |
| Going to a dance/disco | ———— |
| Showing your body in a non-sexual context (e.g. swimming) | ———— |
| Touching and being touched (outside your family) | ———— |
| Situations involving sexual intimacy | ———— |
| Others (please specify) ————————————— | |

B   *In pairs*
Independently answer the above questionnaire, then share and discuss with your partner.

C   *In a training group*
The trainer introduces the concept of shyness, possibly including illustrations from his or her own life. Trainees then answer the questionnaire either in the training group or as homework. They may next be encouraged to discuss their answers in pairs. Then the trainer conducts a plenary sharing and discussion session in which trainees' rights to privacy (shyness!?!) are respected.

## SENDING MESSAGES WITH YOUR VOICE AND BODY

Talking about yourself is not just a matter of *what* you say but *how* you say it. Similarly good listening to others means not just hearing their words but also being sensitive to their vocal and bodily messages. Often *how* you communicate is much more revealing than *what* you communicate which may be more concealing than revealing. For instance, Ian may be saying that 'Everything is all right', but at the same time look very unhappy, talk with a choked voice, and fight back the tears. Cindy may say 'I am not afraid', but laugh and smile nervously, move around in an agitated way, and breathe shallowly and rapidly. In these instances how Ian and Cindy *are* speaks much more loudly than what they *say*.

When talking about yourself, your communications consist of verbal messages and vocal and bodily 'framing messages' which may or may not match the verbal messages. As you have grown up you may have learned to mask many of your feelings by choosing not to express them with either your words, or your voice or your body. Sometimes, however, you may be deceiving yourself more than others since the meaning of your words points in one direction and your vocal and bodily messages point in another. Professional actors and actresses consciously try to suspend your disbelief by controlling the verbal, vocal and bodily messages of the characters they are playing. Much of the skill of people like Jane Fonda and Dustin Hoffman lies in their mastery of vocal and bodily signals.

**Table 4.1** *Some dimensions of vocal communication*

| Dimensions | Illustrative characteristics |
|---|---|
| Volume | Loudness, quietness, audibility |
| Pace | Fast, slow, ease of following |
| Stress | Monotonous, melodramatic |
| Pitch | High pitched, low pitched, shrill, deep |
| Enunciation | Clear, mumbled, slurred |
| Intensity | Very intense, light-hearted |
| Accent | National, regional, social class variations |
| Speech disturbances | Stammering, repetition |

Table 4.1 illustrates some dimensions of vocal communication. These dimensions provide a commentary on each utterance you make. Much emotional content is conveyed by vocal characteristics. For example, you can say 'I love you' either in a flat and monotonous voice or in a clear voice, with intensity, and with an emphasis on the love and the you. In the earlier example Ian was talking with a choked voice at the same time as saying 'Everything is all right', thus suggesting that everything was not all right.

**Exercise 4.2   Talking with your voice**

This exercise can be performed in a number of different ways.

A   *On your own*
1. Write out an assessment of your vocal communication on each of the dimensions listed in Table 4.1.
2. Specify goals for yourself involving changing your vocal communication to make yourself a better communicator.
3. Practise changing your vocal communication in real life to attain your goals.

B   *In pairs*
1. Speaking as close to your usual manner as possible, hold a conversation with your partner for 3 to 5 minutes. It may help to audio-record the conversation. At the end of this period, on each of the dimensions listed in Table 4.1, give feedback to each other and discuss. Both of you may wish to illustrate your feedback with examples from the recording.
2. Both you and your partner work together to specify goals for each of you involving changing your vocal communication to make yourselves better communicators.
3. Try to improve your vocal communication by practising in your deficit areas with each other.
4. Practise changing your vocal communication in real life to attain your goals.

C   *In a training group*
One option is to break the group down into pairs and perform the exercise as in B above, then come back together at the end for a plenary sharing and discussion session. Another option, especially if trainees have had some prior contact, is to get one person to assess his or her vocal communication in the Table 4.1 dimensions, then to get the other trainees to provide feedback on how they see that person's vocal communication. Each trainee should have the opportunity to be the focus of attention. The trainer then encourages both the setting of goals for improving vocal communication and also the practice of skills inside and outside the group.

Table 4.2 illustrates some dimensions of bodily communication. People in relationships continuously attribute thoughts and feelings to each other on the basis of vocal and bodily communication. Consequently, you need to learn to make good vocal and bodily choices as well as to avoid making poor ones. For example, the extent to which your vocal and bodily communication matches your words is

**Table 4.2**  *Some dimensions of bodily communication*

| Dimension | Illustrative characteristics |
|---|---|
| Eye contact | Staring, looking down or away, signalling interest |
| Facial expression | Expressive of thoughts and feelings, vacant, smiling, hostile |
| Hair | Length, styling |
| Gesture | Amount, variety, e.g. arm movements |
| Grooming | Neat, unkempt, tidy, untidy, clean, dirty |
| Smell | Body odour present, deodorised, fragrant, pungent |
| Touch | Part of social ritual, illustrating companionship, sensuality, aggression |
| Physique | Thinness, fatness, muscularity |
| Physical distance | Near, far, ability to touch |
| Trunk lean | Forwards, backwards |
| Trunk orientation | Facing, turned away |
| Posture | Upright, slouched |
| Degree of tension | Tightness, relaxation |
| Fiddling | Fiddling with hair, fingers etc. |
| Perspiration | Sweating, absence of sweating |
| Breathing | Regular, shallow and rapid |
| Blushing | Presence or absence, location of blushes |

highly relevant to how *genuine* you are perceived to be by others. If you give out mixed signals they may not be sure which is the real you. Furthermore, if the messages you send with your voice and body do not match your words, you leave your listener with the task of unravelling what you mean, thus increasing the likelihood of being misunderstood. An analogy is that of communicating in code. Your listener is then left with the task of decoding your meaning. Indeed the fact that your vocal and bodily communication does not match your words may indicate that you too are confused.

**Exercise 4.3   Talking with your body**

This exercise can be performed in a number of ways.

A  *On your own*
   1. Write out an assessment of your bodily communication on each of the dimensions listed in Table 4.2.
   2. Where appropriate, specify goals for yourself involving changing your bodily communication to make yourself a better communicator.
   3. Practise changing your bodily communication in real life to attain your goals.

B *In pairs*
   1. Seated, hold a conversation with your partner for from 3 to 5 minutes. It may help to video-record the conversation. At the end of this period, on each of the dimensions listed in Table 4.2 give feedback to each other and discuss. Both of you may wish to use the video-recording to illustrate feedback.
   2. Both you and your partner work together to specify goals for each of you involving changing your bodily communication to make yourselves better communicators.
   3. Try to improve your bodily communication by practising in your deficit areas with each other.
   4. Practise changing your bodily communication in real life to attain your goals.
C *In a training group*
   One option is to break the group down into pairs and perform the exercise as in B above, then come back together at the end for a plenary sharing and discussion session. Another option, especially if trainees have had some prior contact, is to let one person assess the messages his or her body sends on some of the Table 4.2 dimensions (for example eye contact, facial expression, degree of tension), then to get the other trainees to provide feedback on how they see that person's bodily communication. Each trainee should have the opportunity to be the focus of attention. The trainer then encourages both the setting of goals for improving bodily communication and also practice in the group and homework outside it.

---

## DISCLOSING YOURSELF

Whereas the previous section emphasised vocal and bodily communication, this section focuses more on the use of words in disclosing and sending messages about yourself. It covers talking for yourself, disclosing personal information, expressing feelings and defining yourself in a relationship.

### Making 'I' statements

In a chapter entitled 'How to talk so kids will listen to you' in his book *Parent Effectiveness Training*, American psychologist Thomas Gordon makes a useful distinction between 'You-messages' and 'I-messages'.[5] 'You-messages' focus on the other person: for example '*You* stop that' or '*You* shouldn't do that'. 'I-messages' are centred in the sender rather than the receiver: for example, 'I cannot rest when someone is crawling on my lap' or 'I don't feel like playing when I am tired'. In 'I messages', senders clearly *own* their messages and talk for themselves.

You communicate more openly and honestly in relationships if you speak for yourself. A clear way of speaking for yourself is to make statements starting with the word 'I' when you choose to disclose your feelings, thoughts and actions. This can have a number of advantages. First, you are more likely to be acknowledging that 'I' and 'You' are separate people and that what I think or feel about you is my perception and not necessarily what you are. Second, you are prepared to take responsibility for your own feelings, thoughts and actions. Third, 'I' statements tend to engender less defensiveness than 'You' statements with their connotations of blame.

There are a number of ways in which you may avoid making 'I' statements. For instance, you may make statements starting with words like 'You', 'People', 'We', 'That', 'There' and 'It'. Also, sometimes you may dilute making an 'I' statement by asking a question and hoping that the answer expresses what you wish to express. Talking about yourself entails talking *for* yourself.

Exercise 4.4 is designed to increase your awareness and skills in talking for yourself. Both the pairs and training group parts of the exercise include the use of a ball to highlight the point of the exercise. Many of you learn better if the exercises are made entertaining. There is much to be said for incorporating play or games, at appropriate times, into relationship skills training. Learning the skills can be fun too.

---

**Exercise 4.4   Talking for yourself: making 'I' statements**

This exercise can be done on your own, in pairs or as part of a training group.

The exercise encourages you to assume responsibility for your feelings, thoughts and actions through 'owning' them by using 'I' statements.

*Examples*
● Owning a feeling:
  Ron and Karen are having a row.
  Ron's non-'I' statement: 'You are the end.'
  Ron's 'I' statement: 'I feel hurt and angry.'

- Owning a thought:
  Betty and Steve go to a play which Betty enjoyed.
  Betty's non-'I' statement: 'What did you think about the play?'
  Betty's 'I' statement: 'I thought the play was excellent.'
- Owning an action:
  Julie has dropped a plate when her mother arrives.
  Julie's non-'I' statement: 'It just broke.'
  Julie's 'I' statement: 'Mum, I've just broken a plate. I'm sorry.'

A  *On your own*
  1. Change each of the following non-'I' statements into 'I' statemens. Write out your answers.
     (a) 'Would you like the salt?
     (b) 'People round here are getting fed up with you.'
     (c) 'You made me drive too quickly.'
     (d) 'You shouldn't play your stereo so loud.'
     (e) 'Brown-eyed people are more attractive than blue-eyed people.'
     (f) 'There is going to be some celebrating round here tonight.'
     (g) 'That is a tall story.'
     (h) 'Go to hell.'
     (i) 'Your father/mother does not like your new girlfriend/ boyfriend.'
     (j) 'Would you like to buy that painting?'
     (k) 'They made me tell a lie.'
     (l) 'We don't seem to want to participate in this group.'
     (m) 'A lot of people find you attractive.'
     (n) 'It just happened that my girlfriend is pregnant.'
  2. To what extent do you find it difficult to talk for yourself?
  3. In what specific ways do you avoid talking for yourself?

B  *In pairs*
  *Either* each of you independently write out your 'I' statements for each of the above non-'I' statements, then discuss.
  *Or* get hold of a ball (for example, tennis, football or beach). Partner A throws the ball to Partner B and answers the first statement above by saying either 'I would like the salt' or 'Pass me the salt please'. Partner A talks direct to Partner B as he/she does this. Partner B repeats this procedure with the next statement and so on.

C  *In a training group*
  The trainer discusses the importance of owning your thoughts, feelings and actions. Trainees may answer the questions either singly, in pairs, with or without the ball variation, or as a homework exercise. The trainer then conducts a plenary sharing and discussion session. Alternatively, the exercise can be conducted throughout on a whole group basis. The trainer explains that the person with the ball must throw it to someone and then make an 'I'

statement direct to them. Afterwards the person holding the ball throws it to someone else and makes an 'I' statement direct to them and so on. The 'I' statements can entail changing the non-'I' statements given above into 'I' statements. Otherwise group members can provide their own 'I' statements.

---

**Revealing personal information**

Revealing information about yourself can be intentional or unintentional. Here the assumption is that you have a choice about what personal information to reveal and how and when to do so. There are both risks and gains to revealing personal information about yourself, albeit sometimes more imagined than real. The risks include: being rejected; being misunderstood; lack of confidentiality; having your disclosures used against you; disclosing too much too soon; and being unable to handle the consequences of your disclosures. However, there are considerable gains to revealing personal information. These include: lessened loneliness and alienation; greater self-acceptance; greater self-knowledge; increased possibilities for friendship and intimacy; defining yourself rather than being defined by default; standing up for yourself; and greater control over your life.

There are a number of considerations relating to the *appropriateness* of revealing personal information and, indeed, of any form of disclosing and expressing yourself. One obvious criterion is whether revealing the personal information helps you attain your goals in a relationship. Another related criterion is whether your disclosure is suitable for a particular occasion or social context in which you find yourself. Below are some *dimensions of appropriateness* that apply virtually any time you wish to talk about yourself.

- *Amount.* The quantity of information that you disclose.
- *Topic area.* The area or areas in which you talk about yourself.
- *Breadth.* The range of areas that you disclose.
- *Depth.* The degree of intimacy of your disclosures.
- *Timing.* When to make a disclosure in a relationship.
- *Target person.* The person or persons to whom you reveal personal information.
- *Situational context.* The occasion or social context in which you reveal information.

Virtually all of us find some areas of personal information more difficult to reveal than others. Indeed some categories of people, such as gay people, may not only find it difficult to disclose their sexual preference, but also they have to manage their own and others' reactions once they have disclosed their 'stigma'.[6] Even those of you who would not ordinarily consider yourselves shy are likely to have some areas of personal information that you regard as more private than others.

Exercises 4.5 and 4.6 are designed to make you more aware of some possible barriers in yourself toward revealing personal information. Though some of your barriers may represent conscious choices, others may be the result of learnings that have not been thoroughly examined by you. As such you may be failing to reveal personal information out of habit rather than having the freedom of choice to reveal what is appropriate in any situation in which you find yourself. Frequently, you may engage in only partial disclosure. This is a way of controlling your relationships with others by controlling the amount of information that they receive about you. You are not blatantly lying, but instead just telling partial truths or 'economising on the truth'.

---

**Exercise 4.5   Talking about yourself: disclosing personal information**

This is an exercise, best done on your own, about how threatening it would be for you to disclose and discuss personal information (a) on a one-to-one basis with a specific acquaintance or friend of your choosing and (b) with the members of your training group (if relevant).

Threat involves the degree to which you anticipate feeling uncomfortable and being thought less of as a result of discussing in some detail your thoughts and feelings about yourself in the areas below. Rate each area on the following scale and, if any area is not true for you, rate it as though it were to be true for you.

4   Impossible, much too threatening
3   Very threatening
2   Moderately threatening
1   Slightly threatening
0   Not threatening at all

| Personal information areas | Threat rating, if you were to disclose to: | |
| --- | --- | --- |
| | Friend/acquaintance | Training group (if relevant) |
| Positive thoughts/feelings about my parents | | |
| Negative thoughts/feelings about my parents | | |
| Positive thoughts/feelings about either spouse/partner or boyfriend/ girlfriend | | |
| Negative thoughts/feelings about either spouse/partner or boyfriend/ girlfriend | | |
| My feelings of loneliness | | |
| My feelings of inadequacy | | |
| My feelings of depression | | |
| Achievements in my work | | |
| Failures in my work | | |
| Achievements in my personal relations | | |
| Things I like about my body | | |
| Things I dislike about my body | | |
| How I use my leisure time | | |
| My feelings about death | | |
| My political preferences | | |
| My sexual behaviour | | |
| My religious beliefs | | |
| My thoughts/feelings about old people | | |
| My intellectual capacity | | |
| Times I have lied/cheated | | |
| My financial position | | |
| Things that make me happy | | |
| Things that make me angry | | |
| Things that make me afraid | | |
| People who have liked me | | |
| People who have disliked me | | |
| My childhood | | |
| My adolescence | | |
| My sexual preferences | | |
| My fundamental values | | |
| My overall opinion of myself | | |

Circle all ratings you have made that are 2, 3 or 4. Why do you consider that these items are threatening for you to disclose?

To what extent are you concealing or revealing this 'threatening' information in your current personal relationships?

In what ways, if any, would you like to change the amount to which and areas in which you currently conceal or reveal personal information?

## Exercise 4.6   Sharing your secrets

This is a group exercise. The trainer gives each group member a standard piece of paper and mentions that nobody is allowed to divulge that they have a specific secret. The trainer then asks group members to print a one-sentence statement about themselves that they would ordinarily consider to be too threatening for the group to know. Each piece of paper is then folded twice, collected by the trainer, and shuffled. The 'secrets' are then distributed so that nobody has his or her own secret. If anyone has, the secrets should be reshuffled. The trainer uses the following procedure. First, he or she gets a member to read out someone else's secret; second, that member is asked to say how he or she would feel and think if the secret were true of him or her; and third, the remaining group members are asked to disclose how they would feel and think if the secret were true of them. The procedure is repeated for each secret. The trainer encourages members' exploration of their reactions and ensures that no-one is ridiculed because of his or her secret. Additionally the trainer highlights people's responsibility for the choices they make regarding whether to reveal or conceal personal information.

## Expressing feelings

There are a number of skills attached to handling your feelings in relationships. The previous chapter covered listening to your feelings, identifying them and building up a repertoire of feelings words. Here the focus is on the actual sending of feelings messages to others. A later chapter emphasises learning how to regulate your feelings, especially anger, by regulating your thinking.

Expressing feelings involves letting what is going on inside you be released and revealed outside. Thus it involves the translation of your inner sensations into outer expressions. Sometimes, however, the translation process is virtually immediate, like your startle reaction to a loud noise. On other occasions expressing your feelings is less reflex and can involve conscious choice as to whether and how you reveal them. It is always important to acknowledge and to be attuned to the inner flow of your feelings. However, there are instances where it is either inappropriate to express your feelings or you need beware about expressing them in the wrong way.

In the previous chapter some reasons were given of why it is important to be responsive to your feelings in relationships. Below are some reasons why it can be important to *express* your feelings.

● *Knowing what you feel.* It is often hard to know what you feel until you express your feelings. Also, expression of feelings is often a process in which, after some feelings are expressed, others emerge.

● *Catharsis.* You may need to purge yourself of certain feelings by expressing them. For example, sometimes release of bottled up anger in a relationship can help you to express the more fundamental affection underlying your anger. In any event, continuously bottling up your feelings can be very bad for your health. Your suppressed feelings may contribute to bodily symptoms as ulcers and heart attacks.

● *Letting others know what you feel.* Sharing what you feel with others can be pleasurable and enjoyable. It gives them a chance both to react to your feelings and also to share theirs. Furthermore, they do not have to mindread you to know what you feel, with all the attendant possibilities for misunderstanding. Constructive expression of feelings in a relationship can both let others know your wants and wishes as well as be an important part of the assessment and management of problems and conflicts.

● *Affirming the other person.* By being real and genuine in a relationship you not only affirm yourself but you affirm the worth of the other person as well. They can be trusted with your greatest gift, namely the giving of yourself in a sharing relationship. Not expressing or inappropriately expressing your feelings can diminish yourself, the other person and the relationship.

Apart from those instances where they are reflex reactions, you are responsible for how you express your feelings. Perhaps the first step here is to be able to identify and 'own' your feelings. Then you have numerous choices about how you can express them. Sometimes this may involve inhibiting the way you currently express feelings. For example, Sergio and Tricia each need to learn to become more *flexible* in the way they express their feelings. Sergio's difficulty is that he is impulsive. Instead of getting in touch with what he really feels, he has a 'knee-jerk' reaction in which he blurts out the first thing that comes to his mind. Tricia's difficulty is that she finds it very easy to express nurturance and affection, but very difficult to express assertion and anger. Thus she only communicates part of what she is feeling. The extent to which she expresses the range of her feelings has been affected by her gender conditioning.

Exercise 4.7 has been designed to help you become more aware of the extent to which you are a *chooser* regarding *how* you express your feelings. The exercise has been designed to increase your skills at making choices concerning your sending of verbal, vocal and bodily feelings messages. Ideally your expression of feelings should: (a) represent what you truly feel; (b) be genuine in terms of its vocal, bodily and verbal dimensions; (c) show a sensitive awareness of its likely impact on the receiver; (d) be appropriate to what you are trying to express; and (e) be appropriate to its social context. Having provided this idealised set of criteria, it should be pointed out that no-one is perfect. In expressing feelings, frequently just having a good try is more than adequate. Some answers to Exercise 4.7 are suggested at the end of the chapter.

---

**Exercise 4.7   Talking about yourself: expressing feelings**

This exercise can be done on your own, in pairs or as part of a training group.

The purpose of the exercise is to help you explore the words, phrases, and vocal and bodily communication with which you can express your feelings. The means by which you express feelings differs according to their intensity.

*Example*

Louise is feeling *sad*.

*Words* she might use include: 'I feel sad, low, unhappy, depressed.'

*Phrases* she might use include: 'I feel under a cloud', 'I've got the blues', 'I feel that life's on top of me'.

Her *vocal communication* might include: sighing, speaking slowly, having a monotonous tone, speaking quietly.

Her *bodily communication* might include: unsmiling face with corners of mouth turned down, crying, blowing her nose and rubbing her eyes, averting her gaze, slouched body posture.

A   *On your own*

    1.   For each of the following feelings, write down:

        (a)   words

        (b)   phrases

(c)  vocal communication and
(d)  bodily communication
which *you* use or could use to express the feeling in *your* relationships.

1.  *Affection*
    Words:
    Phrases:
    Vocal communication:
    Bodily communication:
2.  *Fear*
    Words:
    Phrases:
    Vocal communication:
    Bodily communication:
3.  *Happiness*
    Words:
    Phrases:
    Vocal communication:
    Bodily communication:
4.  *Anxiety*
    Words:
    Phrases:
    Vocal communication:
    Bodily communication:
5.  *Anger*
    Words:
    Phrases:
    Vocal communication:
    Bodily communication:
6.  *Friendliness*
    Words:
    Phrases:
    Vocal communication:
    Bodily communication:
7.  *Assertion*
    Words:
    Phrases:
    Vocal communication:
    Bodily communication:
8.  *Trust*
    Words:
    Phrases:
    Vocal communication:
    Bodily communication:

2.  Which feelings, if any, do you have difficulty expressing in your relationships? What is the nature of the difficulty?

B *In pairs*
*Either* independently write out your answers to Section A above,
then discuss together.
*Or* work with your partner and formulate answers for each feeling,
then explore any difficulties each of you may have in expressing
feelings. Role-play better ways of expressing feelings.

C *In a training group*
The trainer introduces the concept of being genuine in expressing
feelings. Trainees can complete Section A either singly or in pairs,
either in the group or as a homework exercise. This is followed by a
plenary sharing and discussion session. The trainer may both
demonstrate and teach group members in ways of expressing
feelings they find difficult. This may involve role-playing expression
of feelings in relevant situations. Alternatively, the exercise can be
conducted on a whole group basis from the start.

---

**Defining yourself**

A key element of the personal responsibility approach to relationships is that through your choices you define yourself both for
yourself and for others. Thus you not only uncover and release your
potential to relate, but you *make* your relationships. The way you
define yourself through your disclosures is a vital part of your
contribution to making your relationships. Relationships are not only
for good or ill, even good ones can be improved.

Exercise 4.8 is intended as a consolidation exercise for this chapter.
The exercise is basically about change. It asks you to review the
adequacy of your current choices about how you are defining yourself
in a relationship. Are there the choices that are most beneficial to
you, the other person and the relationship? Hopefully, as a result of
your learnings from this chapter, you can identify some areas and
ways in which you could be defining yourself differently. Try some of
these out in real life. After all, the aim of practical relationship skills
training is to improve the quality of your day-to-day relationships.

---

**Exercise 4.8   Defining yourself in a relationship**

This exercise can be done on your own, in pairs or as part of a training
group.

A *On your own*
Take any relationship that is currently important to you, for

example, to a boyfriend or girlfriend, marital partner, parent or a close friend. Already you have made a number of choices about how you relate to that person. Now write down:

(a)  the personal information; and

(b)  the feelings;

that to date you have chosen to reveal and express in this relationship. Assess whether you would like to define yourself differently to that person – would you meet more of your needs, would you meet more of their needs, would you be more honest and authentic, would you improve the relationship? If you would like to define yourself differently to the other person:

1.  what additional personal information might you choose to reveal?
2.  how would you go about revealing this information?
3.  what additional or different feelings would you choose to express?
4.  how would you go about expressing these feelings?
5.  set yourself specific goals for changing how you define yourself in the relationship.
6.  if appropriate, draw up an action plan stating how and when you intend achieving your goals.

This exercise may be repeated for other relationships. Furthermore, you might wish to review and improve the ways in which you define and reveal yourself to people in general.

B  *In pairs*

*Either* independently write out your answers to the above exercise, then discuss.

*Or* Person A listens as Person B explores how he/she might define himself/herself differently in a relationship, then reverse roles. After this exploratory phase, Persons A and B work together to set goals for each other and to develop appropriate action plans.

C  *In a training group*

The trainer introduces the idea that people not only *have* selves, but also *make* their selves through their choices. Two important ways in which people make or define themselves in their relationships are through the personal information they reveal or conceal and through the feelings they express or fail to express. The trainer can get the group to do the exercise in Section A above either singly or in pairs, either in class or on a homework basis. The trainer then conducts a plenary sharing and discussion session. He/she is sensitive to trainee reticence about disclosure in front of the group. Where appropriate, the trainer may coach individual trainees in how to reveal and express more of themselves in their outside relationships. This may include working to alter trainees' thoughts about talking about themselves.

## CONCLUDING INNER SPEECH

Below is a sample of inner speech that summarises the main points in this chapter.

I have a choice about how I talk about myself in relationships. I do not just have a self but I can make and define a self to others. If I am shy I can identify and work to improve those areas in which I am shy.

Talking about myself means developing my skills in at least three areas. First, in disclosing personal information to another. Second, in expressing my feelings. Third, in defining the sort of person I want to be and communicating this to another. Each of these areas entails making choices concerning the verbal, vocal and bodily messages I send. Thus not only *what* but also *how* and *when* I disclose matters.

Having good skills at talking about myself is important in starting, developing and maintaining my relationships. It helps others to know me. It helps me to know myself. Also, it makes it easier to manage problems and difficulties that occur. Talking about myself is best achieved in democratic relationships in which there is a mutual commitment to openness, genuineness and sharing.

## REFERENCES

1. This quotation was hung on a bedroom wall in a house I once viewed. I do not remember seeing a source cited.
2. Jourard, S.M. (1964) *The Transparent Self*. Princeton: Van Nostrand.
3. Derlega, V.L. & Chaikin, A.L. (1975) *Sharing Intimacy: What We Reveal to Others and Why*. Englewood Cliffs, NJ: Prentice-Hall.
4. Zimbardo, P.G. (1977) *Shyness*. Reading, Massachusetts: Addison-Wesley.
5. Gordon, T. (1970) *Parent Effectiveness Training*. New York: Wyden.
6. Goffman, E. (1963) *Stigma: Notes on the Management of Spoiled Identity*. Harmondsworth: Penguin.

## ANSWERS TO EXERCISE

*Exercise 4.7*
The following are some suggestions. There are many variations in the way people show their emotions and, consequently, many possible answers.

1. *Affection*
   Words: fondness, tenderness, love, goodwill
   Phrases: 'I love you', 'You're the greatest', 'I adore you'
   Vocal communication: warm low voice, laughter, clear enunciation, relaxed pace
   Bodily communication: direct eye contact, physical closeness, arm round shoulder, kiss

2. *Fear*
   Words: fright, terror, apprehension, alarm
   Phrases: 'I'm scared stiff', 'I'm absolutely terrified', 'I'm frightened out of my wits'
   Vocal communication: quiet, mumbled, stammering, screaming
   Bodily communication; withdrawal, tense body posture, eyes wide open, running away

3. *Happiness*
   Words: contentment, pleasure, joy, well-being
   Phrases: 'I'm on cloud nine', 'I'm over the moon', 'I feel on top of the world'
   Vocal communication: relaxed, clear, light hearted, laughter
   Bodily communication: smiling, bright eyes, expressive gestures, relaxed posture, open trunk orientation

4. *Anxiety*
   Words: worry, uneasiness, concern, apprehension
   Phrases: 'I feel uneasy about the future', 'I'm full of apprehension', 'I feel tense all the time'
   Vocal communication: rapid speech, mumbling, lowered voice, stammering
   Bodily communication: blushing, sweaty palms, withdrawal, tense posture

5. *Anger*
   Words: hostility, rage, displeasure, resentment
   Phrases: 'I'm hopping mad', 'I'm absolutely furious', 'I could murder him/her'
   Vocal communication: loud, intense, shrill, harsh
   Bodily communication: clenched fists, strained face, blazing eyes, physical violence (e.g. pushing and shoving, hitting)

6. *Friendliness*
   Words: sympathy, goodwill, closeness, liking
   Phrases: 'I really like you', 'We get on well together', 'You're my mate'
   Vocal communication: relaxed, clear, easy to hear, well modulated
   Bodily communication: physical closeness, pat on back, kiss, smile

7. *Assertion*
   Words: insistence, affirmation, confidence, positiveness
   Phrases: 'I'm insisting on my rights', 'I'm going to stand up for myself', 'I deserve respect'
   Vocal communication: clear enunciation, firm, relaxed, easy to hear
   Bodily communication: open stance, good eye contact, relaxed body posture, standing tall

8. *Trust*
   Words: rely on, depend on, have confidence in, believe in
   Phrases: 'I place total confidence in you', 'I would go tiger hunting with you', 'I can bank on you'
   Vocal communication: relaxed, easy to hear, firm
   Bodily communication: good eye contact, open stance, physical closeness, relaxed posture

# 5 Starting and Developing Relationships

Simply stated, relationships can be seen as having the potential for four stages: getting started, being developed, being maintained and being terminated. The only stages common to all relationships are the first and last. Some relationships go from getting started to being terminated within seconds, whereas a successful marriage will only be terminated by the death of one of the partners. Relationships vary in the degree to which either or both parties choose to invest themselves in their development and maintenance.

## STARTING RELATIONSHIPS

Let us look at two young women who go to the same party where neither knows anybody else well.

> Kay arrives at the party having made a big effort to overcome her nerves about going at all. Though attractive, she thinks that people do not find her so. On arrival at the party she is given a drink and introduced to a group of people. She listens to them politely, but never makes a contribution of her own. When later a young man called Alan tries to engage her in conversation, she becomes very quiet. She appears tense and lacking in warmth and vitality.

> Sara goes to the party excited and determined to do her best to have a good time. She is not afraid to go up to people whom she thinks look interesting and introduce herself. When in conversation she appears interested in what others are saying and participates in a lively unforced way. Since she wants to meet new people she moves around. Even if she does not find someone with whom to develop a relationship further, she will have enjoyed herself and helped others to do likewise.

Both Kay and Sara are attractive. Assuming it is a reasonably good party, both should be able to make an enjoyable time for themselves. However, Sara has much better getting started skills than Kay. Consequently the chances of Sara finding people who wish to see her again are greater than those of Kay. Kay is far from alone in finding it difficult to manage in situations involving groups of new people. Below we focus on some of the skills that Kay, and possibly you too, might use to help yourselves reach out and make contact with others.

**Some barriers to getting started**

Many barriers to getting started in relationships exist in your mind. These barriers are faulty ways of thinking that constrict your choices. For instance, in the above example, Kay's doubts about her attractiveness and excessive concern with others' evaluations of her have the effect of tensing her up. This makes it more difficult for her to choose to be outgoing. Furthermore, the way you think about relationships affects not only whether or not you make contact but also how and with whom. Below are some areas in which your thinking might be adversely influencing your ability to start relationships.

● *Responsibility for making the first move.* Some of you may play a passive rather than an active role when meeting new people. It is as though you are waiting for events to happen to you rather than taking an active part in shaping events. Sometimes this passivity is reinforced by social rules. For instance, females are expected to be less forward and to take less risks in making initial contact than males. The women's movement is challenging this double standard in its attempt to achieve more equal and open relationships. Some of you may like to take more responsibility for making the first move, but are too anxious or lack the requisite getting started skills.

● *Rigid internal rules.* All of you carry a rule-book in your heads concerning appropriate behaviour for yourselves and for others. If your rules are rigid rather than flexible they can interfere with your choices. For instance, you may have barriers to relating based on other people's age, nationality, race, socio-economic status, eye colour, length of hair, whether they remind you of an unpleasant person in your past and so on. These unrealistic internal rules greatly reduce the number of people to whom you can relate. A common unrealistic internal rule is to make perfectionist demands on others. They must look as though they are going to be the perfect boyfriend, girlfriend, lover, mate or else they do not merit attention. In short, being too rigid about the way others 'should', 'ought' or 'must' be can create huge difficulties in getting started in relationships.

● *Fear of others' evaluations.* You may be tyrannised by your fears of what other people think of you. Usually these fears incorporate being found wanting in some way and thus getting rejected. Furthermore, there is often a secondary fear about not being able to cope with the pain and humiliation of rejection. Though realistically what others think of you is important if you want to start a relationship with them, you are never going to be able to please everyone. Fear of others' evaluations may partly be based on the implicit demand that everyone *must* love and approve of you all the time. If this demand is not fulfilled, the fear may be fuelled by a tendency to see rejection as a catastrophe and a reflection on your total worth as a person.[1] For many young people, fear of others' evaluations can also involve a wish not to displease their parents on whom they are probably also financially dependent. Also your friends and acquaintances can exert pressure on you to conform.

● *Anticipating loss rather than gain.* People vary greatly in their attitude to risk-taking. Past circumstances in your life may be colouring the degree of confidence that you bring to the present and future. Sometimes you may be so involved in seeing the potential negative events or losses that might arise from a course of action that you fail adequately to take into account the potential positive effects or gains. New relationships involve risk and have the potential for both loss and gain. Realism is necessary and the risks require accurate assessment. When starting relationships there is only a limited amount of information available. A more accurate assessment of gain and loss can only be made when you know each other better. The saying goes 'Nothing ventured, nothing gained'. However, this does not preclude assessing the risks and gains involved both at the start of and during a relationship.

Exercise 5.1 is designed to help you explore barriers you may have to starting relationships. The exercise mainly focuses on your possible mental barriers or areas of unrealistic thinking. Its purpose is to increase your freedom of choice about starting relationships.

---

**Exercise 5.1    Exploring barriers to starting relationships**

This exercise can be done on your own, in pairs or as part of a training group.

A   *On your own*
Rate each of the statements below on the following scale:
5   Strongly agree
4   Agree

3   Neither agree nor disagree
2   Disagree
1   Strongly disagree

| Statement | Your rating |
|---|---|
| 1.   Males should always initiate relationships with females. | |
| 2.   Females who ask males out for a date are pushy. | |
| 3.   Males are always after sex rather than a real relationship. | |
| 4.   Basically what females want out of males is a meal ticket. | |
| 5.   I never go out with anyone unless there is a good chance of a lasting relationship. | |
| 6.   If someone isn't near perfect, I don't want to get to know him/her better. | |
| 7.   I act cool because I find it very hard to say no when someone asks me out. | |
| 8.   I generally wait for other people to initiate relationships with me. | |
| 9.   I judge people very quickly on first impressions. | |
| 10.   What my friends think about people with whom I go out is very important to me. | |
| 11.   My parents have strong views regarding my friends. | |
| 12.   If I try to start a relationship I am very afraid of being rejected. | |
| 13.   I am a passive person when it comes to relationships. | |
| 14.   I am not very good at showing someone that I like them. | |
| 15.   I don't know what to say to new people. | |
| 16.   I think new people are judging me all the time. | |
| 17.   I put on a phony front when meeting new people. | |
| 18.   I tense up with new people. | |
| 19.   I don't know how to go about meeting people. | |
| 20.   I am very set in my ways and not prepared to take risks. | |

Make a list of all the items you have rated 4 or 5. These items may indicate barriers for you in starting relationships. What do you think?

B   *In pairs*
    *Either* answer the above questions independently, discuss with

your partner, then summarise any major barriers to starting relationships that you may have.

*Or* together discuss your answers to the items on the questionnaire, then summarise any major barriers to starting relationships that each of you may have.

C *In a training group*

The trainer asks group members to fill in the questionnaire independently. Each trainee is then asked to write down a summary of any major barriers to starting relationships that they may have. The trainer then conducts a plenary sharing and discussion session. The trainer not only facilitates discussion but also helps trainees to formulate more realistic ways of thinking about starting relationships. A variation of this exercise is to ask group members to circulate and pay an appropriate compliment to every person to whom they talk during a 5 minute period. The trainer then facilitates a discussion of their thoughts and feelings before, during and after the exercise.

---

Getting started skills may involve *making* as well as *taking* opportunities to initiate relationships. In the earlier examples, both Kay and Sara were already at the party, so their task was to take the opportunity presented by their invitations. An example of the need to make opportunities is if you come to a new city not knowing anyone. Individuals handle such a challenge with different degrees of initiative and success. Another situation in which you may need to make opportunities is if you find your current circle of friends constricting. You may feel that you have quantity rather than quality in your life.

Realistically some of you may be in very difficult circumstances for meeting new people: for instance, being isolated in the country. Often, however, there are opportunities to be made. The mental barriers already mentioned may block some of you. Particularly important is an attitude of personal responsibility for making things happen in your life rather than waiting for others or luck to do so. Expanding your range of social opportunities may involve hard work. There is a story about a spectator going up to international golfer Gary Player after he had played an excellent shot to near the hole from a difficult bunker and saying: 'Gee, Mr Player you're a lucky golfer.' Player replied: 'You know something. The more and more I practise, the luckier and luckier I get.' Expanding your range of potential relationships may also entail being open to meeting different kinds of people, overcoming fears of others' evaluations and focusing on the gains and not only on the risks of meeting new people.

Though Exercise 5.2, on increasing your chances of meeting new people, may not apply to all of you, it has relevance for many. Even those of you who are satisfied with your present relationships may find that conscientiously working through the exercise opens up some new and pleasing horizons.

---

**Exercise 5.2   Increasing your chances of meeting people**

This exercise may be done on your own, in pairs or as part of a training group.

A   *On your own*
    Write down your answers to the following questions:
    1.   How good are you at putting yourself in situations where you are likely to meet new and interesting people?
    2.   List all those situations as specifically as possible (viz. in home, work, school and recreational settings) where you might meet new and interesting people.
    3.   In what ways could you be behaving more effectively than you are now to expand the range of your social contacts?
    4.   If relevant, draw up a plan for improving your social life by increasing your chances of meeting new and interesting people. Your plan should be realistic, specific and contain: (1) a clear statement of goals; (2) specific steps to meet your goals; and (3) a time schedule.

B   *In pairs*
    *Either* independently answer the questions above, then discuss with your partner.
    *Or* work through the above questions together, including helping each other to draw up a plan for improving your respective social lives by increasing your chances of meeting new and interesting people.

C   *In a training group*
    The trainer discusses the importance of trainees placing themselves in situations where they can increase their chances of meeting people with whom to form relationships. The trainer goes through the first three questions with the group as a whole. Trainees are then asked to write down independently their plans for meeting new people, prior to the trainer conducting a plenary sharing and discussion session. The trainer is sensitive to those shy about participating. Alternatively, the trainer can get trainees to answer the questions either on their own or in pairs followed by a plenary sharing and discussion session.

---

**Making contact**

A group of you in a room together for the first time can either be a collection of separate existences locked within your own skins or you can start to make contact with each other. There are different stages of making contact. Here the main focus is on helping you to make effective choices when first meeting people. This is the important time in which you make and receive first impressions. During this period, you may plant the seeds for relationships to grow later. Alternatively, you may curtail opportunities either by choice or by mistake.

In the previous chapter we introduced the idea that sending messages about yourself involves bodily and vocal as well as verbal communication. How you look and how you sound can be as important as what you say. When getting started in relationships you need to communicate: (1) liking of the other; (2) absence of threat; (3) interest in the other; and (4) some initial definition of yourself. In short, you need to communicate that you are a rewarding rather than a negative person with whom to relate. However, you can still break away at an appropriate moment from people who are not particularly rewarding for you.

Table 5.1 shows some of the dimensions of being a rewarding person on initial contact. Making contact with new people is more likely to occur if you move around at, say, a party rather than allow yourself to get stuck in one location. Furthermore, if someone looks interesting, you increase your chances of meeting them if you go over to them rather than wait for them to come to you. The head and face play an important role in rewarding others. Smiling can indicate liking of the other and absence of threat. However, smiling can be overdone and then appear like a phony mask. A person can pick up whether your facial and other aspects of your bodily communication are congruent with what you say. Lack of genuineness or incongruence is likely to distance others from you. A reasonable amount of eye contact should be maintained. Too little eye contact may indicate bashfulness or lack of interest. A high degree of eye contact may be seen as domineering or possibly indicating sexual attraction. Of course, you may be choosing to convey the latter. Head movements, such as nodding, are one way of showing others that you are listening to them. This assumes that you are not nodding off to sleep!

Touch is often built into initial contacts through the handshake. There is variation according to gender, with a firm handshake generally considered more appropriate for men than women.

**Table 5.1** *Conversational openers and ice-breakers – bodily and vocal communication*

| | | |
|---|---|---|
| *Bodily communication* | | |
| Proximity | – | going over to someone who looks approachable; standing or sitting close but not too close |
| Eye contact | – | looking in another's direction; possibly meeting their eyes and/or winking |
| Facial expression | – | smiling to indicate liking |
| Head movements | – | head nods to indicate interest |
| Touch | – | shaking hands; touching another lightly on the arm to attract attention |
| Posture | – | relaxed |
| Trunk lean | – | if anything slightly forwards rather than backwards |
| Trunk orientation | – | facing or otherwise being open to the other |
| Clothes | – | relevant to the social context and to how you wish to define yourself |
| Grooming | – | appropriate for the occasion |
| *Vocal communication* | | |
| Volume | – | easy to hear |
| Pace | – | relaxed |
| Enunciation | – | clear |

However, times change and females may increasingly want to shake hands firmly. How you stand or sit can either indicate openness to another or create distance. An extreme example of creating distance is turning your back on them. Facing another openly and leaning slightly toward them can be rewarding through demonstrating attention. Having a relaxed body posture reduces threat. Lastly what you wear and how you are groomed conveys numerous messages, both accurate and sometimes inaccurate, as to what you are like.

So far we have focused on bodily communication. Vocal communication is also important. You can choose to be loud, easily heard or silent. Sometimes, without being fully aware, you may show your nervousness by speaking very quickly or by slurring your words. Even those without notable speech impediments may need to work on improving the quality of their speaking voices. For instance, British Prime Minister Margaret Thatcher reputedly has been coached to speak in a less high pitched and strident fashion. Vocal communication is a crucial way of conveying your feelings. Again, as with bodily communication, *how* you say it needs to match *what* you say for you to appear genuine. A clear, easily audible, relaxed, genuine and friendly speaking voice can be very useful both in starting and in developing relationships.

Getting started and breaking the ice in relationships is easier if you have developed a repertoire of appropriate opening remarks. You can choose from these conversational openers and ice-breakers those that are appropriate to the differing situations in which you find yourself. Making initial contact is usually done by way of small talk as you 'feel' each other out psychologically to see if you wish the contact to continue and on what level. *Safe talk* is another way of viewing *small talk*. The level of disclosure is usually low in terms of intimacy. Trust and mutual acceptability has yet to be established. However, in situations where you are unlikely to meet again, a 'strangers on a train' phenomenon may occur in which disclosures may be surprisingly intimate.

Table 5.2 lists numerous ways in which verbally you can get started in conversations. The table lists openers, ice-breakers and suggestions for safe talk. It is by no means exhaustive. Some of you may

**Table 5.2**   *Conversational openers and ice-breakers – verbal communication*

Openers and ice-breakers include the following:

Introduce yourself:
    'Hello, I'm (or 'my name is') _____'
Offer something:
    'Can I get you a drink?'
    'Would you like some peanuts?'
Exchange basic information:
    'What brings you here?'
    'Where do you live?'
    'What line of work are you in?' etc.
Pass comments relevant to the occasion, possibly followed by a question:
    'I like this hot weather. Do you?'
    'It's a great party. Do you agree?'
    'I've just arrived. What's happening?'
Give compliments, again possibly followed by a question:
    'I like your dress.'
    'You are a really great dancer.'
    'I like your dress. Where did you get it?'
    'You are a really great dancer. Where did you learn?'
    'I like your sense of humour.'
Bring up topical subjects:
    'What do you think of the election?'
    'What do you think of the new Arts Centre?'
    'Have you been watching _____ television series?'
Try self-disclosure:
    'I feel nervous because this is the first time I've been here.'
    'I'm so relieved and happy. I've just heard that I have passed my exams.'
    'I went and saw the film _____ yesterday and really enjoyed it.'
Encourage others' conversation:
    'That's interesting'    'Uhm uhm'    'Tell me more'
    'Really'    'Did you?'    'Oh'

have your favourite opening gambits which have worked well for you in the past. If so, why change? Others of you may wish to build up your repertoire so that you make initial contact with others better.

Exercise 5.3 is designed to help those of you who wish to change. The exercise encourages you to pin-point your skills deficits in initiating conversations, set yourself goals, practise, implement your skills in real life, and monitor and evaluate your progress. Some of your present behaviour in getting started may represent well established habits. Consequently you may need to work hard to change your behaviour, including resisting being discouraged by setbacks along the way. Mistakes and errors are best viewed as part of the learning process.

---

**Exercise 5.3  Developing your skills at initiating conversations**

This exercise can be done on your own, in pairs or as part of a training group.

A  *On your own*
Look at Tables 5.1, on bodily and vocal communication, and 5.2, on verbal communication, and write out a list of the skills you need to develop or improve when meeting new people.

Having identified these skills, practise them with a cassette-recorder and/or in front of a mirror. Then try out the skills in real life situations and monitor and evaluate your progress.

B  *In pairs*
Either together or independently refer to Tables 5.1 and 5.2 and write out a list for each of you of the skills you need to develop for meeting new people. Practise the skills on your respective lists with each other. Then try out the skills in real life. Consider meeting again both to monitor and evaluate your progress and also to practise the skills further if necessary.

C  *As part of a training group*
The trainer takes the group through Tables 5.1 and 5.2 and models the skills where appropriate. Either independently, in pairs or as a homework exercise trainees are encouraged to identify the meeting people skills they need to develop. When the group meets with the trainer again, he/she sets up role-play situations in which trainees are coached and practised in the skills relevant for them. A video-recorder and playback may be used as part of the feedback process. Trainees are then encouraged to try out their skills in real life and to monitor and evaluate their progress. The group may meet again for further discussion, coaching and practice.

---

### Searching for common ground

Social psychologist Philip Zimbardo writes: 'Friendships are usually based on: being physically close; being involved in mutual activities; similar attitudes, values, background, personality, and interests; and expressing mutual liking.[2] Thus, more often than not, meeting new people entails you in searching for common ground. This is partly to find safe talk with which to fill or structure time. In general, people find silences awkward when they do not know each other well. However, this searching for common ground is also part of the exploration of whether you later wish to become friends, lovers or marital partners. It can entail finding out specific factual information, for instance a shared hobby or a mutual friend. It can also include discovering emotional information that is possibly more implicit than explicit: for instance mutual liking, compatibility and closeness. In initial contacts a process of coordination takes place in at least two ways: you test out whether or not you wish to continue the contact and you also coordinate the direction and intimacy of your disclosures.

You cannot *not* communicate. Your voice, works and body are always sending out messages. However, you can choose what and how you reveal and define yourself to others. Furthermore, the way you reveal and define yourself will influence not only the level of intimacy of others' disclosures, but also how they react to yours. The late Erving Goffman was very aware of the extent to which people engage in impression management.[3] The way you present yourself and your activities to others guides and controls the impressions others form of you. An analogy may be made to the theatre where the players are engaged in manipulating the audience's impressions. However, suspending others' disbelief can interfere with the starting and developing of relationships. They may perceive you as insincere. Consequently you are faced with a set of choices when first meeting people concerning how open and honest to be about yourself at each stage in the conversation.

Exercise 5.4 is designed to make you more aware of your position as a *chooser* in what you say about yourself when starting relationships. The exercise is designed so that it does not probe beyond a safe level of intimacy. It tries to get you focusing on your thoughts and feelings both as you reveal yourself and as others reveal themselves to you.

**Exercise 5.4   Getting acquainted: choosing what to say about yourself**

This is a group exercise.

The trainer hands out a 5×8 card to each group member. Trainees are asked to print how they like to be called in the top right-hand corner (e.g. GINA, RICK). In the upper left-hand corner, they list three pieces of factual information about themselves (e.g. age, marital status, birthplace, place of residence etc.). In the bottom left-hand corner they list three adjectives that describe them as a person (viz. likeable, sporty, disorganised). In the bottom right-hand corner they list three of their main recreational activities (viz. dancing, tennis, gardening). The trainer may also fill out a card.

Participants are asked to pin their cards to the front of their clothes. Trainees then go around holding conversations in pairs about their cards as if getting acquainted at a party. They are encouraged to circulate and meet as many people as they comfortably can. The trainer ends the 'party' part of the exercise and holds a plenary sharing and discussion session. Trainees are helped to become more aware of how they control the nature and intimacy level of their disclosures. Also, they may gain in awareness of (a) the effects their own disclosures have on how others see them, and (b) how their own perceptions of others are altered by what others disclose to them.

## Coping with shyness

Meeting new people can engender considerable anxiety for some of you. This is a form of stage fright in which you wonder if you can perform or are performing adequately. The criteria for adequacy may be whether you meet your *own* standards or whether you obtain *others'* approval. Shyness can be viewed as a form of social anxiety. The term social anxiety is used here to describe feelings of anxiety in social situations. The effects of social anxiety, as with stage fright in the theatre, can be both positive and negative. Social anxiety *helps* or *facilitates* when it makes you more alert and task-orientated. It *hinders* or *debilitates* when it interferes with your performance.

For many of you, meeting new people is stressful and demanding. Social anxiety is the feeling resulting from the transaction between you and your situation. Note that social anxiety does not result directly from the stressful situation, but involves the transaction between you and the stressor. For instance, the same situation may be seen as stressful by one person and not by another. Furthermore, your perception of a situation as stressful relates to your thoughts and coping skills relevant to it.

Unrealistic internal rules are one category of thoughts that engender social anxiety. Four such unrealistic rules are:

1.  I *must* be liked and approved of by everyone I meet.
2.  I *must* never reveal anything about myself that might be viewed negatively.
3.  I *must* never make a mistake in social situations.
4.  If anything goes wrong it is not only a *catastrophe* in itself, but a reflection of *my total inadequacy as a person*.

If you think the above thoughts before or in social situations, then you are likely to find yourself tensing up in ways that block making contact. These rigid internal rules mean that each encounter with a new person is one in which you lay your sense of personal adequacy on the line. Such rigid internal rules need to be identified, rationally assessed and, to the extent that they are unrealistic, disputed and discarded. Furthermore, the rules need to be reformulated so that they offer you realistic guidelines for the future.

More realistic reformulations of the previous rules are:

1.  Though I might prefer to be universally liked, it is unreasonable and unnecessary to demand that this be the case. I can meet my needs for friendship and affection if I only meet some people who like me and whom I like.
2.  Nobody is perfect. If I am to start and develop honest and open relationships I need to reveal my vulnerability as well as my strength.
3.  To err is human. Everybody makes mistakes. Though I would prefer not to make mistakes, I can use them as learning experiences.
4.  I am a worthwhile person just by virtue of being human. Things that go wrong are only likely to be catastrophes if I label them as such and wrongly treat them as a reflection on my total worth as a person.

Exercise 5.5 focuses on managing shyness through identifying unrealistic and reformulating them into realistic internal rules. As mentioned earlier, rules are frequently unrealistic when they contain words like 'must', 'ought' and 'should'. See if you can identify some of the barriers that may be contributing to your being tense in social situations. You may find it helpful to review your answers to Exercise

5.1 in doing this. Then see if you can arrive at confidence-engendering reformulations of these rules or, at the very least, reformulations that help you contain your anxiety.

---

**Exercise 5.5   Coping with shyness: developing realistic internal rules**

This exercise may be done on your own, in pairs or as part of a training group.

A   *On your own*
1. Make a list of any major unrealistic internal rules which contribute to your being uncomfortably anxious when meeting new people.
2. Rationally assess and dispute these rules.
3. Reformulate each rule so that it offers realistic guidelines for the future.
4. Cassette-record the reformulated rules and play them back to yourself at least once a day for the next two weeks.

B   *In pairs*
*Either* do the first three questions above independently, then discuss together before cassette-recording your reformulated rules for homework.
*Or* work through the above exercise together from the start.

C   *In a training group*
The trainer illustrates how altering unrealistic internal rules can help trainees manage their anxiety when meeting new people. The trainer then takes the whole group through the exercise, including if possible making up individual cassettes of reformulated rules for each trainee's homework. Working with the whole group rather than subgrouping seems preferable for this exercise since it involves a large element of teaching, demonstration and coaching.

---

Using task-oriented inner speech is another way of coping with shyness.[4] The idea is that much of the time you engage in an internal dialogue or perform self-talk. You may use task-oriented inner speech *before*, *during* and *after* specific stressful situations involving meeting new people. For instance, imagine that you either go to a party full of strangers or out on a date with a new person. The object is to get you helping yourself to contain, cope with and lessen any uncomfortable feelings of anxiety that you may have. Also, to stop you behaving on account of your anxiety in ways that distance you from others.

Possible task-oriented inner speech sentences that you might tell yourself *before* the stressful social situation include:

'This anxiety is a sign for me to use my coping skills.'
'Now calm down. Develop a plan to manage the situation.'
'Let's rehearse my realistic internal rules in relation to this situation.'
'I'm a strong person who has coped with difficult situations like this in the past.'

Possible task-oriented inner speech sentences that you might tell yourself *during* the stressful social situation include:

'Now calm down. Take your time. Breathe slowly and regularly.'
'Relax. I can manage it if I just take one step at a time.'
'I don't have to be perfect. All I have to do is the best I can.'
'As I acknowledge my anxiety and use my coping skills, I can feel the tension draining away.'

Possible task-oriented inner speech sentences that you might tell yourself *after* the stressful situation include:

'Each time I cope it seems to get easier.'
'I'm proud of the way I'm learning to manage my fears.'
'I've shown myself that I can do it now.'
'Why did I get so uptight? It simply wasn't justified.'

Shyness can have many causes. Consequently developing realistic internal rules and using task-oriented inner speech are but two approaches to the problem. Sometimes shyness may be the consequence of poor relationship skills, for instance not having a repertoire of conversational openers. If so, you need to work on the relevant skills deficit. Also, shyness may stem from your having received much rejection whilst growing up. If so, you may require a series of individual and/or group counselling sessions to provide you with the nurturance and support that you missed.

Exercise 5.6 has been designed to give you some practice at task-oriented inner speech. It is a useful skill to develop with relevance to many stressful situations, both social and otherwise.

---

**Exercise 5.6   Coping with shyness: using task-oriented inner speech**

This exercise may be done on your own, in pairs or as part of a training group.

A   *On your own*
    1.   What self-talk contributes to any shyness you may experience when meeting new people?

2. Identify a specific situation involving meeting new people that you find stressful. Write out at least three task-oriented inner speech sentences for each of
   2.1. before
   2.2. during, and
   2.3. after the situation.
3. Practise your task-oriented inner speech with a cassette-recorder or in front of a mirror (you may speak aloud) prior to using it in the actual situation.

B *In pairs*
*Either* do questions 1 and 2 above independently, then discuss together. Afterwards role-play each of your stressful situations, but remember to use inner as well as outer speech.
*Or* work through the above exercise together from the start, including role-playing each of your stressful situations using inner as well as outer speech.

C *As part of a training group*
The trainer illustrates how using task-oriented inner speech can help trainees cope with their shyness when meeting new people. The trainer may work with the whole group: (a) in identifying anxiety-engendering self-talk; and, especially, (b) in developing realistic task-oriented inner speech for before, during and after their stressful situations. The trainer may set up within the group role-play situations in which trainees practise their task-oriented inner speech. Additionally, the trainer may encourage practice outside the group as well as the use of the skills in real life situations.

---

## DEVELOPING RELATIONSHIPS

Having spent some time on the skills of starting relationships, we now examine how to develop them further. When you make contact with another you are a chooser who, in general, wishes to maximise the rewards and minimise the costs of your time together. The development of intimate relationships is a process of social coordination in which, independently and together, each of you decides progressively to invest more of yourselves. If either of you decide that the costs of the relationship are greater than the rewards, the relationship becomes uncoordinated. If this lack of coordination remains unresolved, the relationship will not progress. Sometimes both of you wish a relationship to end, in which case the ending is coordinated. The development of less intimate friendships also involves a process of coordination, though progressing to less deep levels.

**Revealing progressively more intimate information**

One of the main ways in which you feel each other out psychologically is through making progressively more intimate disclosures. The
process involves you in matching the intimacy level of each other's
disclosures prior to disclosing at a still more intimate level. In other
words, you move beyond safe talk to talk that has increasingly more
risk attached to it. The main risk is that of rejection or of being
esteemed less as a result of your disclosures. Having your confidences
divulged may also be another major fear. In short, two important
ways that you can develop a relationship are either by *first making* a
more intimate disclosure or by *matching* a more intimate disclosure
when another has taken the first risk. This does not mean that you do
not listen to each other, but just talk about yourselves all the time.
Rather you both listen and talk. However, when you talk about
yourselves, you coordinate the deepening of the level of intimacy of
your disclosures, if that is what you both wish. Many relationships,
for instance those between sporting colleagues, may reach a plateau
involving relatively little intimacy. This may still meet the needs of
those involved since these may be more task-oriented than person-
oriented relationships. Even some long-standing marriages lack
genuine intimacy of disclosure.

There are a number of explanations for why the progressive
matching of the intimacy level of disclosures develops relationships.
One explanation is that your disclosure is a reward given to another
indicating liking. This needs to be reciprocated if the relationship is to
remain equitable or in balance. The underlying assumption here is
that humans strive for equity in their relationships. Another
explanation emphasises the meaning of the way disclosures are
received. If your disclosure is met with acceptance by another, this
not only establishes them as less threatening and more alike, but also
gives them permission to make a similar disclosure. Consequently,
through both not rejecting each other's disclosures as well as disclosing
about yourselves, trust gets established at a deeper level.

Exercise 5.7 has been designed to increase your awareness and
skills regarding developing relationships through the progressive
matching of more intimate disclosures. Relationships tend to develop
as both participants feel able to be more open about themselves to
each other.

**Exercise 5.7   Progressive matching of disclosures**

This exercise can be done in pairs or as part of a training group.

A   *In pairs*
Below are a number of topic areas in which you might choose to reveal information about yourself.

| | |
|---|---|
| Income | Sexual behaviour |
| Present employment | Personal weaknesses |
| Level of education | Your nickname |
| Marital status | Being out of control |
| Birthplace | Feeling helpless |
| Place of residence | Blaming others |
| Age | Major mistakes |
| Favourite hobby | Health |
| Favourite TV programme | Feelings about death |
| Religious beliefs | Homosexual tendencies |
| Friends of same sex | Unemployment |
| Friends of opposite sex | Authority figures |
| Parents | Racial views |
| Fears | Satisfaction with work |
| Lying and cheating | Satisfaction with home life |
| Enemies | Admirers |
| Being angry | Shameful actions |
| Being depressed | Guilt feelings |
| Being happy | People you admire |
| Being confused | Political views |
| Ambitions | Masturbation |
| Feelings of inferiority | Feelings of superiority |
| Feeling attracted | An intimate relationship |
| Intelligence | Your views about your body |

Each of you has an idea of how threatening it would be for you to disclose about these topic areas to your partner. Given time, you could probably list the above items in a hierarchy of how threatening it would be.

Engage in the disclosure of progressively more intimate or threatening information with your partner strictly obeying the following rules.

1. Start with non-threatening information and *gradually* disclose more threatening information in each round.
2. No one discloses anything that they do not want to and there is no pressure brought on anyone to do so.
3. In the first round Partner A makes a personal disclosure. Partner B attempts to match the intimacy level of the disclosure with a

similar disclosure. If possible, Partner B's disclosure should be in the same topic area, though he/she has the option of changing the area if uncomfortable about the initial area of disclosure.

4. In the second round Partner B makes a personal disclosure at a slightly deeper level than that of the previous round. Partner A matches the intimacy level and, if comfortable, the topic area.

5. Partners A and B continue the exercise for as long as they mutually wish, alternating between who discloses first in each round.

6. At the end of the exercise the partners discuss whether they think and feel differently about each other and themselves as a result of the exercise.

B   *In a training group*

The trainer discusses how an important way that relationships develop is through the progressive revealing of more personal information. The trainer may refer the group to their answers to Exercise 4.5 which involved rating areas of personal information in terms of degrees of threat if they were to disclose it. The trainer can demonstrate the concept of reciprocity by getting the group to practise matching the intimacy level of illustrative personal statements. Trainees are then asked to perform the pairs exercise above. This is followed by a plenary sharing and discussion session. If time, trainees can repeat the pairs exercise with another partner.

---

### Acknowledging vulnerability and strength

Though it overlaps with progressively disclosing more intimate information, acknowledging vulnerability is another way in which you can develop your relationships. Some of you may feel the need to present yourselves in a positive light all the time. The effect that this 'boasting' can have on others is at least threefold. First, they fail to get to know you properly since you wear a mask. Second, they find themselves in a negative exchange with you since they are the only people in the relationship who can be vulnerable and make mistakes. Third, because the relationship is unsafe, they are likely to inhibit being open about themselves with you.

Feeling safe enough to acknowledge what you like about yourself and consider your strengths can also develop relationships. Issues of timing and balance are important. For instance, if you start by saying positive things about yourself, others may consider that you are boasting. However, if you have already acknowledged some vulnerability, acknowledging your strengths may be perceived as being free to be more open, dropping your social mask to reveal positives as well as negatives.[5,6] This also allows the recipient of your disclosures to acknowledge both strengths and weaknesses as well.

Exercise 5.8 encourages you to be more open in revealing your vulnerability and strengths to another as a way of developing your relationship. The exercise assumes that others are inclined to disclose likewise to you.

---

**Exercise 5.8   Revealing strengths and weaknesses**

This exercise may be done on your own, in pairs or as part of a training group.

A   *On your own*
1. List five of your characteristics that you consider strengths and five that you consider weaknesses.
2. How open are you in your relationships about revealing what you see as (a) your strengths and (b) your weaknesses?
3. If appropriate, set yourself goals for being more open in your relationships about your strengths and weaknesses.
4. Try implementing your goals. Monitor and evaluate your progress.

B   *In pairs*
1. Independently, each of you list five of your characteristics that you consider strengths and five that you consider weaknesses.
2. Discuss with your partner as much of your list of strengths as you feel comfortable revealing, then reverse roles.
3. Your partner discusses with you as much of his/her list of weaknesses as he/she feels comfortable revealing, then reverse roles.
4. Discuss how you feel about yourselves and each other as a result of the exercise.
5. If appropriate, set yourselves goals for being more open in your relationships about your strengths and weaknesses. Try implementing your goals. Monitor and evaluate your progress.

C   *In a training group*
The trainer discusses the impact of acknowledging vulnerabilities and strengths on the development of relationships. Trainees are asked to perform the pairs exercise above, prior to the trainer conducting a plenary sharing and discussion session. Trainees may be encouraged to set themselves goals for being more open about their strengths and weaknesses in their outside relationships and, where appropriate, to practise this.

---

**Giving and receiving feedback**

Another way in which you develop relationships is when you feel increasingly safe not only to talk about yourselves, but about each other and the relationship. The need for openness and honesty is a consistent theme underlying this discussion on developing relationships. As with all communication, giving feedback to another is not just a matter of *what* you say, but of *when* and *how* you say it. It can build trust, but it also needs to take into account the state of trust in the relationship. A possible analogy is that between feedback in personal relationships and that in counselling. Especially with highly vulnerable clients, counsellors first need to establish rapport and trust by being safe and accepting people. Later, once their human credentials have been established, the client may be less defensive and more willing to listen to feedback from them. In fact, at this stage clients may perceive counsellors as more helpful and committed if they provide some feedback. Even so, counsellors still need to be sensitive as to how they provide the feedback.

In the process of coordination involved in developing a relationship, you give feedback to each other in all sorts of ways, including your vocal and bodily communication. Here the main focus is on giving verbal feedback. Giving another feedback in a relationship has many purposes. You provide the other person with information, both positive and negative, about where you stand in relation to them and they in relation to you. You open up the possibility for change in their behaviour and, possibly, in your own too. Also, you engage in a form of disclosure which is likely to be matched by them in return. Furthermore, you test the strength of the relationship by observing how they react to your feedback.

In the previous chapter it was mentioned that you communicate more openly and honestly in relationships if you speak for yourself. Consequently you were encouraged to make 'I' statements about your own thoughts and feelings rather than starting with words like 'You', 'People' and 'We'. Exercise 5.9 is mainly designed to focus on helping you develop your skills at giving feedback expressed in 'I' statements. Focus on the *how* of giving feedback as well as on the *what*. Especially if the feedback is negative, try and minimise the degree of threat to the other. Additionally, both as you give and receive feedback, not only observe your behaviour but also listen to your thoughts and feelings.

**Exercise 5.9   Giving and receiving feedback**

This exercise can be done in pairs or as part of a training group.

A   *In pairs*
Work through the following sequence together:
1. Using 'I' statements Partner A tells Partner B his/her *first impressions* (when they first met) of him/her. Partner B listens and, when Partner A finishes, shares any thoughts and feelings he/she may have about the feedback.
2. Partners reverse roles for the *first impressions* feedback exercise.
3. Using 'I' statements Partner A gives Partner B feedback concerning his/her *current thoughts and feelings* about him/her. Partner B listens and then, when Partner A is finished, shares any thoughts and feelings he/she may have about the feedback.
4. Partners reverse roles for the *current thoughts and feelings* feedback exercise.
5. Partners discuss their skills resources and deficits at giving and receiving feedback in their relationships.
6. If appropriate, each partner sets himself/herself goals involving improving his/her (1) giving of feedback and (2) receiving of feedback in a relationship.

B   *In a training group*
The trainer discusses the importance in developing relationships of constructively giving and receiving feedback. Trainees are encouraged to use 'I' statements when giving feedback. The trainer divides the group into subgroups of four. Within each subgroup one person sits in the 'hot seat' facing the other three, receives feedback on their *first impressions* of him/her, shares his/her thoughts and feelings about the feedback, before the next person takes their turn in the 'hot seat'. This first part of the exercise may last 10 to 15 minutes. The trainer may then conduct a brief plenary sharing and discussion session prior to subdividing the group again, possibly with different people in the subgroups, and getting group members to give and receive feedback about their *current thoughts and feelings* about each other. After a further 15 to 20 minutes the trainer conducts another plenary sharing and discussion session. Trainees are encouraged both to examine their skills at giving and receiving feedback in their outside relationships and also to work on improving any deficits they may have.

## Developing trust

Though perhaps less explicit than openness and honesty, the need to develop trust has been another consistent theme in this discussion on developing relationships. Trust means a firm belief in the honesty and reliability of another. It implies a confident expectation of trustworthy behaviour. As you develop relationships, especially close ones, a major underlying question you ask yourself is 'Can I trust this person?' At the point at which the answer becomes negative, the relationship will certainly deteriorate, if not be terminated.

Another way of looking at trust in personal relations centres around your fears of rejection. The question then becomes 'Can I trust this person not to reject me?' Against this criterion, progressive disclosure of more intimate information, revealing vulnerability and strength, and giving and receiving honest feedback all become ways of testing the trustworthiness of the other in relation to you. Though the trustworthiness of a person's behaviour outside your relationship is relevant, what counts most often is how trustworthy they behave to you in particular.

Let us look at the progressive disclosure of personal information as part of a process of trust building. You show some trust in another by making a disclosure that is a little risky. If the other accepts and is supportive about your disclosure, trust is likely to be enhanced. Trust may be further enhanced if the other risks disclosing at a similar level of intimacy. However, if he or she rejects your initial disclosure, you are unlikely to risk deeper disclosures and may even end the relationship. Where both of you have had your disclosures accepted, at least at a relatively safe level, you may feel confident to continue your trust testing and trust building process at a slightly deeper level and so on. Relationships end up at different levels of trust. Also, sometimes people can be trustworthy in relation to certain areas of disclosure, but not in relation to others. The trust testing process is more complex than as presented here.

The development of trust takes time. You both need to obtain a large enough sample of behaviour to find out how much you can trust each other. Initially, you relate to each other wearing social masks. Given time, intentionally or unintentionally, you show more of yourselves. Tuning into vocal and bodily as well as verbal communication can be a valuable means of picking up clues as to each other's trustworthiness. Also, actions tend to speak louder than words.

**Table 5.3** *Some adjectives associated with trust and lack of trust*

| trustworthy | untrustworthy |
|---|---|
| reliable | unreliable |
| dependable | undependable |
| consistent | inconsistent |
| trusting | suspicious |
| honest | dishonest |
| open | closed |
| accepting | rejecting |
| supportive | unsupportive |
| cooperative | competitive |
| generous | selfish |
| kind | mean |
| caring | uncaring |
| just | unjust |
| fair | unfair |
| loyal | disloyal |
| faithful | unfaithful |
| keeps confidences | breaks confidences |
| keeps promises | breaks promises |
| loving | hostile |
| genuine | phoney |
| assertive | unassertive |

Table 5.3 attempts to broaden the discussion of *choosing* to be trustworthy and *choosing* to trust others by indicating a number of adjectives associated with trust. The list incorporates honesty and reliability, the initial two adjectives by which trust was defined. It also incorporates being open about yourself and accepting others' disclosures. It highlights the fact that mean, suspicious, uncaring, hostile, selfish and competitive people are unlikely either to be or to be perceived as trustworthy. In relationships, as in the market-place, a good adage is *Caveat emptor* or 'Let the buyer beware'. The giving of your trust to a person, as with a good purchase, depends on the collection and analysis of reliable information. However, you too have some responsibility for creating the psychological conditions whereby others can be trustworthy. For instance, if you persist in being aggressive, you sow the seeds of your own rejection.

Exercise 5.10 is designed to help you explore the concept of trustworthiness in relation to your own behaviour. Though probably all of you like to consider yourselves as trustworthy, you may not always behave as such. Also, in personal relationships, the concept of trust tends to be very specifically applied to what transpires between the two people involved, regardless of how trustworthy they may be in other contexts.

**Exercise 5.10   Developing trust and being trustworthy**

This exercise may be done on your own, in pairs or as part of a training group.

A   *On your own*
1.   List the ways other people have behaved towards you that have helped you to trust them. If possible, list at least five items.
2.   Take the above list, and rank them in terms of their importance for your being a trustworthy person in your relationships.
3.   If appropriate, set yourself goals for being more trustworthy in your relationships and monitor and evaluate your progress.

B   *In pairs*
*Either* answer questions 1 and 2 above independently, then discuss. If appropriate, work together to set each of yourselves goals for being more trustworthy in your relationships.
*Or* jointly make a list of at least five items of the ways other people have behaved towards you that have helped you to trust them. Then independently rank these items in terms of their importance for your being a trustworthy person in your relationships. Afterwards go over your personal ratings together. If appropriate, work together to set each of yourselves goals for being more trustworthy in your relationships.

C   *In a training group*
The trainer introduces the topic of the importance of being trustworthy in developing relationships. The trainer may either work with the whole group or subdivide the group into pairs, threes or fours to make lists of at least five ways in which other people have shown their trustworthiness to them. This is followed by a whole group session discussing and ranking the five most important way of developing trust in a relationship. If appropriate, trainees are encouraged both to set themselves personal goals for being a trustworthy person in their relationships and also to monitor and evaluate their progress.

---

**The role of touch**

Touch connects human animals with each other in a fundamental way. Because of its possible sexual connotations, there are numerous taboos about touch, especially between males. The role of touch varies from culture to culture. Mediterranean cultures are probably more physically expressive than Northern European cultures and those derived from them, for instance Australia, Canada and the

United States. The focus here is on the role of touch in expressing, developing and maintaining emotional closeness. This may or may not entail sexual contact and, as prostitution clearly shows, sexual contact need not involve emotional closeness.

The human need to touch and be touched is present from birth. British psychiatrist John Bowlby observes that there is much evidence to support the view 'that food plays only a marginal role in a child's attachment to his mother, that attachment behaviour is shown most strongly during the second and third years of life and persists at less intensity indefinitely, and that the function of attachment behaviour is protection'.[7] Touch plays a vital role in parent–child relationships. It offers security, tenderness and affection. The need for humans to have attachment figures or secure bases persists into adulthood. Touch is a major way in which adults can demonstrate protection, support and caring for each other.

There are many books that both talk about[8,9] and illustrate with pictures and diagrams[10,11,12] the role of touch in sexual relationships. Though developing emotional and sexual intimacy frequently overlap, Exercise 5.11 on touching and being touched emphasises the former more than the latter. For instance, affection and tenderness may be expressed through a warm hug, a kiss on the cheek, a light touch on the hand, holding hands, an arm over the shoulders, a caress on the side of the face, to mention but some ways.

---

**Exercise 5.11   Touching and being touched**

This exercise can be done on your own, in pairs or as part of a training group.

A   *On your own*
1. List as many different purposes of touch in a relationship as you can.
2. List at least five ways of showing affection and tenderness through touch. Try to think of ways other than those listed in the text.
3. Write down your thoughts and feelings about *touching* other people.
4. Write down your thoughts and feelings about *being touched by* other people.
5. How big a part does touching and being touched play in your life? If dissatisfied with your touch behaviour, set yourself goals for improvement and monitor and evaluate your progress.

B   *In pairs*
   *Either* answer the questions above independently then discuss.
   *Or* work through the questions above jointly.
   A variation of this pairs exercise is that you sit opposite each other
   and hold both your partner's hands when answering it.
C   *In a training group*
   The trainer introduces the topic of the role of touch in developing a
   relationship. The trainer gets the whole group to answer together
   questions 1 and 2 above. The group is then divided into pairs to
   answer questions 3, 4 and 5 prior to coming together again for a
   plenary sharing and discussion session. There can be variations on
   when and how to subdivide the group. The trainer encourages
   group members to explore the adequacy of their own touch
   behaviour, the thinking underlying it, and its consequences for
   them. Where appropriate, trainees may also be encouraged to set
   themselves goals and to change their behaviour.

---

## CHARACTERISTICS OF CLOSE PERSONAL RELATIONSHIPS

When talking about developing relationships, it helps to have an idea
of what is an effective close personal relationship. Here we specify
fourteen characteristics of such relationships. These characteristics
cover all of the major skills areas included in this book. Though styles
of relating may differ, in good long-term relationships the partners to
a greater rather than to a lesser degree exhibit the following
characteristics or skills.

● *Assuming responsibility.* Each of you assumes responsibility for
   your own feelings, thoughts and actions in the relationship.
● *Showing respect.* You demonstrate that you accept and value
   each other. You listen as well as talk. You do not put each other
   down.
● *Showing affection.* Liking, appreciation and prizing is openly
   revealed by means of words and deeds. You gain pleasure from
   giving.
● *Showing commitment.* Each of you is committed to the welfare of
   each other and of the relationship. You are trustworthy
   regarding keeping any implicit or explicit contract involved in the
   relationship.
● *Showing caring.* Each of you shows that you are concerned for
   the physical safety and psychological well-being and development
   of the other.

● *Being open and revealing.* Each of you feels prepared to take the risks involved in revealing yourselves openly and honestly. You are prepared to trust each other with your innermost thoughts and feelings.

● *Feeling it safe to give and receive feedback.* Each of you feels safe to comment on the other's behaviour and on what is going on in the relationship. You help each other to stay honest and in touch with one another.

● *Lack of defensiveness.* Each of you does not feel the need to deny and distort incoming information in order to make yourselves feel more psychologically comfortable. Neither of you wish to diminish the other by defining them on your own terms against their interests.

● *Showing understanding.* You understand the other on various levels: through sensitive intuition, through increased knowledge, and through using good listening skills on an everyday basis. You are capable of a deep and loving rather than a surface understanding of each other.

● *Constructive use of anger.* Each of you owns your anger, tries to understand it and to handle it constructively. You do not hurt each other needlessly.

● *Collaborative management of conflicts.* You view conflicts as problems to be worked through together rather than as competitive 'I Win – You Lose' situations.

● *Non-exploiting sex.* Your sexual relations are characterised by mutual consideration and affection.

● *Shared activities.* You enjoy sharing many activities but allow each other the space to have separate as well as joint interests.

● *Spending time together.* Your relationship is important enough that each of you willingly spends the time it takes to make it work well.

Like all relationships, close personal relationships are processes. As such they involve the continuous application of good relationship skills. Their rewards are huge. Their price is constant vigilance.

---

**Exercise 5.12   Assessing how good your relationship is**

This exercise can be done on your own or with your partner. It can also be done in a training group composed of partners.

A  *On your own*
1.  Take a piece of paper and draw a line down the middle. On one side write down how you see yourself behaving in your relationship on each of the dimensions listed below. On the other side write down how you see your partner behaving.
    – showing respect
    – showing affection
    – showing commitment
    – showing caring
    – being open and revealing
    – feeling it safe to give and receive feedback
    – lack of defensiveness
    – showing understanding
    – constructive use of anger
    – collaborative management of conflicts
    – non-exploiting sex
    – shared activities
    – spending time together
2.  Write down what either or both of you could do to improve your relationship.

B  *With your partner*
    *Either* independently write out your answers to the above exercise, then discuss together.
    *Or* jointly work through the exercise together talking about yourselves and giving and receiving feedback. Make sure to give any negative feedback in a constructive rather than a blaming way. Remember to end by focusing on how you can improve your relationship.

C  *In a training group*
    Partners work in pairs followed by a plenary sharing and discussion session.

---

## CONCLUDING INNER SPEECH

Below is a sample of inner speech that summarises the main points in this chapter.

There are many 'barriers in the mind' that may restrict the choices that I have when starting relationships. These include: my attitude towards taking responsibility for making the first move, the realism of my internal rules, my fears of others' evaluations of me, and my insufficiently taking into account the possible gains from the relationship. I may need consciously to make opportunities to meet new people. I increase my effectiveness when meeting new people not only if I possess a good repertoire of opening remarks, but also if I use appropriate vocal and bodily communication. I have a choice concerning the information I reveal about myself to others. Focusing on the realism of my internal rules and using task-oriented inner speech are two ways I can cope with feeling shy.

I have the choice of developing relationships through progressively disclosing more intimate information. I can also develop relationships by being open about my vulnerabilities and strengths as well as by being prepared to give and receive feedback. It is important that I be trustworthy if I wish to get emotionally close to others. Furthermore, I may enhance emotional closeness if I am able to integrate into my relationships, where appropriate, the skilled use of touch.

# REFERENCES

1. Ellis, A. (1980) 'Overview of the clinical theory of rational-emotive therapy'. In R. Grieger & J. Boyd (eds.) *Rational-emotive Therapy: A Skills-based Approach.* New York: Van Nostrand Reinhold.
2. Zimbardo, P.G. (1977) *Shyness.* Reading, Massachusetts: Addison-Wesley.
3. Goffman, E. (1959) *The Presentation of Self in Everyday Life.* Harmondsworth: Penguin.
4. Meichenbaum, D. (1983) *Coping with Stress.* London: Century Publishing.
5. Nelson-Jones, R. & Strong, S.R. (1976) Positive and negative self-disclosure, timing and personal attraction. *British Journal of Social and Clinical Psychology,* **15**, 323–325.
6. Nelson-Jones, R. & Dryden, W. (1979) Anticipated risk and gain from negative and positive self-disclosure. *British Journal of Social and Clinical Psychology,* **18**, 79–80.
7. Bowlby, J. (1979) *The Making and Breaking of Affectional Bonds.* London: Tavistock.
8. Masters, W.H., Johnson, V.E. in association with Levin, R.J. (1975) *The Pleasure Bond.* New York: Bantam.
9. Brown, P. & Faulder, C. (1977) *Treat Yourself to Sex.* Harmondsworth: Penguin.
10. Comfort, A. (1972) *The Joy of Sex: A Gourmet Guide to Lovemaking.* London: Quartet.
11. Comfort, A. (1973) *More Joy of Sex: A Lovemaker's Companion.* London: Quartet.
12. Oliver, S. & Gorrie, J. (1982) *Touch Love.* Sydney: The Amazing Aquarian Dream Factory.

# 6    Defining and Asserting Yourself

In your relationships you constantly make the choices that create and define you both to yourself and to others. You always define yourself, for good or ill, in the ways you: talk about yourself, start and develop relationships, assert yourself, listen, manage your feelings and work on conflicts. Just as you cannot avoid communicating, you cannot avoid making the choices that define you.

The capacity to assert yourself is an important part of defining yourself in relationships. Asserting yourself includes being able to initiate relationships and talk about yourself openly, so this chapter should not be viewed independently of the preceding ones. There are at least three different viewpoints on assertion, which for the sake of convenience are labelled here the psychological, the religious and the existential or personal responsibility.

In the psychological viewpoint, assertion can be defined as the capacity to express your wants and feelings and to stand up for your rights without unnecessarily violating others' needs. A distinction is sometimes made between inhibition and submission, aggression, and assertion.[1,2] Inhibition involves bottling up thoughts and feelings, while submission entails acquiescing in behaviours with which you disagree. Aggression implies hostility and unnecessarily violating others' needs. Aggression and inhibition both stem from feelings of threat and powerlessness, indeed aggression often comprises the outpouring of pent-up and previously unreleased feelings. Assertion implies the appropriate expression of your needs, feelings and rights.

The psychological view of assertion is increasingly taking into account that unrealistic thoughts can provide barriers to assertion. To date it appears insufficiently to have taken into account that many people require to become more in tune with their underlying feelings or animal nature to be able to assert themselves appropriately. Also, it insufficiently takes into account that your self is something that needs to be made and created and not just asserted. Furthermore, the psychological viewpoint heavily emphasises obtaining your rights in face of other people's poor behaviour.

Whereas the psychological view of assertion emphasises obtaining your rights, the religious view, which in this case is Western

Christianity, emphasises fulfilling responsibilities to God and to your fellow humans. The assumption is that humans are vulnerable people for whom assertion entails not only emphasising their more but also inhibiting their less Christian qualities. One of the main articles of Christian teaching is The Ten Commandments which are mainly expressed as a series of 'Thou shalt nots . . .'. Without wishing to go into detail, the religious view of assertion has a number of shortcomings, including a tendency to induce unnecessary guilt. Guilt feelings can apply even to assertion itself, since it may be regarded as insufficiently self-effacing. However, here two positive aspects of the religious view of assertion are stressed. First, it acknowledges that you have to assert your *own* desirable qualities and not only just resist the undesirable behaviours of *others*. Second and related to the first, there is an assumption that assertion in a relationship entails responsibilities as well as rights, caring as well as being cared for and giving as well as receiving.

The existential or personal responsibility view of assertion is that the whole of life is a process in which you make the choices that define yourself. Here assertion in a relationship is virtually synonymous with personal responsibility or making the choices that are conducive to your survival and fulfilment. These choices may entail acknowledging significant *feelings*, disciplining *thinking* as well as *acting* effectively. The personal responsibility view of assertion merges the psychological emphasis of standing up for your rights and avoiding others' undesirable behaviours with the religious view of being aware of others' needs and asserting your own desirable behaviours. In short, the personal responsibility view of assertion focuses on the need for people to be positive and constructive human beings who can meet both their own and others' needs in their relationships. Though this also is a psychological view of assertion it is perhaps more balanced and less superficial than the psychological viewpoint presented earlier.

Below are some important categories of defining and asserting yourself.

- *Acknowledging your own thoughts and feelings.* There is always a risk in assertion that you are out of touch with your *own* true feelings. Consequently rather than assert your real self you may assert a self which is based on the unexamined internalisation of others' thoughts and feelings, for instance, those of your parents.
- *Thinking realistically.* There are numerous faulty thoughts that may inhibit assertion. Many of these are related to gender, for

instance men not showing affection and women not standing up for their rights.

● *Talking about yourself.* Being able to start, develop and maintain relationships through appropriate mutual sharing of personal information with another.

● *Communicating what you want.* Being sufficiently in touch with yourself to discover what you want and being able to communicate this clearly to others. Neither saying 'no' when you mean 'yes' nor unnecessarily waiting to be asked. Being prepared to take initiatives in saying, negotiating and doing what you want.

● *Being positive towards others.* Being able to make a positive impact on your own and others' lives through your words and actions toward them. Being able to say and show that you have positive feelings toward them and care for their happiness and fulfilment as unique human beings.

● *Absence of defensiveness.* Being able to own up to mistakes and avoid blaming others for your troubles.

● *Being able to stand up for yourself.* This entails the capacity to share negative thoughts and feelings about others, set limits, not say 'yes' when you mean 'no', end relationships appropriately and not allow others to manipulate you into falsely defining yourself on their rather than on your own terms.

● *Using the right amount of strength.* Having sufficient respect for yourself and for the other person that you know the appropriate amount of 'muscle' to use in situations in which you assert yourself. Not unnecessarily either threatening other people or being destructive by lowering their self-esteem.

● *Knowing your own and others' limits.* Being realistic in choosing when not to assert yourself. For instance, the situation might not be that important to you, you may not be ready, the risks might outweigh the gains etc.

Exercise 6.1 is designed to provide you with an initial assessment, in the areas mentioned above, of your skills at defining and asserting yourself. While a few of these skills, for instance developing relationships through revealing personal information, have been covered already, most will be further developed in the remainder of this chapter. A further insight into your assertion behaviour may be gained from reviewing your answers to Exercise 4.1 on 'How shy are you?' What are your feelings and physical reactions when you are being non-assertive? What are your thoughts, both about yourself and concerning others' thoughts about you? How do you behave when you are non-assertive? What people and situations are associated with lack of assertion? There is a large overlap between shyness and lack of assertion.

---

### Exercise 6.1  Assessing how good you are at defining and asserting yourself

This exercise may be done on your own, in pairs or as part of a training group.

A  *On your own*

Assess how good you consider your skills in each of the following areas of defining and asserting yourself. Use the rating scale below:

5  Very poor
4  Poor
3  Neither poor nor good
2  Good
1  Very good

| *Areas* | *Your rating* |
|---|---|
| 1. Being aware of your significant feelings and wishes. | |
| 2. Being free from unrealistic thoughts that impede self-definition and assertion. | |
| 3. Being able to engage in inner speech that is helpful rather than harmful. | |
| 4. Being able to develop intimate relationships through appropriately revealing personal information. | |
| 5. Being able to admit vulnerabilities and strengths. | |
| 6. Being able appropriately to touch and to be touched. | |
| 7. Being able to express wants and wishes clearly. | |
| 8. Being able to discard constricting limits and to say 'yes'. | |
| 9. Being able to take initiatives. | |
| 10. Being able to express positive thoughts and feelings to and about others. | |
| 11. Being able to act positively towards others. | |
| 12. Being able to own up to mistakes and to avoid being defensive. | |
| 13. Being able to express negative thoughts and feelings towards others. | |

14. Being able to set limits and to say 'no'.
15. Being able to end relationships appropriately.
16. Avoiding colluding in others' attempts to have you define yourself falsely to suit their own needs.
17. Using the right amount of strength when you assert yourself.
18. Being able to avoid being unnecessarily destructive.
19. Appropriately handling others' feedback and criticism when you are assertive.
20. Knowing when not to assert yourself.

List all those items that you have rated 5, then those rated 4, then those rated 3. This should give you some idea both of what you consider your skills deficits in asserting and defining yourself and also of their severity.

B *In pairs*

Independently fill out the above questionnaire and make a list of your skills deficits, then discuss.

C *In a training group*

The trainer discusses the concepts of self-definition and assertion. He/she briefly introduces each item in the questionnaire prior to getting the group to rate their skills for that area. Trainees independently make up their list of skills deficits. The trainer may then get them to discuss their responses in pairs or small groups. This is followed by a plenary sharing and discussion session.

## Bodily and vocal messages

When being assertive, your bodily and vocal messages can add to or detract from your overall message. For instance, a firm tone of voice may communicate to others that your verbal assertion is to be taken seriously, while a weak tone dilutes it. Assertion is not only a matter of presence of desirable verbal, vocal and bodily messages, but also involves absence of undesirable messages. Above all vocal and bodily messages that are aggressive and 'put-downs' of others are to be avoided.

Table 6.1 indicates some bodily and vocal components of assertion. It has been included at the beginning of the chapter to increase your awareness of something that is pertinent to all aspects of assertion. When doing all the later exercises, bear in mind that making appropriate vocal and bodily choices comprises an essential part of the development of your assertion skills.

**Table 6.1**  *Some bodily and vocal components of assertion*

| | |
|---|---|
| *Bodily messages* | |
| Eye contact | – looking another directly in the eyes; ability to maintain eye contact when being assertive |
| Facial expression | – showing your positive and negative emotions when appropriate; being genuine, for instance not smiling when you are angry |
| Body posture | – not slumping |
| Gesture | – using hand and arm movements to help express yourself in a constructive fashion |
| Proximity | – not avoiding people, not 'hitting and running' |
| Absence of negative bodily communication | – head shaking, door slamming, fist shaking, finger pointing |
| Absence of distracting bodily communication | – hair pulling, fiddling with fingers |
| *Vocal messages* | |
| Volume | – reasonably loud |
| Tone | – firm, not putting on a 'little girl' or 'little boy' voice |
| Speed | – not too fast |
| Inflection | – presence of inflections that emphasise assertion; absence of inflections that indicate aggression and are 'put-downs'. |

## Mental barriers

In the previous chapter mental barriers to starting relationships were explored. Many of the same issues regarding responsibility for making the first move, rigid internal rules, fear of others' evaluation and anticipating loss more than gain are relevant to being assertive during as well as at the start of relationships.

Table 6.2 lists some illustrative mental barriers to assertion. These unrealistic thoughts are frequently indicative of lack of respect on two levels. First, they may imply that you do not fully respect yourself and hence lack flexibility in reacting to people and situations. Second, they can indicate lack of respect for other people. For instance, one of the main reasons you may give for not asserting yourself is 'I must not hurt others'. This is often a defensive rationalisation to avoid acknowledging anxiety about getting into conflict and being rejected. Thus you may not respect yourself enough to be completely honest about your motives. Furthermore, you may not respect other people's responsibility for their own feelings and lives. Consequently, you inhibit giving honest feedback that may help rather than hinder your relationships. For instance, if a person continuously irritates you by interrupting you it may be better for both of you if you draw it to their attention rather than hide behind a fear of hurting them. Your vocal and bodily messages will also be important indicators of the degree of respect you have for yourself and others. Clumsy or aggressive vocal and bodily communication can needlessly hurt others.

All the mental barriers listed in Table 6.2 are capable of blocking your freedom of choice regarding defining and asserting yourself. The rigid demands on self do not allow you the flexibility to respond creatively to emerging situations. The fears about others' reactions, if overdone, can get you so focused on yourself that you are unable to be fully aware of others and react to them appropriately. The fears

**Table 6.2**   *Some mental barriers to assertion in relationships*

*Demands on self*
I must be nice
I must avoid conflict
I must be self-effacing
I must be liked
I must be feminine
I must be masculine
I must not wear the pants
I must not have wishes of my own
I must not be selfish
I must not hurt others
I must not seem vulnerable
I must not show anger
I must not show liking
I must keep a stiff upper lip
I must not make the first move
I must not make a mistake
I must not admit a mistake
I must not take a risk
I must not ask for what I want

*Fears about others' reactions*
Others might reject me
Others might criticise me
Others might consider me unfeminine
Others might consider me emotional
Others might think I am pushy
Others might consider me uptight
Others might not understand my point
Others might take advantage of me
Others might like me
Others might give me what I want

*Fears about my reactions to others' reactions*
I can't handle rejection
I can't handle conflict
I can't handle uncertainty
I can't handle causing pain
I can't handle being liked
I can't handle getting what I want

about your inability to cope with others' reactions strengthen this tendency.

This chapter focuses on two broad categories of assertion, being positive and coping with negative behaviour. Mental barriers are not only relevant to the latter. There are numerous mental barriers that prevent people from expressing and showing the positive side of themselves.

---

**Exercise 6.2   Exploring your mental barriers to assertion**

This exercise can be done on your own, in pairs or as part of a training group.

A   *On your own*
Using Table 6.2 as a guide write out any mental barriers you may have to asserting yourself in each of the following categories. Relate to specific situations in your relationships as appropriate:
(a)   demands on yourself
(b)   your fears about others' reactions
(c)   your fears about your reactions to others' reactions.

B   *In pairs*
*Either* independently work through the above exercise, then discuss.
*Or* work through the above exercise together from the start.

C   *In a training group*
The trainer introduces the topic of the relationship between thinking and assertion. The trainer gets the whole group to answer the questions, but then encourages individuals to identify those unrealistic thoughts most applicable to them. The trainer can help individual trainees reformulate unrealistic into more realistic thoughts. Alternatively, the trainer may divide the group into subgroups to do the exercise prior to holding a plenary sharing and discussion session.

---

## BEING POSITIVE

Much of the early psychological literature on assertion centred on standing up for your rights. Though this is important in developing and maintaining relationships, it is not the whole story. Indeed relationships where people are perpetually sensitive to real and imagined violations of their rights are disturbed rather than happy.

Increasingly, expressing positive feelings has entered the literature on assertion. For instance, in one book on assertion for women, the definition of assertion is fourfold: expressing positive feelings, expressing negative feelings, setting limits and 'self-initiation', or the ability to take initiatives.[3] Furthermore, the underlying assumption is that of the 'androgynous' person who is able to express all significant aspects of herself regardless of whether they have traditionally been considered masculine or feminine.

Many relationships run into difficulty when those involved are unable to be positive about expressing their wants and wishes, taking initiatives, expressing liking and being likeable. Frequently, this absence of positive behaviour creates an emotional climate where negative behaviours are more likely to occur since one or both partners feels that they are being inadequately listened to and appreciated. Thus, assertion may play an important role in developing and maintaining your relationships. Expressing liking and being positive may help prevent others' negative behaviour. Earlier it was suggested that people strive for equity in their relationships and have a tendency to match or reciprocate each others' behaviours. Expressing liking and being positive towards others in a relationship increases the likelihood of their behaving similarly toward you.

### Stating what you want

Some of you may find it hard to acknowledge the legitimacy of your own wants and wishes. For instance, the 'perfect mother' may feel that she has to spend all her time serving the needs of her husband and children rather than attending to her own. Related to this is the difficulty some have in acknowledging your true wants and wishes because you were brought up in childhood to suppress them. This may be a matter of either denying the wants and wishes altogether or diluting their strength. Still another problem relates to those of you who, while acknowledging your wants and wishes, remain silent about them or present them so diffidently that they are ignored. A variation of this is asking a question so that it elicits a desired response: for instance, 'Do you want to go to the movies?' may be a coded way of saying 'I want to go to the movies'. Even more unfortunate are those of you who state or agree with the opposite of what you want through fear of rejection. For instance, you agree that you want to see movie B when you really want to see movie A.

Stating what you want does not deny others the right to state what they want. Rather, in a relationship where there is mutual respect, it may enhance their ability to state what they want. Your vocal and bodily messages can be extremely important. Stating your wishes can be done in a way that threatens giving the message 'I want this or else . . .'. Alternatively, it may convey more a preference to be considered than a demand to be obeyed.

Stating what you want has been included in this section on being positive because the ability to listen to yourself and then state your wants and wishes can benefit not only you but also your relationship. It allows you to express your needs. It allows the other to listen to your needs without having to mindread you. It gives both of you the possibility of discussing your respective needs where they differ. In short, if appropriately done, it enhances the honesty and vitality of your relationship.

Exercise 6.3 looks at situations in which you may have been inhibited, aggressive or assertive in expressing your wants and wishes. When doing the exercise remember that wants and wishes are best expressed as I-statements. For instance, Jane wants Peter to show her more affection. An inhibited expression of this might be either remaining silent about the want or, in a weak voice, saying 'You do love me, don't you?' An aggressive way of stating this is: 'You are always thinking of yourself. You just don't know how to make a woman happy.' An assertive way might be: 'I love it when you come over and hug me and show your affection. It's something I really want.'

---

**Exercise 6.3   Expressing your wants and wishes**

This exercise can be done on your own, in pairs or as part of a training group.

A   *On your own*
  1. If possible, write down a recent situation in your relationships in each of the following categories:
      1.1.   where you have been *inhibited* in expressing your wants and wishes;
      1.2.   where you have been *aggressive* in expressing your wants and wishes;
      1.3.   where you have been *assertive* in expressing your wants and wishes.
  2. How could you have chosen to behave differently so as to have been assertive in each of the situations above where you were either inhibited or aggressive?

3. If appropriate set yourself goals for improving your effectiveness at expressing your wishes and wants in your relationships. Monitor and evaluate your progress.

B *In pairs*
*Either* independently write out your answers to questions 1 and 2 above, then discuss together.
*Or* each identify recent situations in which you have been (a) inhibited, (b) aggressive and (c) assertive in expressing your wants and wishes. Role-play how you actually behaved and then role-play acting assertively in each of the situations in which you were inhibited or aggressive.

C *In a training group*
The trainer discusses the difference between inhibition, assertion and aggression in expressing wishes and wants. He/she helps the group to identify recent situations for themselves in each category. Where the trainees are willing, these situations are shared with the group. The trainer then uses demonstration, behaviour rehearsal and coaching to help trainees express their wants and wishes assertively. Video-feedback may also be used.

---

Stating what you want can also involve avoiding saying 'no' when you mean 'yes'. For instance, shy people, who may be desperate for human contact, sometimes turn down offers either to go out on a date or to go to a party and then regret it later. Also, stating what you want can involve responding to others' advances in such a way that they can read you loud and clear. Later we deal with the capacity not to say 'yes' when you mean 'no'. Here the emphasis is on getting those of you who have trouble saying 'yes' when you mean 'yes' to have the courage to state what you really want. Acknowledge your resistances to saying 'yes', explore their realism and assess their consequences for your happiness and fulfilment.

**Taking initiatives**

Initiatives need to be taken not only in starting relationships, but in developing and maintaining them. Taking initiative in a relationship means assuming responsibility for making things happen, rather than waiting for others to do so. It can also involve taking responsibility for expressing thoughts and feelings first rather than waiting for permission to do so.

Many women feel that they are controlled by men in their relationships. They consider that they are expected to behave passively, wait for the male to take a lead and not have their own competence and authority acknowledged. In reality, both genders allow themselves to be controlled by their role expectations not only of each other but of themselves. There are certain areas where traditionally women expect and are expected to take the lead: for instance, cooking, looking after the house, and being a harmoniser in family relations. There are certain areas where traditionally men expect and are expected to take a lead: for instance, being the breadwinner, looking after the car, and in bed.

These are, however, areas of double standard for both genders. For instance, men risk much less disapproval for taking heterosexual initiatives than women. Women risk much less disapproval for taking the initiative in showing their feelings. Indeed, all the traditional divisions of what is 'masculine' and what is 'feminine' are sets of double standards. For each gender there are different permissions and prohibitions pertaining to appropriate thoughts, feelings and actions.

Exercise 6.4 has been designed to help you explore the extent to which, in male–female relationships, you impose a set of rigid expectations on yourself and on your partner. These expectations make it more difficult for each of you to take the initiatives that make for a democratic relationship based on choice rather than on having to rely upon tradition.

---

**Exercise 6.4   Taking initiatives: exploring double standards**

This exercise can be done on your own, in pairs or as part of a training group.

A   *On your own*
  Below are a number of areas in male–female relationships where either or both of you may take the initiative.

  Asking for a date
  Ordering a meal
  Paying the bill after eating out
  Arranging to go to a movie
  Arranging a vacation
  Providing transportation
  Driving

Showing affection
Asking for support
Touching
Making love
Doing housework
Doing household repairs
Choosing living accommodation
Decorating living accommodation

1. Assess the degree to which you are prepared to take the initiative in each of these areas in a male–female relationship.
2. Assess the extent to which you have a double standard between yourself and the other gender in regard to taking initiatives in each of these areas.
3. Assess the degree to which any double standards you have block rather than help your own and the other person's happiness and fulfilment.
4. If appropriate, set yourself goals for acting differently. Monitor and evaluate your progress as you try to attain your goals.

B   *In pairs*
    *Either* independently do the above exercise, then discuss.
    *Or* work through the above exercise together.
C   *In a training group*
    The trainer introduces the idea of being free in male–female relationships to take initiatives regardless of gender. The trainer subdivides the group into pairs, threes or fours and gets these subgroups to work through the above exercise together. This is then followed by a plenary sharing and discussion session.

---

As traditional gender roles get challenged, along with some confusion there is an increasing tendency for males and females to discuss where to take initiatives in relationships. When you are in an established relationship, one of you, often nowadays the female, may wish to redefine your role. This can have both opportunities and risks for the stability of your relationship. Here being assertive may entail the strength to persist in new kinds of behaviour. Also, showing understanding of and tolerance towards the resistances exhibited by and the adjustments required of your partner.

**Communicating positively**

An area where some of you may find assertion difficult is in expressing positive sentiments towards others. Frequently you may remain unaware of the extent to which you accentuate others' negative and ignore their positive aspects. From birth humans hunger for recognition, warmth and approval. All too often their needs remain frustrated or only partially fulfilled. This may be a matter not only of others insufficiently expressing positive feelings towards them, but also of their insufficiently expressing positive feelings towards others. Not surprisingly a research study has shown that distressed relationships, as contrasted with happy ones, show a lack of reciprocity of pleasing behaviours.[4]

Communicating positively towards others can be done both by words and actions. Saying you like or love someone, paying them compliments, and expressing gratitude and appreciation are all ways in which you can verbally communicate your positive feelings. Appropriate vocal messages are essential. A verbal message of affection gets totally negated if said in a flat and disinterested voice.

Communicating positively towards others also involves acting positively toward them. Communication of positive feelings by words alone can lead to mistrust if not accompanied by deeds. There are numerous ways of acting towards other people in ways that make them happy and are perceived as helpful. Part of the art of this is tuning in to the other person sufficiently well so that you do what *actually* makes them happy rather than what you think *should* make them happy. In the latter instance, if you have incorrectly identified their needs, they may not produce the desired happiness for you. This seeming lack of appreciation may worsen rather than improve your relationship.

What are some of the blocks that you may need to overcome if you are to have the choice of communicating more positively in your relationships? You may have deep-seated feelings of insecurity which cause you to see others in a more negative and threatening light than is justified. Indeed it is said that such people project their hatred of themselves onto others. Here counselling may be indicated. Having positive feelings about yourself is fundamental to having positive feelings about others. Some of you may be unfortunate enough to be in relationships with disturbed and aggressive partners. Consequently, you may need to review whether or not to stay in the relationship. However, often blocks to communicating positively are less intractable. They involve mental barriers which, once identified, can be altered. One of the biggest unrealistic rules is probably 'I must receive from someone before I can give to that person'. Masters and Johnson, the noted American pioneers into the treatment of sexual problems, encourage their patients to adopt a 'give-to-get' philosophy.[5] Even this philosophy has an implicit demand that the other give in return. Though it is preferable that the receiver give in return, it is undesirable to make it a demand. The reason for this is that you may resent not having your demand met. This could interfere with future positive communication on your part. Thus a 'give-to-give' philosophy has much to recommend it.

Other mental barriers to communicating positively involve the perceived psychological costs of this behaviour. For instance, if you express positive feelings toward another you may be: rejected; perceived as soft, insincere or manipulative; taken advantage of; or perceived as giving way in a power struggle. Also, you may deepen the relationship in a way you find hard to manage. The realism of such psychological costs needs to be carefully reviewed and set against the possible gains from asserting yourself through positive communication. Positive actions towards others may involve time, money and effort. Again the costs of such actions need to be set against the rewards to yourself, the other and the relationship from behaving positively.

Exercise 6.5 on expressing liking and being likeable is designed to help you explore whether you are assuming sufficient personal responsibility for communicating positively in your relationships. The exercise is not about seeming positive or a superficial niceness. Rather it is about ways in which you can authentically assert yourself as a constructive and positive human being.

---

**Exercise 6.5   Expressing liking and being likeable**

This exercise can be done on your own, in pairs or as part of a training group.

A   *On your own*
   Write out your answers to the following questions:
   1.   In your relationships how good are you at verbally expressing positive thoughts and feelings towards others?
   2.   In your relationships how good are you at acting in ways that are designed to be helpful and/or to give pleasure?
   3.   What, if any, are some of the mental barriers or unrealistic thoughts you possess that interfere with your expressing liking and being likeable?
   4.   Take a specific relationship in your life and assess whether it could be improved by your asserting yourself more in expressing liking and being likeable. If so set yourself goals for acting

differently and monitor and evaluate your progress as you try to achieve your goals.

B *In pairs*
*Either* independently answer the above questions, then discuss.
*Or* work through the above questions together from the start.

C *In a training group*
The trainer introduces the importance in developing and maintaining relationships of asserting yourself by expressing liking and being likeable. Each question above is introduced by the trainer, then trainees answer it independently, in pairs, or in small groups followed by a whole group discussion on that question. The trainer helps group members to see the range of their choices in expressing liking and being likeable. Additionally, mental barriers are identified and reformulated. Lastly, the trainer uses demonstration, behaviour rehearsal and coaching to help trainees develop specific skills in this area.

---

## COPING WITH NEGATIVE BEHAVIOUR

It is possible to view much of life as a contest in which people strive to impose their behaviour and their definitions of situations on others. Furthermore each of you has a picture of yourself that implies not only how you relate to others, but how others should relate to you. Consequently defining yourself may require having the courage to stand up to others' negative behaviour and to their attempts to define you on their terms rather than your own.

A personal responsibility view of assertion is that it entails a number of choices. For instance, in coping with negative behaviour you need to make *choices* in the following areas.

● *What is my contribution to creating the negative situation?* It is all too easy to attribute the responsibility for negative events outside of yourself. Consequently your assertion may need to be focused less on changing the negative behaviour of another rather than on changing your own behaviour so that they do not react negatively to you. Furthermore, your definition of behaviour as negative may stem from the rigidity and lack of realism of your thinking.

● *How defensive am I being?* When your view of yourself is threatened it may be very tempting to strike back under the guise of assertion. For instance, if someone gives you negative feedback about an aspect of your behaviour, you need to assess whether they may have a point. Especially where strong emotions are involved, you may be labelling your behaviour as assertive whereas in reality it is aggressive.

● *Is it worth being assertive?* One issue here is whether you feel sufficiently involved in a relationship to choose to be assertive. Another issue may be how realistic it is to be assertive in a situation where you know another person to be highly threatened and potentially destructive if challenged. Though there are great rewards to being openly assertive, there also may be realistic risks. It is naive to expect that assertion, however well performed, always leads to a happy outcome. The consequences both of your assertion and of your failure to be assertive need to be carefully considered.

● *Do I have the requisite skills?* Asserting yourself to cope with others' negative behaviour can be difficult. There are six possible areas of deficit in which you may need to build up your skills.

1. *Being aware.* Being aware of when you have the choice of responding and acting in an assertive manner. This can be more difficult than it sounds where others are putting subtle pressures on you to define yourself on their terms.
2. *Overcoming your mental barriers.* Increasingly realising and reformulating the kinds of thoughts that prevent you from asserting yourself. Many of these were listed in Table 6.2.
3. *Managing your anxiety.* Situations in which you have to cope with others' negative behaviour can be stressful. Task-oriented inner speech before, during and after may be helpful.
4. *Knowing what to say.* Being able to express yourself verbally by means of 'I' statements.
5. *Knowing how to say it.* Possessing assertive and avoiding non-assertive vocal and bodily communication.
6. *Acting appropriately.* If necessary, backing up your words with actions.

Table 6.3 illustrates inhibited, aggressive and assertive ways of coping with others' negative behaviour. In the inhibited examples you may be less than honest and pay the price by feeling bad about yourself and others. In the aggressive examples the emotional temperature is unnecessarily raised by the use of 'You-blame' rather than 'I-rational' statements.[6] In 'I-rational' statements people state how they feel and why they feel that way in a calm and rational fashion. 'You-blame' statements engender defensiveness by being accusatory statements which are 'put-downs' of others.

**Table 6.3** *Inhibited, aggressive and assertive ways of coping with negative behaviour*

1. *Perceived negative behaviour:* You invite someone to dinner and they arrive an hour late without contacting you.

| Inhibited | Aggressive | Assertive |
|---|---|---|
| 'It's all right. Good to see you.' | 'Damn you. Now the dinner is spoiled.' | 'I'm concerned at your being so late without contacting me. Was there a reason for this?' |

2. *Perceived negative behaviour:* You study for an exam and your neighbour plays his/her record player very loud.

| Inhibited | Aggressive | Assertive |
|---|---|---|
| You thump the table and curse to yourself. | 'Turn that bloody record player down. Don't you realise other people have work to do.' | 'I'm upset because I can't concentrate with your record player so loud. Would you please turn it down.' |

3. *Perceived negative behaviour:* You live with somebody who rarely does the washing up.

| Inhibited | Aggressive | Assertive |
|---|---|---|
| You keep doing the washing up, but resent it deeply. | 'You lazy idiot. Do you think I like acting as your servant all the time?' | 'I'm annoyed because you always leave the dishes to me and this is a lot of extra work. I want us to work out an arrangement so we share this chore.' |

The assertive examples are based on 'I-rational' statements following an F.E.R. (Feeling, Explanation, Request) format, though not slavishly in that order. F is how you feel. E is your explanation of why you feel that way. This should specify the behaviour that you find negative. R is your request that either the negative behaviour be ended or, at the very least, that it be explained.

Pamela Butler's concept of 'muscle' is helpful in considering how to make 'I-rational' assertive statements.[7] Basically, muscle entails taking into consideration how forceful to be. As a rule of thumb, assertion should be achieved with the minimum level of forcefulness necessary to achieve its objective. There are two main reasons for this. First, the greater the use of muscle the more chance there may be of eliciting defensive resistances that block you from getting what you want. Second, even if you do get what you want, the more muscle you use the greater is the chance that you will leave a residue of resentment. This unfinished business on the part of the other may later interfere with your relationship. Using too much muscle can be

**Table 6.4**   *A grid for looking at the choices involved in inhibited, aggressive and assertive behaviour*

| | Your goals | Your thoughts | Your feelings | What you say | How you say it | Your actions |
|---|---|---|---|---|---|---|
| *Inhibited behaviour* | | | | | | |
| *Aggressive behaviour* | | | | | | |
| *Assertive behaviour* | | | | | | |

the strength of weakness rather than the strength of genuine strength. As such it moves your assertion into the direction of aggression.

Table 6.4 provides a grid for looking at the *choices* involved in inhibited, aggressive and assertive behaviour. In assertive behaviour: your goal is clearly defined and sensible; your thinking is disciplined, realistic and goal-oriented; your basic feeling is that of adequacy and you keep in check any self-defeating feelings; your verbal message is clear; your voice and body messages back up your verbal message with an appropriate degree of muscle; and, if necessary, so do your actions. Inhibited and aggressive behaviour is deficient, to a greater or lesser degree, on each of the above dimensions.

**Standing up for yourself**

Exercise 6.6 on speaking out for yourself is designed to give you some knowledge and skills for handling situations where another person in a relationship behaves in a way that bothers you. In formulating your assertive responses, you may find it helpful to stick closely to the following guidelines.
1.   Make an 'I-rational' statement.
2.   Use the F.E.R. format.
3.   Use the minimum amount of muscle necessary for achieving your goal.
4.   Pay close attention to voice and body messages.
5.   Think of any actions you may need to take to back up your assertive message.

**Exercise 6.6    Speaking out for yourself**

This exercise can be done on your own, in pairs or as part of a training group.

A  *On your own*
Think of at least one situation in your current or previous relationships where you have been faced with the need to cope with other people's behaviour that you perceived negatively. Refer to Tables 6.3 and 6.4 and for each of your situations write out an inhibited, aggressive and assertive response.

B  *In pairs*
*Either* independently write out your responses to the above exercise, then discuss.
*Or* each identify at least one situation in your current or previous relationships where you were faced with negative behaviour. For each situation role-play how you actually behaved. Then, if you were inhibited or aggressive, rehearse an assertive response.

C  *In a training group*
The trainer discusses the difference between inhibition, aggression and assertion in dealing with perceived negative behaviour. He/she helps the group to identify situations in their lives that they are finding difficulty in handling. Group members are asked to role-play these situations. The trainer then uses demonstration, behaviour rehearsal and coaching to help trainees cope assertively with perceived negative behaviour. Video-feedback may also be used. Alternatively, the trainer gets the group to do the above exercise on their own, followed by a plenary sharing, discussion and role-play session.

Exercise 6.7 is designed to help you define the limits of your personal space and to stop other people from intruding. While it overlaps with Exercise 6.6 on speaking out for yourself, its emphasis is much more on saying 'no' when you mean 'no': for instance, not going out with someone, not allowing certain physical advances, not going to a play or movie, not letting someone stay later than you want, not lending something, and refusing an unreasonable request for work. Earlier Exercise 6.3 encouraged you to express what you do want. Exercise 6.7 focuses on communicating clearly what you do not want. Use 'I-rational' statements, the minimum necessary muscle and assertive vocal and bodily messages. Explain what you do not want to the extent that you consider it appropriate. Sometimes, after indicating what you do not want, it can be helpful to say what you do want. This can provide a more positive basis for discussing and negotiating your differences.

---

### Exercise 6.7  Setting limits and saying 'no'

This exercise can be done on your own, in pairs or as part of a training group.

A  *On your own*
Think of at least one situation in a current or previous relationship where you are/have been faced with the need to set limits and/or say 'no'. Take a piece of paper and put a line down the middle. For each situation, to the left of the line write out how you actually behaved. To the right write out an assertive response if you are/ were not satisfied with your original response. Repeat the task with different situations as many times as you find useful.

B  *In pairs*
*Either* independently write out your responses to the above exercise, then discuss.
*Or* each identify at least one situation in a current or previous relationship where you are/have been faced with the need to set limits and/or say 'no'. For each situation role-play how you actually behaved. Then, if you were inhibited or aggressive, rehearse acting assertively.

C  *In a training group*
The trainer discusses the difference between inhibition, aggression and assertion in setting limits and saying 'no'. The trainer uses demonstration, behaviour rehearsal and coaching to help trainees develop the skills of setting limits and saying 'no' in areas where they are experiencing difficulty. Video-feedback may be useful.

---

### Ending relationships

Ending a relationship can be achieved in an inhibited, aggressive or assertive way. To start, you need to be clear that this is what you really want. For example, Jane asks Peter not to come round to her place any more. However, each time he does come she lets him in and has a long conversation with him. Here Jane is giving a very mixed message about ending the relationship.

Some of you may be inhibited about ending a relationship because you take on responsibility for another person's life. For instance, Ken does not come right out and tell Betty that he thinks they have no future because he tells himself he is afraid that she will not be able to handle being on her own. In reality, Ken may be afraid of the confrontation and, after a period of adjustment, Betty might manage very well on her own.

Many relationships end with hurtful rows after which the participants are not on speaking terms. When Lord Byron's relationship to Lady Caroline Lamb broke up he is alleged to have said: 'She has lost the power of communication, but not, regrettably, the gift of speech.' Aggressive endings to relationships can add to the pain of parting for either or both of you. Furthermore, they can negate the good times that you may have had in the relationship.

There are several factors which may make it difficult to end a relationship assertively, especially if you are married, have children and have shared property. Here the focus is on ending non-marital relationships assertively. Already you may have set some limits in the relationship: for instance, by restricting the intimacy level of your disclosures and by limiting the amount of physical contact. Even if you have not, many of the guidelines suggested earlier still apply to ending virtually any relationship: whenever possible the use of 'I-rational' rather than 'You-blame' statements; the minimum use of muscle; and assertive vocal and bodily messages that reinforce rather than undermine your verbal message.

Though sometimes relationships end abruptly, most often there is some prior indication that they are in trouble. If both of you are coordinated in your wish to end the relationship, this eases the ending. Where you are the person who initiates the ending of the relationship, it is generally better to come right out and say what you want rather than fudge the issue. You may either be asked or feel it appropriate to give an explanation for your decision. Alternatively you may be the recipient of a tirade of abuse. In either event you may be able to show your strength by doing minimal damage to the self-esteem of the person with whom you have been involved. Ending a relationship assertively entails showing respect for yourself and the other person rather than being brutal and ruthless. Though you may well be contributing to another's pain, you have a responsibility for your own happiness and fulfilment. Provided you have not raised another's expectations dishonestly, part of the implicit contract in your relationship was probably that either of you could withdraw and seek your happiness elsewhere.

---

**Exercise 6.8   Ending relationships: saying goodbye**

This exercise may be done on your own, in pairs or as part of a training group.

A   *On your own*
1.   Write out what you think are the main considerations in ending a relationship assertively.
2.   Do you experience or anticipate any special areas of difficulty in ending a relationship.
3.   If relevant, pick a relationship that you have ended or would like to end. Take some paper and in one column write out how you did behave or are behaving to end it. In a second column write out an assertive way to end the relationship.

B   *In pairs*
*Either* independently write out your answers to the above questions, then discuss.
*Or* each identify a situation where you have needed/need to end a relationship. Role-play how you actually behaved or intend to behave. If this is inhibited or aggressive, discuss and rehearse an assertive ending to each of your relationships.

C   *In a training group*
The trainer discusses differences between inhibition, aggression and assertion in ending relationships. Trainees are asked to provide illustrative examples from their own lives. The trainer uses demonstration, behaviour rehearsal and coaching to help trainees develop the skills of ending relationships assertively. Video-feedback may be useful.

---

## AVOIDING COLLUSION

Geoff uses his anger as a way of getting what he wants. Mike obscures the issue to avoid dealing with you directly. Vera finds that her tears are a very effective means of getting others to bend to her wishes. Joan withdraws affection if people do not give her the feedback that she wants. In all the above instances people are using various devices – anger, mystification, tears, withdrawal of affection – to get what they want at someone else's expense. They are successful to the extent that others, knowingly or unknowingly, collude in allowing them to succeed.

The above are instances of people using specific interventions to manipulate or control others. Another possibility for collusion is where a whole relationship has underlying assumptions that place pressures on one of the parties to define themselves and behave to their own disadvantage. One example of this is that of parents' relationships with their late adolescent or young adult children. Here the parents may place their children under pressure to please them in choice of friends, job etc. Another example is that of a male–female relationship where the male is discouraging the female from pursuing her career. In both the above instances, people are attempting to influence if not control the behaviour of others. Again they are successful to the extent that others, knowingly or unknowingly, collude in allowing them to succeed.

People are frequently using power-plays of varying degrees of subtlety to get others to do what they want.[8,9] Sometimes they may be unaware of the way they are using defining situations to their advantage or use interventions like tears to control other people. Behaving assertively entails minimising the extent to which you collude in others' false definitions of you and to which you allow yourself to be manipulated.

Being aware of others' attempts to operate on your self-definition and to manipulate you is the first step in being able to handle their control moves. You then have a number of options. First, being submissive and at least tacitly acquiescing in their false definitions and manipulations. Second, being aggressive and perhaps escalating the tension and emotional temperature by counterattacking. Third, being assertive by quickly yet firmly persisting in your definition of yourself and/or the situation. This option may also include working on your own tendencies to either acquiescence or escalation. Fourth, and this may also be an assertive option if you find you are relating to a highly manipulative person, getting out of the relationship.

Attempts to control and define you may not only come from people with whom you relate closely. Especially for young people, much pressure, both overt and subtle, may come from your peer group. Again you need to become aware of whether and how these pressures block rather than facilitate your happiness and fulfilment. The options listed above apply to relating to groups as well as to individuals.

Exercise 6.9 focuses on avoiding colluding in others' power plays, manipulations and control moves. For some of you it may come as a surprise to think that people, such as your parents or boyfriends or girlfriends, may be defining and manipulating you for their own rather than for your benefit. In all probability, this is not an either/or matter. Though much of the time they may relate to you in your own best interests, they too are fallible human beings who may want you to collude in their distortions of reality and acquiesce in their manipulations. Paraphrasing the theologian Paul Tillich's phrase 'The courage to be',[10] adequately defining and asserting yourself also involves 'The courage not to collude'.

---

**Exercise 6.9    Avoiding colluding in others' power plays**

This exercise can be done on your own, in pairs or as part of a training group.

A  *On your own*
1.  List as many ways you can think of in which others you know have manipulated you, are manipulating you or might manipulate you to define yourself on their terms and to act according to their wishes.
2.  Select one or two situations in which this has, is or might happen. Write out a plan for each situation for stopping colluding in their behaviour and handling the situation assertively. The plan should identify their power plays and your ways of dealing with each one.

B  *In pairs*
*Either* independently write out your responses to the above exercise, then discuss.
*Or* each identify one or more situations in which another person is power-playing you to define yourself on their terms. Together develop a plan for each situation for stopping colluding in their behaviour and handling the situation assertively. Then rehearse and practise your assertive behaviour.

C  *In a training group*
The trainer discusses the notion of power and control in relationships and how it is possible to collude, knowingly or unknowingly, in other people's false definitions of you. He/she helps group members identify situations in their lives where they are being power-played. The trainer uses behaviour rehearsal and coaching to help trainees cope assertively with situations in which they are being manipulated or power-played. Video-feedback may also be used.

---

**Dealing with defensiveness**

In an ideal world, a well thought-through and delivered assertion message would receive respect and merit serious consideration. In the real world, even excellent assertion messages may create problems for the sender. Almost by definition, coping with negative behaviour assertion messages challenges the existing behaviours and self-conceptions of those to whom they are delivered. Regrettably all too many people are highly defensive regarding anything that even remotely threatens their sense of adequacy or self-esteem. Few of you, if any, are not subject to some feelings of threat when your behaviour or customary way of seeing yourself is challenged. However, some of you are more secure than others and thus are less inclined to feel threatened and more able to manage any feelings of threat that you experience.

The results of others' feelings of threat in relation to your assertion can take many forms. Some people may even try to deny your message by pretending that they did not hear you. Others may distort your assertive message and react to it as though it were aggressive. Consequently, they may either withdraw from you and sulk or attack and put you down. Others may simply refuse to accede to your request, however reasonable it may appear to you.

There are at least two agendas when you are faced with other people's defensiveness, lack of co-operation and negative feedback in relation to your assertion. The first agenda concerns how you handle your own thoughts and feelings. Here it can be important to acknowledge that defensiveness is a common initial reaction to assertion. Thus it may neither indicate that you have asserted yourself poorly nor that you may not ultimately succeed in your assertion. Related to this, it may help you if you are clear that you can only be responsible for your own thoughts, feelings and behaviour. If someone reacts negatively to your assertion or is uncooperative, their behaviour is their responsibility not yours, despite their possible attempts to make you feel guilty. Furthermore, the expectation that others will always do what you want is unrealistic and can only contribute to your denigrating yourself if they do not.

The second agenda concerns how you behave toward the other person. One option is to be unassertive by becoming inhibited, compliant, submissive or passive. Another option is to be aggressive. Assuming you consider it in your best interests to persist in the assertion, you still have a number of options. First, you may pause after the negative response and then calmly yet firmly repeat your assertion message. Second you may respond by reflecting or mirroring the other person's feelings and then calmly yet firmly repeating your assertion message. Below is an example of this:

Pete: I'm upset because I can't concentrate with your record-player so loud. Would you please turn it down.

Fred: Why the hell are you complaining?

Pete: I realise you're angry at my request, but I really do want to concentrate on my study and would be grateful if you could turn your record-player down.

Fred: (still not too pleased) – O.K.

In the above instance, acknowledging Fred's feeling may help him to be less defensive. He may consider that at least you have understood his feelings.

A third option in the face of another person's defensiveness or resistance is to use more muscle. For instance, you may use a firmer voice to convey to Fred that you mean business. Also, you may strengthen your verbal message by saying: 'I'm serious, please turn your record-player down.' You may specify a negative consequence for Fred if he persists: for instance, 'If you don't turn your record-player down, I'm not going to lend you my records any more.'

A fourth option in the face of another's resistance is to try to negotiate a mutually acceptable solution to the differences that exist. In the above example you might negotiate with Fred times when he can play his record-player and times when you can study. The skills of managing conflict are covered in greater depth later in this book.

Exercise 6.10 focuses on dealing with others' defensiveness. One of its purposes is to counter any naive optimism you may have that being assertive is always going to be easy and get you what you want. As you focus on developing strategies for dealing with defensiveness remember that there are two main agendas: the *inner*, managing your own thoughts and feelings, and the *outer*, how you actually behave towards the other person.

---

**Exercise 6.10  Coping with defensiveness, resistance and negative feedback**

This exercise can be done on your own, in pairs or as part of a training group.

A  *On your own*
 1. Write down all the major ways others might try to make it difficult for you to persist in each of the following:
    (a)  speaking out for yourself;
    (b)  setting limits and saying 'no';
    (c)  ending relationships;
    (d)  avoiding colluding in their power plays.

2. Develop strategies for persisting in your assertion and for handling others' defensiveness, resistance and negative feedback as best you can.

B   *In pairs*
*Either* independently write out your responses to the above exercise, then discuss.
*Or* each identify an important situation where you consider that you might have difficulty persisting in your assertion. Discuss strategies for handling each situation and role-play persisting in your assertion despite defensiveness, resistance and negative feedback.

C   *In a training group*
The trainer discusses some of the difficulties trainees may face when they assert themselves to cope with others' negative behaviours. Trainees are encouraged to present situations in which they consider that they may have difficulty persisting in their assertion. The group discusses strategies for coping in those situations. The trainer then uses demonstration, behaviour rehearsal and coaching to help trainees develop skills at coping with defensiveness, resistance and negative feedback when they assert themselves. Video-feedback may help.

---

## CONCLUDING INNER SPEECH

Below is some inner speech that summarises the chapter.

Defining and asserting myself in relationships entails my being in touch with my own feelings. I need to reinforce my verbal assertion messages with assertive vocal and bodily messages. The way I think can interfere with my ability to be assertive. I need to be realistic about the demands I make on myself and about my fears concerning both others' reactions and my ability to handle their reactions.

Being assertive entails expressing myself positively as well as being able to cope with others' negative behaviours. I can assert myself by communicating my wants and wishes clearly, by taking initiatives, and by consciously making the effort to be likeable and to express liking. As such, assertion entails my being a constructive and positive human being.

Much of life resembles a contest in which I have to cope with others' negative behaviour. I need to be aware of any contribution that I may be making to the difficulties. In general my assertion messages should be: 'I-rational' statements; using an F.E.R. (feeling, explanation, request) format; showing the minimum necessary amount of muscle; and backed by good voice and body messages. Coping with others' negative behaviours may involve me in: speaking out for myself; setting limits and saying 'no'; ending a relationship; and not colluding in others' power plays and manipulations. I may encounter defensiveness, resistance and negative feedback in response to my assertion. There are a number of choices I can make in coping with such behaviour.

# REFERENCES

1. Alberti, R.E. & Emmons, M.L. (1974) *Your Perfect Right* (2nd ed.). San Luis Obispo, California: Impact.
2. Bolton, R. (1979) *People Skills: How to Assert Yourself, Listen to Others and Resolve Conflicts*. Englewood Cliffs, NJ: Prentice-Hall.
3. Butler, P. E. (1981) *Self-assertion for Women* (new ed.). San Francisco: Harper & Row.
4. Margolin, G. (1981) Behavior exchange in happy and unhappy marriages: a family cycle perspective. *Behavior Therapy*, **12**, 329–343.
5. Masters, W.H. & Johnson, V.E. (1970) *Human Sexual Inadequacy*. London: J. A. Churchill.
6. Burley-Allen, M. (1982) *Listening: the Forgotten Skill*. New York: Wiley.
7. Butler, P.E. (1981) *Self-assertion for Women*. San Francisco: Harper & Row.
8. Steiner, C.M. (1981) *The Other Side of Power*. New York: Grove Press.
9. Berne, E. (1964). *Games People Play*. New York: Grove Press.
10. Tillich, P. (1952) *The Courage to Be*. New Haven: Yale University Press.

# 7 Becoming a Good Listener

The next two chapters focus on the skills of listening with understanding and of helping others to talk. Being a good listener is related to being relaxed at talking about yourself. The less energy you spend on worrying what others' reactions to you might be, the more you have to devote to listening to them. Developing your skills as a receiver of information is every bit as important as developing your skills as a sender of information. The observation that you need to assume responsibility for listening well in your relationships may strike you as odd at first. There is a prevalent illusion that, while others may listen poorly, one's own listening is both good and also something that is natural. While, for those not born deaf, the capacity to hear sound is natural, the capacity to understand the meaning of most sounds needs to be learned. Furthermore, listening entails picking up both bodily and vocal messages. It requires the capacity to observe as well as to hear.

Listening is a powerful way of affirming another human being. When children grow up, the quality of listening of the adults around them is vital for their psychological development. Children who have been well listened to are likely not only to feel accepted by others but also to be able to accept themselves. Furthermore, they have had the safety to express and explore their feelings. Thus they have been helped to acquire the capacity of *inner* listening, listening to and trusting their own feelings and reactions, which is an essential part of *outer* listening, listening to others. Additionally, having at least one reliable parent who listens well provides them with a secure base to engage in exploratory behaviour and make personal experiments. Children who have not been adequately listened to are likely to be more out of touch with their feelings, more afraid and anxious, and more aggressive and violent. Just as good listening can affirm the core of another's being, bad listening can disconfirm it. As such, bad listening perpetrated regularly may be viewed as a significant form of psychological violence, even if often unintended.

In adult life listening can also affirm and disconfirm. A frequent complaint in relationships where communication has broken down is that either or both partners no longer listens. People vary in their listening skills. At one extreme there are those whose 'communication only goes one way', they talk but do not listen. More facetiously this has been expressed by American golfer Lee Trevino, himself a big talker, in relation to fellow professional Fuzzy Zoeller that Zoeller should donate his body to medical science since 'His mouth is worn out, but his ears are brand new.'[1] At the other extreme are those who are able to be sensitively attuned to another's thoughts and feelings and to convey this so that the other feels understood. This kind of listening, often called empathic listening, is the hallmark of effective counsellors and therapists.[2] It is a disciplined form of listening which is easier to achieve in a counselling relationship, mainly focused on meeting the needs of the client, than in an everyday relationship where both of you are seeking to have your needs met. Nevertheless disciplined listening is extremely important in everyday relationships where the risks of minor and major breakdowns in communication are ever present.

Some of you choose to listen too much. Though it is always important to listen well, you may have to assert yourself in some relationships to ensure that communication remains two-way and that you do not allow yourself to be what the Australians call 'earbashed'. Also, listening too much can be a form of defensiveness whereby you allow others to take the risks involved in revealing themselves and remain concealed yourself. This misuse of listening impedes rather than facilitates the development of genuine relationships based on mutual disclosure and trust.

Exercise 7.1 is designed to help you become aware of some of the choices that you need to take responsibility for if you are to be an effective listener. Complete the questionnaire before looking at the answers provided at the end of the chapter.

---

### Exercise 7.1 Exploring your views on listening

This exercise can be done in a number of ways.

A  *On your own*
B and C  *In pairs or in a training group*
   One option is to complete the whole questionnaire independently and then discuss together your answers to each item. Another option is to go through the questionnaire independently answering single items, each of which is discussed before moving on to answering and discussing the next item.

*Exercise*

For each statement write down whether you consider it to be true (T) or false (F). Answer every item.

*T or F*

_____ 1. People are brought up to be good listeners.

_____ 2. People's thoughts can interfere with their listening.

_____ 3. Listening is a natural activity.

_____ 4. To be able to listen to others, people need to be able to listen to themselves.

_____ 5. People may resist listening to others who blame and get angry with them.

_____ 6. Being a good listener never requires self-discipline.

_____ 7. People are more likely to talk to people with whom they feel safe and accepted than with those whom they do not.

_____ 8. It is always up to other people to communicate precisely what they want.

_____ 9. People who have something that they can't wait to say listen well.

_____ 10. Some people listen too much because they are afraid of revealing themselves.

_____ 11. An important aspect in developing trust is listening and then keeping confidences.

_____ 12. Talking is more important than listening.

_____ 13. The amount people reveal about themselves is likely to influence the amount others tell them about themselves.

_____ 14. Fatigue never affects the quality of people's listening.

_____ 15. Effective listening entails making a series of correct choices in receiving what is being said.

_____ 16. People who feel very emotional about issues are good listeners.

_____ 17. Listening to others does not involve paying attention to their voice quality and body language as well as to what they say.

_____ 18. Repeatedly not listening to and understanding another can be viewed as a form of psychological violence.

_____ 19. People are more likely to hear messages which correspond with their view of themselves than messages which challenge their view.

_____ 20. People who are very angry are rarely good listeners.

_____ 21. The way in which people listen is not affected by their prior life experience.

_____ 22. People sometimes send mixed messages which are difficult for the listener to understand.

## SOURCES OF INTERFERENCE

In an ideal world, those talking would be readily and easily understood by those listening. In the real world life is not that easy. Two amateur radio operators are similar to two people trying to communicate. When all goes well, the receiver receives the sender 'loud and clear'. However, on a number of occasions, there is likely to be poor reception due to static or interference. The reasons for this interference may be located in the sender's radio, the receiver's radio or both.

**Table 7.1**  *Possible sources of interference located in the sender*

The following talker characteristics may be sources of interference impeding accurate listening.

Lack of clarity regarding the intentions of a message
Material left out by mistake
Material left out because of incorrect assumption that it is known
Message encoded rather than communicated directly
Lack of matching of vocal and bodily with verbal communication
Has vocal and bodily mannerisms that discourage listening
Has heavy accent
Has poor command of language
Has speech impediment, e.g. stammering, slurred speech
Shyness
Anxiety and tension
Anger and aggression
Uses 'You-blame' language
Engaging in competitive power contest
Focuses on awkward topic areas, viz. sexuality

Table 7.1 suggests some sources of interference located in the sender or talker to your receiving a message loud and clear. It may be hard for you to be clear about a message when the sender is not clear or leaves material out, either unintentionally or because it is assumed that you know it already. Even when intentional many messages are not sent loud and clear, but encoded. That requires the receiver to decode the verbal, vocal and bodily components of the message to understand the real communication. A simple example is the use of 'Do you want the salt?' to mean 'I want the salt'. Another example is saying 'I'm not upset' with a choked voice. The more senders communicate in code rather than direct, the more chance there is for misunderstanding on the part of listeners through errors in decoding.

Additionally, if senders have distracting mannerisms and awkward voices this may contribute to poor reception.

Lack of ability to speak good English and being emotional to the point where listeners feel uncomfortable are two further sender-based sources of interference. For instance, a heavy accent, misuse of words and a stammer may each interfere with sending a message fluently. Furthermore, emotions like shyness, anxiety and tension not only distract senders but also receivers. Expressions of hostility, the use of 'You-blame' language, and a competitive rather than a cooperative approach may all contribute to listeners feeling threatened. Lastly, the talkers may focus on topic areas that 'hook into' listening barriers in receivers: for instance, feelings of embarrassment when hearing sexual disclosures.

Part of the skill of becoming a good listener is the ability to overcome many of the sources of interferences located in the other person. However, an even more important part of the skill, though related to coping with external sources of interference, is the ability to assume responsibility for becoming aware of and dealing with your own barriers and filters to listening with understanding. Many of your internal sources of interference are related to your level of confidence. Table 7.2 is a schematic representation of how your level of self-acceptance is reflected in the level of acceptance, and hence quality of listening, you are able to offer to another in a relationship. As the figure implies, the level of self-acceptance of some of you may be so low, because you have been inadequately listened to when growing up, that you need a nurturing counselling relationship to remedy your earlier misfortune.

**Table 7.2** *Relationship between level of self-acceptance and ability to accept others*

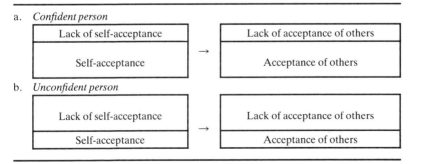

**Table 7.3**   *Possible sources of interference located in the listener*

The following are possible barriers and filters that may impede the listener accurately receiving and understanding a sender's messages.

*Attentional barriers and filters*
Hearing difficulties
Sight difficulties
Physical distractions, viz. noise
Fatigue, illness
Low attention span
Perceived lack of relevance
Carry over of unfinished business
Time pressure
Time lag, daydreaming

*Reception barriers and filters*
Memory difficulties
Limited vocabulary
Low intelligence
Out of touch with feelings
    (and hence inability to tune into another's feelings)
Areas of rigidity/prejudice
Areas of personal need
    (and hence selective listening)
Is reminded of another by sender
Feels shy
Feels emotional
Feels anxious and tense
Feels threatened
Sensitive topic areas, for instance sex, anger
Hears trigger words
Lacks decoding skills
Lacks checking out skills
Leaves out material
Adds material
Substitutes material

*Discouragements to sender*
Has said little about self
Demonstrates poor interest and
    attention
Lacks capacity for helpful responding
Uses 'You-blame' language
Doubts about confidentiality

Table 7.3 depicts possible sources of interference, along with lack of confidence, that are located in the listener. The sender sends a message, even if imperfect, that may then be either received accurately or distorted so that the message ultimately received differs from the message originally sent. In extreme instances, incoming messages are totally denied. There are a number of barriers and filters that affect the degree to which the listener attends. Obvious ones include: poor hearing, poor vision, noise, fatigue, low attention span, time pressure and perceived lack of relevance. Sometimes a major attentional barrier is that the listener has unfinished emotional and possibly intellectual business from a previous encounter. For instance, Sybil who has just had a row with her mother may not be 'all there' when immediately afterwards she meets her boyfriend George. Time lag refers to the possibility that the listener's rate of processing information may be considerably faster than the speaker's rate of speech.[3] This may contribute to loss of attention through, for instance, daydreaming. Alternatively time lag could be used constructively both to understand the material better and to think about how best to respond.

Memory difficulties may have at least two causes. First, receivers have not sufficient discipline to listen precisely so that they can memorise precisely. Second, some people's capacity for retention is worse than others'. Limited vocabulary and low intelligence may interfere with adequate understanding of a speaker's message. Listeners who are distant from their own feelings have some of their sensitivity for tuning into others' feelings blocked. Similarly listeners who have rigid internal rules regarding their own and others' behaviour may be blocked from adequately processing information that runs counter to their thoughts. Often people's listening is distorted by their personal needs. For instance, Janis hates Peter and is all too ready to listen to negative comments about him and to discount positive ones. Sometimes people do not listen accurately because they transfer their reactions to previous people in their lives onto people to whom they are currently relating. Most relationships contain an element of working through what the psychoanalysts call transference as people learn to listen to others as they are rather than in terms of their own previous relationships.

Anxiety and threat are present to a greater or less degree in all relationships. To the degree that people feel anxious and are helped to feel anxious by the sender, there is a greater chance that this anxiety harms rather than helps their listening and subsequent communication. Feelings of shyness, emotional instability and threat, possibly in relation to specific topic areas, may all contribute to poor and defensive listening. For some, just hearing certain 'trigger words' which may be expressed in 'You-blame' language may be sufficient to close their ears. For instance, a wife told by her husband 'You are a fool' may well resist listening to anything further he has to add. In fact, she may either physically withdraw or switch over on to the attack herself.

Sources of interference can also come through listeners' difficulties at decoding senders' messages and through their inability to check out the accuracy of their understanding. Sometimes listeners leave out material, sometimes they add or substitute it. In any of these circumstances the original message gets distorted.

Listening does not take place in a vacuum. It is part of process in which how each of you talks and listens in your relationship has an effect on the other. Listeners who are reluctant to disclose themselves may inhibit others from talking about themselves. Additionally, people may be discouraged from talking if the listener seems bored, cannot respond helpfully, lapses into threatening 'You-blame' language, and is perceived as a 'leaky sieve' in terms of confidentiality. Good listening entails not only receiving accurately what the other has to say but creating an emotional climate in which people feel safe, free and rewarded for talking.

Exercise 7.2 is designed to help you become more aware of how you may be blocking receiving another person's messages loud and clear. How do you introduce static into the communication? What from your side may be preventing you from tuning into and staying tuned into another's wavelength?

---

### Exercise 7.2 Exploring your sources of interference to listening accurately

This exercise may be done on your own, in pairs or as part of a training group.

A   *On your own*
   Write down your answers to the following questions.
   1.   List as many as you can of the *attentional* barriers and filters you have experienced interfering with your capacity to listen?
   2.   Are you aware of instances where *your own and/or another's emotions* have interfered with your capacity to listen? If so, give illustrative examples.
   3.   Are there certain *categories of people* to whom you find it difficult to listen? If so, please specify.
   4.   Are there any special *words, phrases or attitudes* from others that trigger off in you a resistance to listening? If so, please specify.
   5.   Are there any particular *topic areas* regarding which you find it difficult to listen accurately? If so, please specify.
   6.   List any other sources of interference to your listening that you have not mentioned above.
B   *In pairs*
   *Either* independently answer all the above questions, then discuss.
   *Or* work through the above exercise together from the start.
C   *In a training group*
   The trainer introduces the idea of people having internal barriers

that interfere with accurate listening. The trainer may then take the whole group through the exercise question by question. Alternatively the trainer may subdivide the group into pairs, threes or fours, get them to answer the questions, and then end with a plenary sharing and discussion session.

## CHOOSING TO LISTEN WELL

Like all relationship skills, listening consists of a series of choices. Good listeners make good choices, bad listeners make bad choices. Good choices are based on awareness of the decision points when listening. During the remainder of this chapter and throughout the next, we focus on how you can make the choices that are conducive to good listening.

Exercise 7.3 on characteristics of good and bad listeners gets you drawing on your own experience to illustrate what you have found helpful and harmful. Listening is a complex skill and this exercise may highlight some of its component parts. Remember that the characteristics of your good listeners represent good choices or skills resources on their part. The characteristics of your bad listeners represent poor choices or skills deficits. When it comes to listening all of us have deficits to a greater or lesser degree. We need to discipline ourselves constantly to make better listening choices.

---

**Exercise 7.3   Characteristics of good and bad listeners**

This exercise can be done on your own, in pairs or as part of a training group.

A   *On your own*
1.   Think of three people in your past or present life that you consider to be good or superior listeners and another three whom you consider to be poor listeners.
2.   Draw a line down the centre of a piece of paper. In the left-hand column write down all the characteristics that you associate with good listening and in the right-hand column all the characteristics that you associate with bad listening.
3.   In light of the above analysis, assess your own skills, resources and deficits as a listener.

B   *In pairs*
    *Either* independently write out your answers to the above questions, then discuss.
    *Or* jointly work through the above exercise, including together making a list of the characteristics of good and poor listeners. Help each other assess your own skills resources and deficits as listeners.
C   *In a training group*
    The trainer gets the group to answer the first two questions either on their own or in pairs. The trainer then works with the whole group to develop a master list of the characteristics of good and bad listeners. Either on their own or in pairs trainees then assess their own skills resources and deficits in light of the master list. The trainer then conducts a plenary sharing and discussion session.

---

### Being safe and accepting

Many of the characteristic ways in which you respond to others in everyday conversations are *not* particularly helpful in encouraging them to talk. A distinction is sometimes made between a therapeutic conversation, where the therapist listens carefully to the client, and a social conversation, cynically described as 'Two people taking turns to exercise their egos'. Counsellors and therapists are trained to make the choices that help their clients feel safe and accepted. This includes avoiding the kinds of behaviour and remarks prevalent in everyday conversations that create threat and otherwise act as a disincentive to the talker.

Earlier in this book it was emphasised that talking about yourself and revealing personal information involves risk. You are offering something of yourself and this may be rejected. The amount that you are likely to reveal is related to the level of safety, acceptance and trust in the relationship. When you are a listener, the boot is on the other foot. The amount that others reveal to you relates to how safe and accepting the talker perceives you to be.

If people are going to talk to you they need psychological space. Such space is both quantitative and qualitative. If you are not physically accessible or, when you are, you monopolise the conversation or keep interrupting you are scarcely giving another the *quantity* of space in which to talk. However, you can also preclude them from having the *quality* of psychological space they need by choosing to respond in ways that show a lack of respect for the importance of *their* thoughts and feelings. Below are some characteristic ways in which people communicate to others that they are not really safe and free to be and talk about themselves. This is not to say that some of the following ways of responding are never appropriate in relationships. Rather that you need be aware of the possible negative consequences for the talker if you choose to respond in any of these ways.

*Directing and leading*
Taking control of what the other person can talk about.

> 'I'm interested in what's going right for you, not what's going wrong.'
> 'I would like you to talk about your relationship with your mother.'
> 'Let's focus on how you get on at work.'

*Judging and evaluating*
Making evaluative statements, especially ones that indicate that the other is falling short of your own standards.

> 'I don't think you should be seeing her.'
> 'You've made a real mess of your life.'
> 'You are not very good at expressing yourself.'

*Blaming*
Assigning responsibility for what happens to another in a finger-pointing way.

> 'It's all your fault.'
> 'You started it.'
> 'I'm all upset now because of you.'

*Getting aggressive*
Making statements that are designed to cause pain and put the other person down.

> 'Can't you ever do anything right?'
> 'You fool!'
> 'Idiot!'

*Moralising and preaching*
Patronisingly telling another how they should be leading their lives.

> 'You should always respect your parents.'
> 'Honesty is the best policy.'
> 'Sex is not everything in life.'

*Advising and teaching*
Not giving the other space to arrive at their own solutions to their

concerns. Appearing to know best how they should lead their lives.

> 'My advice to you is to drop him.'
> 'No wonder you're lonely. You need to go out and meet people.'
> 'You need to spend more time outdoors.'

### Not accepting another's feelings
Telling people that their feelings should be different from what they are.

> 'You shouldn't be feeling so sorry for yourself.'
> 'Come on. Buck up. Don't let yourself get so depressed.'
> 'I don't see why you're so happy.'

### Inappropriately talking about yourself
Talking about yourself in ways that interfere with another's disclosures.

> 'You have troubles. Let me tell you mine.'
> 'I think I'm a good listener. A lot of people tell me that.'
> 'I am going to tell you my experience so that you can learn from it.'

### Interrogating
Using questions in such a way that the other feels threatened by unwanted probing.

> 'Do you masturbate?'
> 'Tell me all about your previous relationships.'
> 'What are your weaknesses?'

### Reassuring and humouring
Trying to make others feel better more for your sake than theirs. Not really acknowledging their true feelings.

> 'We all feel like that sometimes.'
> 'You can get by . . . I know you can.'
> 'Look, I've made you laugh. It can't be that bad.'

### Labelling and diagnosing
Playing the amateur psychologist and placing a label or diagnostic category on another.

> 'You have a hysterical personality.'
> 'You're paranoid.'
> 'You're a real neurotic.'

*Over-interpreting*
Offering explanations for others' behaviour which bear little relationship to what they may have thought of by themselves.

> 'I think that you are afraid of men and that is why you don't go out more.'
> 'Your indecision about getting a job is related to your fear of failing to live up to your father's standards.'
> 'The fact that you were not loved as a child makes it hard for you to show your affection for me.'

*Distracting and being irrelevant*
Confusing the issue by going off in another direction or creating a smokescreen.

> 'Let's go someplace else.'
> 'Let's change the subject.'
> 'Do we have to talk about this? Why don't we have some fun?'

*Faking attention*
Insincerely pretending to be more interested and involved in what is being said than you are.

> 'That's so interesting.'
> 'I would never have believed it.'
> 'Oh, really.'

*Placing time pressures*
Letting the other know that your availability for listening is very limited.

> 'I've got to go soon.'
> 'You had better be brief.'
> 'I'm very busy these days.'

Exercise 7.4 aims to get you exploring which of your present ways of responding interfere with your ability to be the sort of person to whom others want to talk. The common mistakes listed above not only make it more difficult for others to talk to you, but they also make it more difficult for them to listen to themselves.

---

**Exercise 7.4   How safe are you to talk to?**

This exercise may be done on your own, in pairs or as part of a training group.

A *On your own*
1. Rate each of the following items according to how often you respond that way in your relationships. Use the scale below.
   4 Very frequently
   3 Frequently
   2 Occasionally
   1 Almost never
   0 Never

   | *Characteristic* | *Your rating* |
   |---|---|
   | 1. Directing and leading | _____ |
   | 2. Judging and evaluating | _____ |
   | 3. Blaming | _____ |
   | 4. Getting aggressive | _____ |
   | 5. Moralising and preaching | _____ |
   | 6. Advising and teaching | _____ |
   | 7. Not accepting the other's feelings | _____ |
   | 8. Inappropriately talking about yourself | _____ |
   | 9. Interrogating | _____ |
   | 10. Reassuring and humouring | _____ |
   | 11. Labelling and diagnosing | _____ |
   | 12. Over-interpreting | _____ |
   | 13. Distracting and being irrelevant | _____ |
   | 14. Faking attention | _____ |
   | 15. Placing time pressures | _____ |

2. Look at the items that you have rated 2, 3 or 4 and assess the impact of each of these behaviours on your relationships.

B *In pairs*
*Either* independently do the above exercise, then discuss.
*Or* work through the above exercise together from the start.

C *In a training group*
The trainer introduces the concept of being a safe person with whom to talk. The trainer ensures that the group understands what the items on the questionnaire mean. Trainees then complete the questionnaire either independently or in pairs followed by a plenary sharing and discussion session.

---

Another set of choices that distinguishes good from poor listeners relates to your vocal and bodily communication. You can freeze and threaten people by using unaccepting bodily communication when they speak. For instance, when Mary reveals to Bill that she is upset at getting a poor grade in an exam, he raises his eyebrows and looks down his nose at her in a way she finds intimidating. When Angie talks to Lois about herself Angie looks interested and makes good eye contact. When Lois tries to talk about herself to Angie, Angie's face is much less expressive, she makes less eye contact and she seems tense and impatient. The message to Lois is that Angie is much more interested in talking about herself than in hearing about her. Another example is that of Bill who wants to break to his friend Ivan the good news of his engagement to Hazel. However, Ivan is so down in the mouth that Bill feels it better not to confront Ivan's depression with his happiness.

Seeming not to be genuine when you are listening breeds a feeling of insecurity in the talker. Assessing the matching of words with vocal and bodily communication is a major way in which people gauge each other's sincerity. If you say you are interested and look bored, the latter message will likely be the one that registers with your listener. If you say you are happy at another's good news but seem to force a smile, then they may be reluctant to share their feelings further.

Exercise 7.5 looks at how you may be encouraging and discouraging people from talking to you through your vocal and bodily communication. Which of those behaviours are rewarding and which might be viewed as put-downs?

---

**Exercise 7.5   Encouraging and discouraging non-verbal communication**

This exercise can be done on your own, in pairs or as part of a training group.

A  *On your own*
1. Look at the non-verbal behaviours below. Imagine yourself in the speaker's role. Put an E before all those behaviours on the part of your listener which you would find rewarding or encouraging and a D before all those behaviours which you would find unrewarding or discouraging.

| | | | | |
|---|---|---|---|---|
| _____ | 1. | Picks nose | _____ | 7. Sits on same level as you |
| _____ | 2. | Calm manner | | |
| _____ | 3. | Leans far back | _____ | 8. Bounces a leg |
| _____ | 4. | Head very close to yours | _____ | 9. Waves arms |
| | | | _____ | 10. Voice easy to hear |
| _____ | 5. | Tugs at ear | | |
| _____ | 6. | Looks towards you | _____ | 11. Stares at you |

|  | 12. | Looks out of window |  | 22. | Looks clean |
|---|---|---|---|---|---|
|  | 13. | Relaxed seating position |  | 23. | Comfortable speech pace |
|  | 14. | Slouches |  | 24. | High pitched voice |
|  | 15. | Raises eyebrow |  | 25. | Body posture open to you |
|  | 16. | Looks alert |  |  |  |
|  | 17. | Smiles |  | 26. | Shuffles about |
|  | 18. | Sits higher than you |  | 27. | Has vacant look |
|  |  |  |  | 28. | Has warmth in voice |
|  | 19. | Shuts eyes |  |  |  |
|  | 20. | High pitched voice |  | 29. | Whispers |
|  |  |  |  | 30. | Looks anxious |
|  | 21. | Leans slightly towards you |  |  |  |

2. Assess whether you have any bodily and vocal behaviours which discourage others from talking to you.

B   *In pairs*
As below.

C   *In a training group*
Independently answer the questionnaire then discuss together, including assessing your own bodily and vocal behaviours which might discourage others from talking to you.

---

How you think about yourself and others influences how safe and accepting you are likely to appear to them. In Table 7.2 an attempt was made to relate people's acceptance of themselves to their acceptance of other people. If you have numerous rigid internal rules about the way you and others 'should', 'ought' or 'must' be, these are likely to get communicated. Their effect may be that talkers edit what they say possibly to avoid conflict and to retain your approval. Consequently, while you may think that you are being a good listener this is not really so. Good listening is based on respect for others' experiencing. It avoids contributing to making them feel so threatened that they only tell you what you want to hear. Additionally, if others feel you are a competitive rather than a co-operative person, they are likely to restrict what they say to you. They fear that you might use certain disclosures against them.

Exercise 7.6 focuses getting you to listen to your reactions as others make various disclosures to you. Your internal reactions are partly related to what they say, but partly also to your thoughts concerning how both you and they should be. For instance, if you think you should always come first, the fact that someone gets a promotion over you might generate feelings such as depression, anger and envy rather than pleasure in their achievement. These negative feelings might make it hard for you to tune into and listen to their feelings. Similarly, if you have the internal rule that 'no one should be homosexual', the admission of gayness by someone might generate feelings of disgust or sadness or, if a parent, of 'What have I done wrong?' Such feelings might well interfere with your relating and listening to the other as they are rather than as you would like them to be. The purpose of the exercise is not to say whether your reactions are right or wrong. Rather it is to get you exploring how your thoughts and feelings might interfere with your being a safe and accepting listener.

---

### Exercise 7.6 Listening to your reactions

The following exercise may be done on your own, in pairs or as part of a training group.

A *On your own*
After reading each of the following vignettes, write down the sorts of feelings that the disclosures might generate in you. Identify any that might interfere with your effectiveness as a listener.

B *In pairs*
Go through each vignette, first giving yourself time to listen to your own reactions, then discussing your reactions together.

C *In a training group*
As for B above. The trainer can then get group members to share any experience they may have had of their own thoughts and feelings getting in the way of their listening. Also, the trainer can get them exploring current and prospective situations where the quality of their listening is at risk.

*Exercise*
Imagine that you are the recipient of the following disclosures and/or feedback. How would you feel? Would you be a safe and accepting listener?

1. A close friend of the same gender states: 'I've been feeling pretty low recently. I try not to show it, but there are times I get so depressed that I feel suicidal.'
2. A colleague at work says: 'I've just had wonderful news. I have been appointed to head the unit that we are in. I can't believe my luck.'

3. A friend of the same gender says: 'I've finally decided to come out. I'm gay and have been so for as long as I can remember.'
4. Your partner of the opposite gender says: 'I have been seeing a lot of _____ recently. We enjoy each other's company but there is nothing more to it than that.'
5. A friend of either gender says: 'How could you have done that to me? I feel really hurt and angry. You made an agreement with me and now you've broken it.'
6. A male acquaintance says: 'I think I'm pretty good looking. I'm successful with women and all I want to do is have fun with them. No obligations, no ties, just fun.'

---

### Understanding another's world

If people to whom you relate are to feel that you receive them loud and clear you need the ability to 'get inside their skins', 'walk in their shoes', and 'see the world through their eyes'. The skill of really listening to and understanding another person is based on your choosing to get into their internal rather than remain in your external frame of reference. At the heart of listening is a basic distinction between 'you' and 'me', between 'my view of me' and 'your view of me' and between 'your view of you' and 'my view of you'. Now 'my view of me' and 'your view of you' are both inside or internal viewpoints, whereas 'your view of me' and 'my view of you' are both outside or external viewpoints.

To the extent that I understand 'your view of you' I am inside your *internal frame of reference*. If I then respond in a way that illustrates an accurate understanding of your viewpoint, I am responding *as if inside* your internal frame of reference. If, however, I choose not to understand 'your view of you' or lack the skills to do so, I remain in the *external frame of reference* in regard to your world. Furthermore, even if I have understood you accurately, I may still choose to respond from my frame of reference, which is external to you, rather than as if inside your frame of reference. In short, if I respond to you as if inside your frame of reference, I respond to you from where you are. If I step outside your frame of reference in my response, I am responding in an external way. Such responses reflect more where I am or think you should be than where you are.

All of the previously mentioned ways of responding that might interfere with the talker feeling safe and accepted by the listener were from the external frame of reference. Furthermore, it is probable that much of the bodily and vocal communication that you listed as discouraging in Exercise 7.5 indicated that the listener was not fully in your frame of reference. Below are some illustrative *external frame of reference* responses by a listener.

> 'I'm interested in what's going right for you, not what's going wrong.'
> 'You should always respect your parents.'
> 'My advice to you is to drop him.'
> 'You have troubles. Let me tell you mine.'

The internal frame of reference involves you in understanding talkers on their own terms. This involves careful listening and allowing talkers the psychological space to tell their own story. Furthermore, it entails if necessary accurately decoding any message that may not have been clearly sent. This includes understanding vocal and bodily communications. In the following examples, the assumption is that the listener responds as if inside the talker's *internal frame of reference*.

> 'Though you don't like to show it, you've been feeling very depressed recently and even contemplated suicide.'
> 'You are thrilled that you've just got this promotion and can't believe your good fortune.'
> 'You are pretty scared at the thought of being unemployed.'
> 'You have mixed feelings about the wedding ceremony and will be glad when it is out of the way.'

Exercise 7.7 is on identifying whether the listener has responded as if from the talker's internal frame of reference. The answers to Exercise 7.7 are provided at the end of the chapter.

---

**Exercise 7.7  Getting inside another's frame of reference**

This exercise may be done in a number of ways.

A  *On your own*
  This exercise consists of a number of statement–response excerpts from different relationships. Three responses have been provided to each statement. On a piece of paper write IN or EX for each response according to whether you consider it is *as if inside* the speaker's internal frame of reference or from a frame of reference *external* to the speaker.

B  *In pairs*
  *Either* independently make your ratings for the responses to all statements, then discuss.

*Or* independently rate the responses to one statement at a time, then share and discuss your answers.

C  *In a training group*

The trainer introduces the concept of the internal versus the external frame of reference. Trainees independently rate the responses to one statement and then share and discuss their answers before moving on.

*Example*

Husband to wife

Husband:  I'm worried about the kids. They always seem to be out late these days and I'm beginning to feel that I scarcely know them.

Wife:  (a)  If you took a bit more interest, then you might get to know them better.

(b)  You feel concerned both that the kids are out late a lot and also that you are becoming more distant from them.

(c)  You are a good father and deserve better than this.

Suggested answers and comments:

(a)  External. This is what the wife is thinking.

(b)  Internal. This demonstrates acceptance and understanding of the husband's viewpoint.

(c)  External. This is reassurance coming from where the wife rather than her husband 'is at'.

*Exercise*

1.  Girlfriend to boyfriend

Girlfriend:  I really like your Mum. She is a really sharp person. I hope I can be as youthful as her when I'm her age.

Boyfriend:  (a)  Mum likes you too.

(b)  Wait until you get to know her better.

(c)  You think Mum's great and admire her youthfulness.

2.  Child to parent

Child (crying):  I have just had a fight with Eric. I think he is a bully. I hate him!

Parent:  (a)  You poor boy.

(b)  Big boys don't cry.

(c)  You are really upset with that bully Eric.

3.  Student to teacher

Student:  I am finding the workload very heavy. I feel depressed because I'm having practically no social life.

Teacher:  (a)  You're feeling down with the combination of too much work and too little social life.

(b)  You have to work hard if you are going to pass these exams.

(c)  I had to study hard too when I was your age.

4. Friend to friend
   Friend A: Let's go to the beach this weekend? I want to enjoy the fine weather while it's here. I'm sure you will enjoy it too.
   Friend B: (a) I'm not so certain.
   (b) You're keen to go to the beach while the sun shines and know I will enjoy it too.
   (c) I think that is an excellent idea.

---

Though understanding the talker's world is always important, responding as if you are inside it is not always the best way of responding. For instance, in Exercise 7.7 response 4(b), 'You're keen to go to the beach while the sun shines and know I will enjoy it too' is as if inside the internal frame of reference response. However, response 4(c), 'I think that is an excellent idea', both shows a good understanding of the sender's message at the same time as also answering the question posed. In this instance the combination of understanding the speaker's internal frame of reference, yet responding from your own external frame of reference is the most appropriate response.

There are different levels of understanding another's world. When first meeting people you will only have relatively little opportunity to understand their frame of reference. However, if you are a safe person with whom to talk and do not have too many preconceptions, as time goes by you will develop a much fuller understanding of their world. This additional information is likely to be helpful in putting what they say in context. Furthermore, a good way of viewing an intimate relationship is that both parties understand each other's worlds and that this mutual understanding is acknowledged and appreciated.

**Disciplining your listening**

Research conducted by the author and a colleague on beginning British counsellor trainees indicated a widespread tendency to respond from the external frame of reference.[4,5] This was partly a matter of the trainees having poor responding habits. However, deficits in the accuracy with which they received the messages probably contributed to the results. There is no reason to believe that the listening skills of these British trainees were any worse than those in the population at large. Poor listening skills are a widespread phenomenon. This is not helped by so few people being trained to listen properly. Being a good listener across a range of relationships is not easy. They entail different levels of involvement, roles, emotional styles and expectations. Already we have indicated many of the possible sources of interference.

You need to make a conscious choice to work on disciplining your listening and helpful responding skills. You have picked up a number of bad habits already. You may have been unaware of many of these in the past. Indeed you may still be unaware of some. The illusion that we are good listeners and can remain so without much effort is hard to dislodge.

Exercises 7.8, 7.9 and 7.10 each emphasise the discipline and precision with which you listen. These exercises do not ask you to decode vocal and bodily communication. They stress the precision with which you have heard and are able to relay back the verbal or literal content of another's communication. You may find it helpful to cassette-record the exercises so that you have a record against which you can check the precision of your responding.

Exercise 7.8 is a straight repetition exercise, with one variation. You are to use the second person singular in all instances where your talker has used the first person singular. Exercise 7.9 is designed to ensure that you have listened and understood before you make your contribution to a conversation. Exercise 7.10 forces you to listen carefully so that you can summarise another person's frame of reference. Repeat the exercises as many times as you consider it necessary to discipline these aspects of your listening.

---

**Exercise 7.8   Staying in another's frame of reference**

This is a pairs exercise, though it may also be performed in a training group.

Person A talks about himself/herself for 3 to 5 minutes pausing after each sentence to allow Person B to respond. Person B's task is to repeat precisely everything that Person A says, but to switch all use of the first person singular into the second person singular: for instance, 'I feel' becomes 'You feel'. Start with very brief sentences before moving on to longer sentences. After the first part of the exercise partners discuss their reactions to what transpired and then reverse roles. The exercise can be done for progressively longer periods if felt appropriate. Participants are encouraged to try and become much more conscious of when they are responding from either the internal or the external frame of reference in their outside lives. Also, of the effect of these different kinds of responses on the people with whom they relate.

---

## Exercise 7.9  Checking out another's frame of reference

This is a pairs exercise, though it may also be performed in a training group.

You hold a conversation with your partner in which each of you talks in brief sentences. Each sentence is repeated by the listener, though using the second instead of the first person singular. Listeners can only become active talkers by adding something new to the conversation *after* they have checked out through repetition that they heard accurately the last sentence spoken. If a talker does not consider the listener has been sufficiently accurate, he/she raises his/her index finger. If the listener cannot correct the accuracy of their response on their own, the speaker helps them before continuing the exercise. This exercise can last 5, 10 or 15 minutes. When finished partners should discuss their thoughts and feelings about what transpired during the exercise. Participants are encouraged to become more conscious of whether they listen accurately prior to talking in their everyday lives.

## Exercise 7.10  Summarising another's frame of reference

This exercise may be done in pairs or in a training group.

A  *In pairs*
You listen while your partner talks to you either about how he/she assesses his/her relationship skills or about some other area in which he/she is interested. When your partner is talking you may use bodily communication but not talk yourself. At the end of 2 minutes summarise what your partner has been saying from his/her frame of reference, including using the first person singular. Switch into his/her chair as you do this. Your partner listens but does not talk while you summarise and then provides feedback on the accuracy of your summary. Then reverse roles. This exercise may be repeated with longer turns: for instance, 3, 5 and even 10 minutes. Use of an audio-cassette helps you check on accuracy.

B  *In a training group*
The trainer acts as listener–summariser and demonstrates the exercise with one of the trainees. Then the group might be divided into twos or threes to do the exercise. If the group is divided into threes one person should act as observer while the others are the talker and the listener–summariser. All three give feedback at the end. The trainer should visit each group and ensure that there is a real focus on disciplined listening. After the pairs or subgrouping, there might be a plenary session of the whole group in which trainees are encouraged to explore their listening abilities. Again use of an audio-cassette is helpful during the exercise for checking on accuracy.

**Demonstrating your attention and interest**

To be a rewarding person with whom to talk you need to convey your attention and interest. Sometimes this is referred to in the counselling literature as attending behaviour.[6] In Exercise 7.5, on encouraging and discouraging non-verbal communication, the main focus was on avoiding negative messages. Here the focus is more on sending positive messages. Some of the main nonverbal ways you can demonstrate your interest and attention as a listener are as follows.

1. *Physical availability.* People who are always off to the next event in their busy lives choose not to find time to listen adequately to those to whom they relate. Close relationships require an investment of time. If this is not forthcoming, sooner rather than later either or both parties are likely to feel that they are not being adequately listened to. If you are rarely or never available to listen you have withdrawn much of your interest and attention from the other person.

2. *Relaxed body posture.* A relaxed body posture is likely to convey the message that you are emotionally available. If you sit in a tense and uptight fashion the listener may consciously consider or intuitively feel that you are so bound up in your own personal agendas and unfinished business that you are not fully accessible to them. Depending on how done, crossed arms, crossed legs, a stiff body posture, finger drumming and leg bouncing may all indicate tension. However, beware of slumping or slouching.

3. *Physical openness.* Physical openness means facing the speaker not only with your face but with your body. You need to be either right opposite the other person or sufficiently turned towards them that you can receive all their significant facial and bodily messages.

4. *Slight forward lean.* This especially applies when you are sitting rather than standing. If you lean too far forward you look odd and others may consider you are invading their personal space. If you lean back, others may find this distancing. A slight forward trunk lean can both encourage the talker and avoid threat, especially at the start of relationships.

5. *Good eye contact.* Good eye contact means looking in the other's direction so that you allow the possibility of your eyes meeting reasonably often. Staring at the other threatens. Looking down or away too often may indicate that you are tense or uninterested. Good eye contact also means that you see the important facial messages sent by the other.

6. *Appropriate facial expressions.* A friendly relaxed facial expression, including a smile, initially demonstrates interest. However as the other talks, your facial expressions need to show that you are tuned into what they say. For instance, if the other is divulging material that makes them feel sad, a look of concern may be much more indicative of paying good attention than a smile.

7. *Use head nods.* Each head nod can be viewed as a reward to the talker giving the message that you are paying attention. Head nods need not signify that you agree with everything they say, but rather that you are interested.

As your relationships develop, people get to know whether and when you are attending to them. For instance, the talker may know from past experience that when you lean back you are not withdrawing attention. However, based on the experience of innumerable hours training people to listen, all too often people's bodily communication is much poorer than they think. Consequently you may need to become more aware of your current behaviour as a step in remedying any skills deficits you possess. Exercise 7.11 gives you the opportunity to explore how you use your body when you are a listener. If possible, video-record your sessions. Not just being told, but actually seeing how your bodily communication comes across may sharpen your awareness and increase your motivation for any changes required.

---

**Exercise 7.11 Demonstrating attention and interest with bodily messages**

This exercise may be done on your own, in pairs or as part of a training group.

A *On your own*

Write down as many ways you can think of for demonstrating, by means of bodily messages, attention and interest when you listen.

B *In pairs*

Partner A talks for 3 minutes while Partner B demonstrates attention and interest by means of bodily communication, but does not talk. Both partners are seated. Partner A should focus on: relaxed body posture, physical openness, slight forward lean, good eye contact, appropriate facial expressions, and use of head nods. At the end of 3 minutes Partner A gives Partner B feedback on his/her demonstration of attention and interest as a listener. Partners then reverse roles. If possible video-record each 3-minute session and play it back to illustrate the feedback. This exercise may be repeated with progressively longer sessions.

C *In a training group*
The trainer goes through ways of using bodily communication as a listener to show attention and interest. The trainer then demonstrates showing attention and interest through bodily messages with one of the trainees who talks for 3 minutes. The trainer then subdivides the group into threes – listener, talker and observer – and trainees are given the opportunity to be each. Where feasible, the trainer enables trainees to get video feedback in how they use their bodies when they listen. At the end of the subgroups the trainer holds a plenary sharing and discussion session. Trainees are encouraged to practise in their everyday lives using good bodily communication when listening to demonstrate attention and interest.

---

## Permissions to talk and continuation expressions

*Permissions to talk* are comments that indicate that you are prepared to listen. They can occur at any time in a relationship. These statements are 'door openers'. The message contained in all of them is: 'I'm interested and prepared to listen. I give you the opportunity of sharing with me what you think and feel.' A good time to use a permission to talk is when you sense someone has a personal agenda that bothers them, but finds difficulty sharing it with you. Examples of permissions to talk are:

'Is there something on your mind?'
'Would you like to share it with me?'
'Would you like to talk about it?'
'I'm happy to listen to what you have to say?'
'I'd like to hear your viewpoint?'

*Continuation expressions* are designed to keep other people talking. The message they convey is: 'I am with you. Please go on.' Continuation expressions can be used for good or ill. On the one hand they can reward people for talking to you from their frame of reference. On the other hand, they may range from crude to subtle attempts to take others out of their frame of reference by shaping what they say. For instance, you may say 'Tell me more' whenever someone says what you want to hear, yet remain silent when they do not. Continuation expressions can also be bodily messages, with perhaps the main one being the head-nod. Below are some examples of verbal and vocal continuation expressions:

| | |
|---|---|
| Um-hmm | Indeed |
| Please continue | Well |
| Tell me more | And |
| Go on | So |
| I see | Really |
| Oh | Right |
| Interesting | Ah |
| Then | Yes |

You can develop a repertoire of permissions to talk and continuation expressions. By using them well you will convey positive messages to others about your willingness to give them time, space, attention and interest.

## CONCLUDING INNER SPEECH

I need to assume responsibility for the quality of my listening. Listening is a disciplined skill. There are many sources of interference that can impede my effectiveness. Three broad categories of possible listening difficulty for me are: not paying attention, not receiving messages accurately, and behaving in ways that discourage the other from talking.

I can choose to listen well. It is important for me, where appropriate, to be perceived as safe and accepting. This includes being aware of verbal and nonverbal ways of responding that can threaten and show lack of respect for talkers. I also need to listen to my own thoughts and feelings when others talk. This both gets me more onto their wavelength and also helps alert me to my own listening barriers.

Effective listening always requires me to do my best to understand the other's world or frame of reference. Then I have the choice of either responding as if in the other's internal frame of reference or from my frame of reference. Elements of disciplined listening include the ability to stay in, check out and summarise another's frame of reference. I can choose to discipline my body language to demonstrate attention and interest. Being an effective listener includes encouraging others by means of permissions to talk and continuation expressions. I can help myself by possessing a good repertoire of these.

## REFERENCES

1. Quoted in *The Weekend Australian*, August 25–26, 1984.
2. Rogers, C.R. (1980) 'Empathic: an unappreciated way of being', pp. 137–163 in C.R. Rogers *A Way of Being*, Boston: Houghton Mifflin.

3.  Burley-Allen, M. (1982) *Listening: The Forgotten Skill*, New York: Wiley.
4.  Nelson-Jones, R. & Patterson, C.H. (1974) 'Some effects of counsellor training', *British Journal of Guidance and Counselling*, **2** (2), 191–199.
5.  Nelson-Jones, R. & Patterson, C.H. (1976) 'Effects of counsellor training: further findings', *British Journal of Guidance and Counselling*, **4** (1), 66–73.
6.  Ivey, A.E. (1971) *Microcounseling: Innovations in Interview Training*, Springfield, Illinois: Charles C. Thomas.

## ANSWERS TO EXERCISES

*Exercise 7.1*

| 1. F | 2. T | 3. F | 4. T | 5. T | 6. F | 7. T | 8. F |
|------|------|------|------|------|------|------|------|
| 9. F | 10. T | 11. T | 12. F | 13. T | 14. F | 15. T | |
| 16. F | 17. F | 18. T | 19. T | 20. T | 21. F | 22. T | |

*Exercise 7.7*
1.  (a) external; (b) external; (c) internal
2.  (a) external; (b) external; (c) internal
3.  (a) internal; (b) external; (c) external
4.  (a) external; (b) internal; (c) external

# 8 Helpful Responding

Effective listening requires you to be able to respond helpfully. Helpful responding entails sending verbal, vocal and bodily messages that encourage rather than discourage talkers. Reverting to our radio operator analogy, the receiving operator not only needs to pick up the message of the sending operator loud and clear, but also communicate to the sender that this has happened.

In the previous chapter Exercise 7.4 encouraged you to explore ways that you might be responding unhelpfully. The risk of such responses is that you become unsafe and discourage senders both from talking about and also from listening to themselves. Helpful responding, on the other hand, enables talkers to expand on and develop their own internal frame of reference. You show your respect for them by listening accurately and communicating your understanding. Also, you give them the psychological support and space to make their own decisions and to solve their own problems, especially those not directly affecting you. Even when another's problems directly affect you, as in the case of conflict in your relationship, you can still choose to use your helpful responding skills.

Active listening is another way of viewing helpful responding.[1] Assuming responsibility for your listening entails both receiver and sender skills. If listening only consisted of receiver skills it would be passive. However, effective listening also entails the activity of helpful responding. In this chapter we focus on two important, yet overlapping, groups of choices connected with active listening or helpful responding. These are the choices entailed in responding with understanding and in aiding another person's attempts to solve problems. Both require the listener to understand the talker's internal frame of reference.

## RESPONDING WITH UNDERSTANDING

### Defining responding with understanding

Effective listening entails offering another person a sensitive form of companionship. *Responding with understanding* demonstrates that you are psychologically present in the relationship and open to the other person. The sources of interference entailed in paying attention and in receiving messages have been mastered to the point where you are able to tune in accurately to another's wavelength. Furthermore, not only do you accurately understand, as if from the internal frame of reference, what the speaker tells you, but also you communicate back your understanding with accuracy, simplicity and clarity.

Responding with understanding tends to be called terms like accurate empathy, empathic understanding, empathic responding or just the word empathy in the counselling and psychotherapy literature. In 1975 Carl Rogers published an updating of his views on the process of being empathic.[2] The key elements in Rogers' definition of *empathy* are: entering another's world, sensing meanings both at and below the surface, communicating your understandings, checking out their accuracy, and helping the other person experience themselves more fully and move forward in the experiencing. Thus empathy entails providing an emotional climate of respect and acceptance in which others can feel safe and free to reveal and become more themselves.

In this book the term *reflective responding* is used as a shorthand term for responding with understanding. Reflective responding entails tuning into and, as it were, 'mirroring' the meanings contained in the verbal, vocal and bodily messages of the other. It involves responding with understanding to single or brief series of statements. This requires sensitivity, tact and good timing.

## Assessing reflective responding

Good reflective responding communicates a basic acceptance of the other as a person. It does not mean that you necessarily agree with what they say, but that you acknowledge and understand their statements as representing their frame of reference. Reflective responses are not 'put-downs'. They do not act as stoppers on others' flow of talk and expression of feelings. They do not contribute to others feeling inadequate, inferior, defensive or as though they are being talked down to.

Good reflective responses are made in easily comprehensible language. They have a clarity and freshness of expression. They are accompanied by appropriate vocal and bodily communication, something which the next exercise is unable to incorporate since it is in written form. Implicit in good reflective responding is the fact that you are *working in collaboration with* the other to understand their frame of reference and personal meanings. In such a collaborative effort you need both overtly and covertly to check out the accuracy of your understandings. Furthermore, the emotional climate needs to be sufficiently safe so that others feel secure enough to mention if you are inaccurate. Thus they help you to stay accurate.

In assessing reflective responding it is sometimes helpful to think of a three-link chain: *first statement – reflective response – second statement*. Good reflective responses allow the opportunity for another's second statement to be a continuation of the train of thought contained in their first statement. Bad reflective responses do not.

In light of the above discussion on good reflective responding and the numerous examples of unhelpful responding in the previous chapter, work through Exercise 8.1. Some answers are suggested at the end of the chapter.

---

**Exercise 8.1   Assessing reflective responding**

This exercise may be done in a number of ways.

A   *On your own*
Reflective responding involves your accurately understanding, as if from their internal frame of reference, what another tells you and then sensitively communicating back your understanding in clear language. Take a piece of paper and rate the three responses to each of the initial statements using the following scale.
4   Very good reflective response
3   Good reflective response
2   Moderate reflective response
1   Slight understanding in the response
0   No understanding at all
Write down your reason or reasons for each of your ratings.
B   *In pairs*
With a partner, either rate individual responses or segments of the exercise and then discuss, or go through the whole exercise making independent ratings and then discuss.
C   *In a training group*
See B above, with the difference that the group meets as a whole. The trainer facilitates the sharing and discussion of ratings by group members including sharing his/her own ratings with the reasons for them.

*Example*
Wife to husband
Wife:     With the children nearing the end of their education I want to build more of a life for myself. I don't want to hang around the house all the time. I want to get out and be active.
Husband: (a)  You would like me to suggest what you should do.
         (b)  You have decided to explore your options once the children leave home.
         (c)  With the children growing up you see the need to build more of an independent life for yourself. One that gets you out of the house and allows you to be active.
Suggested ratings and comments:
(a)  1; She has made no such request.
(b)  3; This goes further than her current frame of reference, but is a reasonably good response.
(c)  4; Communicates good understanding.

*Exercise*
1.  Boyfriend to girlfriend
    Boyfriend:  We used to really enjoy ourselves. Now all we seem to do is fight. I wish we could go back to how it used to be. How we are makes me really sad.
    Girlfriend: (a)  You are not the same person any more.
            (b)  I wish we got on better.
            (c)  You're really upset that we fight so much now and long for our previous good times.

2.  Patient to nurse
    Patient:  When I first heard I'd got terminal cancer, my world fell apart. I'm still pretty shaken and frightened at the thought of death.
    Nurse: (a)  You feel scared about dying. Finding out you had terminal cancer was a huge blow and you are still coming to terms with it.
         (b)  The news of your terminal cancer sent you reeling and you haven't recovered yet.
         (c)  Well, we all have to die sometime.

3.  Pupil to teacher
    Pupil:     I've got this problem about getting in all the assignments in time. My mother is very ill and I think I should spend more time with her.
    Teacher: (a)  You want to spend more time with your mother and would like to discuss what to do about your assignments.
          (b)  I'm very sorry to hear about your mother, but reluctant to make any exceptions on deadlines.

      (c)  You are concerned about your mother's illness and feel she has higher priority than your assignments.

4. Girlfriend to boyfriend

   Girlfriend:  I never know where I stand with you. One moment you are saying I'm terrific, then the next moment you are putting me down. I want you to be more consistent.

   Boyfriend:  (a)  Well what about your moods?

                (b)  You are finding my blowing hot and cold hard to take and would like me to be more consistent.

                (c)  I really do like you.

---

## Uses of reflective responding

When people are first introduced to the skill of reflective responding they frequently express reservations.

> 'It's so unnatural.'
> 'People will just think I'm repeating everything they say.'
> 'It gets in the way of my being spontaneous.'
> 'It makes me too self-conscious.'

When learning any new skill, from driving a car to driving a golf ball, there is a period where you are likely to have to concentrate extra hard on making the correct sequence of choices that go to make up the skill. Reflective responding is no exception. If you work and practise at a skill, you ultimately are likely to own it as a 'natural' part of you. It is natural to the extent that it feels natural. One of the main reasons why reflective responding seems so unnatural at first is that unhelpful ways of responding, such as judging and moralising, are firmly installed in many people's relationship skills. Thus you may need not only to learn a new skills resource, but also to unlearn a current skills deficit.

Reflective responding should not be used all the time, but flexibly incorporated into your repertoire of responses. There are many occasions where choosing to use reflective responding is helpful.

- When you need to show that you have understood.
- When you need to check out that you are understood.
- When another person needs to be able to experience their feelings as valid.
- When another is struggling to understand himself or herself.

- When another needs help in expressing thoughts and feelings.
- When another is trying to solve a problem for himself or herself.
- When you need to be clear about another's position in a disagreement.
- When you wish to ensure that the responsibility for a decision or course of action in their lives rests with the other person.
- When you wish to maintain and enhance your relationship by setting aside a regular time for listening to each other.

There are however other occasions when you may gain from choosing either not to use reflective responding or to use it sparingly.

- When you consider someone talks too much and it is time communication became more two-way.
- When it is important that you share your frame of reference.
- When you wish to match the level of intimacy of another's disclosures.
- When someone expresses praise or appreciation to you.
- When you are aware that you are using listening as a means of avoiding defining and asserting yourself.
- When you feel too tired or hassled to listen properly.
- When you are unable to be accepting.
- When you consider another's solution might damage either yourself and/or them.

**Reflecting words**

There is a joke, probably apocryphal, about a well known American counsellor who was counselling a suicidal client in his office near the top of a tall building.

| | |
|---|---|
| Client: | I feel terrible. |
| Counsellor: | You feel terrible. |
| Client: | I feel really terrible. |
| Counsellor: | You feel really terrible. |
| Client: | For two cents I would jump out of that window there. |
| Counsellor: | For two cents you would jump out of that window there. |
| Client: | Here I go. |
| Counsellor: | There you go. |
| Client: | (lands on the pavement below with a thud.) |
| Counsellor: | Thud! |

In the above sequence, the counsellor has mechanically repeated what the client has been saying. As a frustrated husband once said to his wife who did the same 'If I had wanted someone to repeat everything I said after me, I would have married a parrot.' If you are to avoid seeming artificial as you respond reflectively, you need to be able to build up at least two subskills. First, you need to develop fluency in paraphrasing or restating what the client has just said. Second, you need to develop fluency in mirroring the emotional tone and meaning of the other's messages by using vocal and bodily, as well as verbal, responding.

A distinction is sometimes made between reflecting *content* and reflecting *feeling*. Reflecting content refers to mirroring the literal meaning of another's communication. It entails reflecting words. Reflecting feeling refers to mirroring the 'framing' vocal and bodily messages that may communicate the real meaning of the words. The distinction as presented above is artificial in that verbal content, for instance 'I am angry because I have been excluded', often contains feeling words. Nevertheless, in terms of how people respond to each other it can be a valuable distinction, hinging on the degree to which the listener responds to feelings and not just to words. For instance, our tall building counsellor was only responding to words. He did not pick up the desperation of the client's feelings. Indeed, his failure to respond to feelings might have been a significant factor in the client's suicide.

Exercise 8.2 below is designed to make you more aware of the degree to which you have choice in responding to verbal content. Also, it aims to build up your fluency in reflective responding. A brief exercise is insufficient to do this properly. You need to work on this skill afterwards. In the exercise you are required to stay very close to the sequencing and amount of the other's words. This is for teaching purposes. In everyday life you have much choice regarding how much and in what order you respond to another. Frequently your responses will be more succinct than those you are asked to provide in this exercise.

Using clear and simple English work through Exercise 8.2. Some possible paraphrase responses are given at the end of the chapter. However, as you will notice if you perform the exercise in a training group, there are usually several ways of making good restatements of the same statement.

### Exercise 8.2   Reflecting the words – paraphrasing

This exercise may be done in a number of ways.

A   *On your own*
   For each of the following statements, paraphrase the content of the statement in clear and simple language. Use 'you' or 'your' where the speaker uses 'I', 'me' or 'my'.
B   *In pairs*
   *Either* Partner A paraphrases statements 1 and 3 and Partner B statements 2 and 4, then discuss.
   *Or* work together on different ways of paraphrasing each statement.
C   *In a training group*
   The trainer gives trainees time to write out a paraphrase response to one statement at a time. Then the trainer facilitates the sharing and discussion of all trainees' paraphrases, including his or her version.

*Example*

Friend A to Friend B

Friend A:   'I'm saving up to go abroad. If I don't see other countries now when I'm young, I may never get the chance again.'

Possible Friend B paraphrase response: 'You're putting money aside for overseas travel. You feel that you need to explore something of the world before you grow too old, otherwise you may miss the opportunity for good.'

*Exercise*
1.   Mother to son: 'Would you please do more around the house. After a day at the office I'm tired when I come home. You don't seem to realise this.'
2.   Boyfriend to girlfriend: 'You are really cute. When I'm meant to be studying I just can't keep my mind on my work. Look what you are doing to me.'
3.   Priest to widow: 'Your husband was a fine man. His unexpected death was a great shock. We shall all miss him terribly. You have my deepest sympathies.'
4.   Boss to employee: 'I'm pleased with your progress. When we took you on I had my doubts. I'm glad that I've been proved wrong.'

### Reflecting feelings

Reflecting feelings may be viewed as *feeling with* another's flow of emotions and experiencing and being able to communicate this back to the speaker. Beginning counsellors often have trouble with the notion of reflecting feelings, since they just talk about feelings rather than offer an expressive emotional companionship which goes some way to mirroring their client's feelings. Reflecting feelings can be seen as responding to others' music rather than just to their words. To do this properly, you need to be proficient in the following areas.

● Observing another's facial and bodily movements.
● Hearing another's vocal communication.
● Listening to another's words.
● Tuning into the flow of your own emotional reactions to the other.
● Taking into account the content of another's communications.
● Sensing the meanings of another's communication.
● Taking into account the degree of self-awareness of the other.
● Responding in ways that pick up the other's feelings words.
● Using expressive rather than wooden language.
● Using vocal and bodily messages that neither add to nor subtract from the emotions being conveyed.
● Checking out the accuracy of your understanding.

To date in this book the main emphasis has been on sending rather than receiving bodily and vocal messages. For instance, part of Chapter 4 emphasised talking with your voice and body and part of Chapter 7 using your body to demonstrate attention and interest. Here the emphasis is on receiving and understanding the feelings messages contained in another's vocal and bodily messages. For instance, Sandra may say it's 'Just great' that her mother is getting married again at the same time as having a choked voice and sad expression with the corners of her mouth turned down. While the forthcoming marriage may be great for her mother, Sandra's voice and body messages indicate her doubts about how great it will be for her.

Impressionists such as Rich Little in the United States, Max Gillies in Australia and Mike Yarwood in Britain are experts at mirroring the voice and body characteristics of the people they take off. They mirror their subjects by *sending* information like them. Your job as a listener is to *receive* information in a way that shows emotional responsiveness to the sender. As such you need to integrate the mirroring of emotional messages from the speaker into your own style of responding. Much of this can be done by varying your vocal inflection and facial expression. For instance, if a hypothetical suicide-prone friend says 'I feel terrible', you could adjust your voice and facial expression to mirror some sense of desperation. This does not prevent your voice and face also expressing warmth and sympathy.

Reflecting feelings entails expressive listening and responding. The reflection of feelings needs to be accurate in two ways. First, the feelings need to be correctly identified. Second, the level of intensity of the feelings needs to be correctly expressed. At one extreme there is the wooden responder who continuously subtracts from the level of intensity of the speaker. At the other extreme is the melodramatic responder who overemphasises the speaker's intensity of feelings. In North American, Australian and British cultures, if anything, there is a tendency when responding either to ignore or to subtract from the level of intensity of the speaker rather than to overemphasise feelings.

Another consideration in reflecting feelings is whether and the degree to which the speaker is prepared to acknowledge their feelings. For instance, as a listener you may infer that a parent is absolutely furious with an offspring. However, the parent may not be able to handle such an observation since it clashes with their self-image of being an ideal and loving parent. Thus you need to use your judgement in choosing how much feeling to reflect.

Exercise 8.3 focuses on mirroring and reading body language. It aims to sharpen up your powers of observation in regard to picking up other people's bodily messages. Furthermore it gives you the opportunity to check out whether the meanings you attach to the other's bodily signals correspond with what they wanted to convey. Sometimes people are blind to their bodily messages and to the meaning they contain for others. For instance, it is possible for people to be so anxious or threatened that, at the same time as showing their feelings, they deny them to others. Consequently, you may observe more than your partner is prepared to acknowledge. Remember, when mirroring your partner's body language in Exercise 8.3, to mirror the intensity as well as the direction of expression.

---

**Exercise 8.3   Mirroring and reading body language**

This exercise can be done in pairs or in a training group.

A   *In pairs*
Partner A talks to Partner B for 2 minutes. During this period Partner B copies or mirrors all of Partner A's body language. At the end of the 2 minutes Partner B shares how he/she interpreted or read Partner A's bodily signals. Partner A comments on this. Afterwards reverse roles.

B   *In a training group*
The trainer demonstrates the above exercise by acting as Partner B for the first part. He/she then divides the group into threes (Partner A, Partner B, Observer) with trainees being told to rotate until they have played all three roles. The observer always gives feedback before roles are changed. Afterwards the trainer holds a plenary sharing and discussion session. An alternative, which takes less time, is to divide the group into pairs for the exercise and then hold a plenary session.

---

Exercise 8.4 again emphasises the importance, when reflecting feelings, of accurately reading another's body language. However, here there is an added emphasis on accurately reading vocal communication. Children tend to express their emotions very openly. As you grew up you received and internalised numerous messages about which emotions it was appropriate for people of your social characteristics, family background and gender to express where and when. Consequently many emotional messages 'come out sideways' rather than being expressed loud and clear. As such they are encoded and need to be decoded. Even if they are decoded accurately, there is the further issue of whether the sender is sufficiently self-aware to acknowledge them if reflected back.

Exercise 8.4 is about observing feelings from voice and body messages. The first time you do the exercise focus on the more obvious manifestations of anger, friendship, sadness and anxiety. Later on you may wish to list some of the ways a negative emotion like anger may be expressed when it 'comes out sideways' rather than gets expressed directly. For instance, the speaker may both smile and clench his or her fist. In other words, you receive a mixed message that requires decoding. Some answers to Exercise 8.4 are suggested at the end of the chapter.

## Exercise 8.4   Observing feelings from voice and body messages

This exercise can be done on your own, in pairs or as part of a training group.

A   *On your own*
   By filling in the blank spaces, write out what voice and body messages you might observe for each of the following feelings.

| Non-verbal cue | Anger | Friendship | Sadness | Anxiety |
|---|---|---|---|---|
| Tone of voice | | | | |
| Voice volume | | | | |
| Eye contact | | | | |
| Facial expression | | | | |
| Posture | | | | |
| Gestures | | | | |

   Assess your effectiveness at understanding other people's feelings from their voice and body messages.

B   *In pairs*
   *Either* complete the above exercise independently, then discuss.
   *Or* work through the above exercise together from the start.

C   *In a training exercise*
   The trainer gives each trainee a copy of the exercise and gets them to fill it out independently or in pairs. This is followed by a plenary session in which a master answer sheet for the exercise gets drawn up.

What people actually say, the verbal messages, can also give you a considerable amount of information about their feelings. The ability to listen for another's feelings words is an important subskill in reflecting feelings. The following is an example of feelings words being ignored.

> Charles: I have my law exams coming up and it's vital for my career to get a good grade. My whole future depends on it. I'm so worried.
>
> Marcus: Your exams are soon?
>
> Charles: Yes, they are in the last half of March.

Marcus's response has helped Charles to answer from his head rather than in terms of his feelings. The conversation has been steered towards facts rather than feelings.

Below is an example of how the reflection of his feelings might have helped Charles discuss them further.

> Charles: I have my law exams coming up and it's vital for my career to get a good grade. My whole future depends on it. I'm so worried.
>
> Marcus: You're really anxious because you have these make-or-break exams imminent.
>
> Charles: Yes. I can't sleep properly any more and I'm not eating well. I have a constant feeling of tension and wonder what I should do.

Marcus's response has correctly identified Charles's worry and anxiety rather than blocked its discussion. Charles was able to use Marcus's response not only to elaborate his feelings but also as a stepping stone to wondering how he should handle them. Reflective responding *focusing on* Charles's *feelings* is helping him move onto *taking action* to cope with them.

There is, of course, a risk that constant reflective responding focusing on feelings just encourages people to talk rather than act. For instance, Neil may wallow in his feelings of hurt and self-pity when discussing his relationship with Christy which is not going well. However, this does not invalidate the importance of reflecting feelings. It means that judgement is needed in how much and when to use this skill. For instance, a listener might reflectively respond to allow Neil to express his feelings, summarise, and then ask an open-ended question. 'Well. Is there anything you think you could do to help your situation?'

Exercise 8.5 attempts to help you become more disciplined at listening for and picking up verbal messages about feelings. Having identified the feelings words you are asked to provide alternative feelings words. Referring back to Table 3.1, which lists feelings words, may help. Just as you need to build up a repertoire of feelings words to communicate your own feelings accurately, building this repertoire also aids communicating a good understanding of other's feelings. The third part of the exercise gets you formulating reflective responses focusing on feelings. For teaching purposes the format of this exercise requires you to respond to all the feelings expressed by the speaker. In your everyday lives, your reflective responding may be much more selective. For instance, if a speaker mentions three feelings, you may decide only to respond to the one felt most intensely. In formulating your reflective responses in the exercise try to match, rather than to add or subtract from, the level of intensity of the other's feelings. If anything, exaggerate rather than understate your expression of feeling. A good analogy is that of putting when playing golf. If you strike the ball past the hole, unlike if you play short, at least you have given yourself the chance of it going in. Some suggestions for words, phrases and responses are provided at the end of the chapter.

---

### Exercise 8.5   Listening to the music – reflecting feelings

This exercise may be done in a number of ways.

A *On your own*
  For each of the following statements: (a) identify the words or phrases the speaker has used to describe how he or she feels; (b) suggest other words or phrases to describe how the speaker feels; and (c) formulate a reflective response to the speaker focusing on and reflecting his/her feelings, starting with the words 'You feel . . .' Write out your answers.

B *In pairs*
  1. *Either* independently answer, and then together discuss your answers to, one statement at a time.
     *Or* work through the exercise together from the start.
  2. Practise with each other using reflection of feeling responses as part of a conversation or role-play. Make sure to express the appropriate feelings with your voice and body as well as with your words. If anything, exaggerate your vocal and bodily messages as you reflect feelings.

C *In a training group*
  The trainer gives group members time to formulate answers to one statement at a time and then facilitates the sharing and discussion

of group members' answers, including his or her own versions. Trainees are encouraged not only to read out their reflective responses, but also to say them as though they really meant them.

The trainer then demonstrates giving some reflection of feeling responses as part of a conversation or role-play. He/she mirrors feelings vocally and bodily as well as verbally. If anything, he/she hams it up since some group members may need the permission to be more expressive in their responding. The trainer may then work with the whole group by providing each member with the chance to match a feelings expression of his/hers. Alternatively, the group may divide into pairs in which partners practise using reflection of feelings responses as part of conversations or role-plays.

*Example*

Mick to Faye: 'I really enjoyed our date last night. It was just great. Even after so little time I feel very close to you. When can we meet again?'

(a) Speaker's words and phrases to describe his feelings: 'really enjoyed', 'just great', 'very close to', 'can we meet again'.

(b) Other words and phrases to describe how the speaker feels: 'delighted with', 'very pleased with', 'terrific', 'wonderful', 'a deep sympathy with', 'a great affinity with', 'I want to be with you again', 'I wish to see you soon'.

(c) Possible response reflecting the speaker's feelings: 'You feel you had a super time with me last night. Already you feel very comfortable with me and want to see me again soon.'

*Exercise*

1. Tony to Wayne: 'I find being without a job depressing. I'm young and want to get ahead. Right now my prospects look bleak. I struggle not to let it get me down.'

2. Eileen to Tricia: 'I'm keen to be my own woman. It's exciting to think I could be a success. I'm beginning to get much more confidence in myself.'

3. Sophia to Mario: 'I wish my folks got on better. I hate seeing them getting old and being unhappy. Also I don't like stepping into all the tension when I visit them.'

4. Tim to Colleen: 'I'm furious at his interference. Who the hell does he think he is telling me what to do. If I didn't need the job I would tell him to go to hell.'

---

One kind of reflective responding that is often helpful entails reflecting back both feelings and reasons. For instance, in the examples of Charles and Marcus, Charles's main feeling, that of worry, came at the end of his statement. When Marcus replied the second time, he picked up Charles's feeling and placed it at the start of his response. It often helps another to feel understood if you reflect their predominant feeling first. After reflecting the feeling, Marcus used the word *because* as a transition to reflecting Charles's reasons for his feeling. Exercise 8.6 requires you to reflect feelings and reasons in a standard 'You feel . . . because . . .' format. People who are starting listening training often have trouble both identifying feelings and stating them accurately. The exercise tries to make sure you do this first before moving on to reflect the reasons for the feeling. Some possible responses to Exercise 8.6 are provided at the end of the chapter.

---

### Exercise 8.6   Reflecting feelings and reasons

This exercise may be done in a number of ways.

A   *On your own*
For each of the following statements formulate and write out a response which reflects both feeling and reasons using the standard format: 'You feel . . . because . . .'

B   *In pairs*
*Either* independently formulate a response reflecting feelings and reasons for each statement one at a time, then discuss.
*Or* work through the exercise together from the start.

C   *In a training group*
The trainer gives group members time to formulate and write out their response reflecting feelings and reasons to one statement at a time and then facilitates the sharing and discussion of their answers, including his or her own version. He/she encourages members to read out their responses with appropriate vocal and bodily messages.

*Example*
Ted to Ronnie: 'I'm over the moon. I've got my examination results and they have surpassed my wildest hopes. I'm now sure to get into a good university.'

Possible response: 'You feel elated because you've done far better than you have ever dreamed in your exams and now getting a place in a good university is assured.'

*Exercise*

1.   Brenda to Vince: 'I hate being teased. I just hate it. I'm really no different from the other girls and yet they seem to enjoy ganging up on me. It makes me feel so angry and lonely.'

2.   Merle to Dick: 'I've got this neighbour who wants her little boy to play with mine. I would like to please her and yet her boy is very naughty. I feel confused and wonder how best to handle her.'

3. Sally to Trudy: 'Though it's not really what we planned, I'm pregnant. I'm surprised how strongly I feel about having the baby. Fortunately, John wants it too.'
4. Helmut to Ian: 'I get annoyed when people don't understand my relationship with Tom. Sure we are emotionally very close, but what's wrong with that? Some people can't understand intimate friendships between males.'

---

**Making a succession of reflective responses**

There are times when it may be helpful to make a succession of reflective responses in a relationship. One of the big problems here is that there is an expectancy that both partners in a relationship will respond in relatively traditional ways. Though making a succession of reflective responses may be what is most helpful for your relationship, you could inhibit doing so if either you or your partner feels uncomfortable.

Relationships are processes in which the risk of misunderstanding is ever present. There are a number of different ways that reflective responding can be used to strengthen your relationship, especially if both partners possess the skill. One way is that either of you can use reflective responding whenever it seems appropriate to respond to the other's feelings or concerns. Another way is for each of you to use the skill, as part of a systematic managing conflict procedure, to ensure that you understand the other's frame of reference when differences occur in your relationship. Still another way is that either of you may request listening time in which the other uses reflective responding as you communicate your thoughts and feelings or work through a problem and/or decision of your own.

Both of you may choose to build listening time on a regular basis, say once a week, into your relationship. This may have many uses: staying in touch with each other; helping each other tune into yourselves; preventing misunderstandings; identifying misunderstandings and differences; and enjoying each other as separate unique individuals. For instance you could set aside an hour each week, without distractions, to be with each other. You might spend half this time doing what is known as co-counselling. For the first 10 or 15 minutes one of you talks while the other listens and uses reflective responding. Then you reverse roles. The second half hour could be used to discuss any issues that have arisen or anything else you want to discuss. The precise time dimensions are not important.

You are encouraged to use the timing that works for both of you. What is important is that you use listening and reflective responding as a way of helping yourselves, each other and your relationship grow. Evidence abounds, for instance the statistics on marital breakdown, that traditional ways in which people relate to each other are deficient. Perhaps it is time to acknowledge much more clearly the destructive power of bad and the constructive power of good listening in relationships. If that means breaking with tradition in the manner and quality of your listening in your relationships, this may be long overdue.

Below is an example of the use of making a succession of reflective responses in a relationship. Marcus encourages Charles to develop his own thoughts and feelings about his situation in his own words and at his own pace. Sometimes reflective responding helps the other to shift from talking about more distant to talking about more personally relevant and emotionally tinged material. Here it frees Charles to start problem-solving.

Charles: I have my law exams coming up and it's vital for my career to get a good grade. My whole future depends on it. I'm so worried.

Marcus: You're really worried because you have these make-or-break exams imminent.

Charles: Yes, I can't sleep properly any more and I'm not eating well. I have a constant feeling of tension and wonder what I should do.

Marcus: You're wondering how to handle this situation. What with the incessant tension, your poor sleep, and being off your food.

Charles: I'm also losing my concentration.

Marcus: Uhm. Uhm.

Charles: I think I may have been overdoing it. I've been working solidly now for the past month.

Marcus: You think that all work and no play may have taken its toll.

Charles: I'm frightened to ease off, yet my present strategy is proving increasingly ineffective.

Marcus: You feel torn between your fears of easing off and the worsening consequences of continuing to work so hard.

Charles: The more I think about it, the more I realise I am harming rather than helping my chances by too much work.

Marcus: The risks of overwork appear to be increasingly outweighing the gains.

Charles: I need to focus down on what is really important in my work and then block out some time to get fresh again.

In Exercise 8.7 you are asked to reflect both feelings and content as your partner talks. Your role is that of facilitator or making it easy for your partner to talk. You may find that as you do the exercise you are self-conscious and feel wooden. Also, that you are afraid the other person will dry up. This may be partly that you are still striving to achieve fluency in a new skill. It may also be that others are so used to being interrupted, distracted, taught, preached at, advised etc. that they are unused to having the psychological space for listening to themselves before talking. Indeed your partner may take time to use the opportunity you provide. Additionally, your partner may be reticent about disclosing because the trust-building process is in its early stages in your relationship. You are encouraged to persist through these initial difficulties as you develop your listening and reflective responding skills.

---

### Exercise 8.7   Practising reflective responding

This exercise may be done in pairs or in a training group.

A   *In pairs*
Partner A talks about either his/her relationship skills or about some other matter of current concern or interest for 5 minutes. Partner A pauses fairly frequently to let Partner B practise reflective responding. Partner B should focus on feelings and not just on verbal content. Furthermore Partner B should demonstrate bodily and vocal as well as verbal empathy. The overall message should be 'I am with you. Please continue.' If Partner B strays slightly from Partner A's frame of reference, Partner A puts up one finger. If Partner B strays badly, Partner A puts up two fingers!

At the end of the 5 minutes Partner A gives Partner B feedback on how much he/she considered Partner B understood and was emotionally tuned into his/her frame of reference. It may help to audio-record the 5-minute sessions and play them back when giving feedback. Afterwards reverse roles.

This exercise may be varied by allowing a percentage of responses other than reflective ones so that it approximates outside life more closely. Additionally, the exercise may be performed for progressively longer periods. Both partners are encouraged to identify ways in which they can integrate their reflective responding skills into their everyday relationships and then to practise them there.

B   *In a training group*
The trainer demonstrates the above exercise using his/her reflective responding skills while a trainee talks. Afterwards the group is subdivided into pairs to do the exercise. The trainer concludes by

conducting a plenary sharing and discussion session with a focus on how trainees can integrate their reflective responding skills into their everyday relationships. Trainees are encouraged to practise their skills outside the group.

---

## AIDING PROBLEM-SOLVING

A personally responsible way of thinking entails taking a problem-solving approach to life. Helpful responding when others have a problem aids them in taking a realistic problem-solving approach rather than solves the problem for them. Put another way, the person with the problem should be encouraged to keep 'owning' it. You should neither directly take over ownership of another's problem nor allow them to pass all or part of its ownership on to you.

There are grave risks in solving other people's problems for them. For instance, you may help them stay dependent rather than stand on their own two feet. You may have failed to develop and define the problem adequately from their frame of reference. Your solutions may be wrong. The fact that the solutions come from you rather than them may lessen their motivation for implementing them, even to the point of rejecting them altogether. One of the best known psychological games devised by Eric Berne is called 'Why don't you . . . Yes but . . .' in which a would-be helper continuously gets frustrated by the person they are trying to help.[3]

There is an old saying: 'A problem shared is a problem halved.' Just being available to listen may lessen another's anxiety. This allows them to get some emotional distance from and perspective on a problem. Also, it may help them to think more clearly. If you can use your reflective responding skills, as Marcus did with Charles, this may be even more helpful. However, there are additional ways that you could aid another's problem-solving.

Solving or coping with a particular problem consists of two overlapping stages: *understanding it* and *doing something about it.* Your job as a helper of someone else solving their problems is to facilitate the processes of understanding and, if necessary, action. Sometimes just helping another understand and clarify their problem will be sufficient since then they will act on their own. On other occasions people may need assistance in moving from understanding to action.

Table 8.1 lays out some basic skills in aiding another's problem-solving. The table implies a more formal approach than you will necessarily take in your everyday relationships. However, sometimes it is likely to be in the other person's interest to take such a systematic approach.

**Table 8.1** *Some basic skills in aiding problem-solving*

---

*Stage One: Facilitating understanding*
    Permission to talk
    Continuation expressions
    Reflective responding
    Helpful questioning
    Feedback
    Translating descriptive into behavioural statements of problems
*Stage Two: Facilitating action*
    In addition to the skills of Stage One:
    Aiding goal-setting
    Aiding generating and evaluating alternative courses of action
    Developing a plan
    Being a resource during implementation of a plan
    Helping evaluate outcomes

---

Facilitating another's understanding of their problem can be more complex than it appears at first sight. Problems can have many different layers and ramifications. For instance, Marie a woman in her early forties says 'I am bored at home'. Possible considerations here include: how good Marie is at helping herself rather than waiting for others to do so; the expectations that she, her husband and her children have of each other; the work, educational and leisure opportunities that she has available and so on. In short, Marie may need to move from a *descriptive* statement of her problem, namely 'I am bored at home' to a *behavioural* statement. A behavioural statement identifies her current deficits in being able to solve the problem. In this hypothetical example, Marie's current deficits may include: an inability to tell her family that she wants some space for herself; and an absence of information-seeking behaviour that has resulted in her being unaware of all the available educational, leisure and employment opportunities. Thus a general statement of Marie's problem can be changed to one which is much more tangible in terms of identifying the areas in which she needs to work. The reverse-side of a behavioural statement of deficits is a statement of goals.[4] The goals entail developing resources to remedy the deficits. For instance,

Marie's goals could include: being assertive about stating her needs to husband and children, and developing information-gathering skills so that she can make a more informed decision as to how to spend her time.

To provide another example, Pete says 'I am lonely'. That is a descriptive statement of his problem. A behavioural statement might be that Pete lacks specific relationship skills. A statement of goals would target the various skills that Pete requires as goals to be attained. Sometimes attaining a goal involves generation and consideration of alternative courses of action. For example, though Charles's goal may be to take one day a week for recreation before his exams, he still needs to decide how best to do this. Charles needs to review his options and develop a plan. If goals are difficult, people may need support while attaining them. Also, they may need a sounding board as they evaluate their progress.

The remainder of this chapter focuses on three broad categories of skills that you may find useful, in conjunction with reflective responding, when aiding another's problem-solving. These skills are: helpful questioning, describing problems and goals in behavioural terms, and aiding exploration and evaluation of alternative courses of action.

### Helpful questioning

Wrongly used, questions can lead other people to expect you to provide solutions to their problems. The emphasis here is on using questions to aid others in solving their own problems. Thus questions may help them to identify, explore, clarify and develop their understanding of their problem areas. Furthermore, questions can help them decide how best to act. There are a number of questioning errors that you should usually try to avoid.

- *Too many questions*. Conducting an interrogation that may lead to defensiveness.
- *Leading questions*. Questions that put the answer into the other person's mouth: for instance, 'Your dad's a great guy, isn't he?'
- *Closed questions*. Closed questions curtail the other person's options for responding while open questions do not. For instance, 'Do you like domestic or imported cheese?' is a closed question, while 'What cheese do you like?' is an open one.

● *Too probing questions.* Questions that the other person is not ready to answer given the level of trust existing in your relationship.
● *Poorly timed questions.* Questions that interrupt the other person from doing their own work and come at the wrong time in the helping process.

Below are four beneficial ways in which you might use questions to help others explore and clarify their concerns. You will need to use your judgement as to whether the questions are really helping them to solve their problems rather than just meeting your own needs for information. It is often desirable to intersperse the use of questions with reflective responding. This disciplines you to listen to the answers, helps keep the ownership of the problem with the other, avoids creating a climate of interrogation, and allows the other person the psychological space to elaborate on their answers if they wish. The four potentially helpful kinds of questions are as follows:

● *Elaboration questions.* Elaboration questions give the other the opportunity to expand on what they have already started talking about. Illustrative elaboration questions or responses are: 'Would you care to elaborate?', 'Is there anything more?', 'Could you amplify what you've just said?'
● *Specification questions.* Specification questions aim to elicit detail about a problem area. For instance, 'When you say he upsets you, what precisely happens?', 'When?', 'How many times?'
● *Focusing on feelings questions.* These questions aim to elicit the feelings generated by a problem area. In general these questions should be open and tentative since the other person should, but not always will, know his or her feelings better than anyone else. Questions focusing on feelings include: 'How do you feel about that?', 'Would you care to describe your feelings?' 'I'm hearing that you're feeling . . .?'
● *Personal responsibility questions.* These questions imply not only that the other has a responsibility for owning the problem, but also for making the choices that contribute to solving it. These questions aim to establish links between how others initially describe their problems and their role in sustaining and changing them. Questions focusing on personal responsibility include: 'How do you see your own behaviour contributing to the problem?', 'Are there any skills you need to develop in relation to the problems?', 'Are there any ways in which you could be helping yourself more?'

Exercise 8.8 focuses on helping others clarify their problems through the use of questions. Remember to leave the responsibility for solving *their* problems with others. Also, try to avoid the questioning errors mentioned earlier: namely, too many, leading, closed, too probing and poorly timed questions.

---

**Exercise 8.8  Helping clarify problems through using questions**

This exercise may be performed in pairs or in a training group.

A  *In pairs*

Partner A presents a problem, to which he/she is having difficulty finding an adequate solution, to Partner B. Partner B uses reflective responding after *each* statement made by Partner A, but then may ask a question. Partner B's questions should be asked in the following sequence.

1. *Elaboration questions.* Spend a minimum of 2 minutes getting Partner A to elaborate his/her problem by using elaboration questions interspersed with reflective responding.
2. *Specification questions.* Spend a minimum of 2 minutes getting Partner A to provide a more precise specification of his/her concern by using specification questions interspersed with reflective responding.
3. *Focusing on feelings questions.* Spend a minimum of 2 minutes helping Partner A explore his/her feelings about the problem by using focusing on feelings questions interspersed with reflective responding.
4. *Personal responsibility questions.* Spend a minimum of 2 minutes helping Partner A explore his/her contribution to sustaining the problem by using personal responsibility questions interspersed with reflective responding.

Allow Partner A to give you feedback on whether and how your use of questions has helped or hindered him/her in clarifying and understanding the problem better. It may be helpful to audio-record the session to illustrate this feedback. Afterwards reverse roles.

B  *In a training group*

The trainer demonstrates the above exercise by using questions interspersed with reflective responding to help a trainee clarify his/her problem. The trainer then subdivides the group into pairs and gets them to do the exercise. Afterwards a plenary sharing and discussion session is held in which trainees are encouraged to develop questioning skills resources and to eliminate questioning skills deficits in their relationships.

---

## Defining problems and goals in behavioural terms

The ability to define problems and goals in behavioural terms provides the link between the facilitating understanding and the facilitating action stages in aiding another's problem-solving. This requires the analysis and breaking down of problems into the specific behaviours that are contributing to them. Describing problems in behavioural terms should not be done prematurely. Often as the talker stays with a problem it begins to emerge in a new light. However, sooner or later, if the other is to be able to work on altering the problem it needs to be defined in behavioural terms. In particular, this entails working with the other to identify the behaviours and skills deficits that contribute to sustaining the problem.

For instance, in our earlier example, Pete says 'I am lonely'. On exploring his situation with Pete, together you discover that the real problem, or that defined in behavioural terms, is that he lacks three specific skills: (1) the attitude that he is responsible for making things happen in his life; (2) getting started skills with new people, for instance initiating conversations; and (3) the ability to reveal himself to others. You have just stated Pete's problem in behavioural terms, though it could be stated more fully. Consequently, Pete's goals, which are the reverse-side of the skills he lacks, are: (1) acquiring an attitude of personal responsibility; (2) acquiring getting started skills, in particular those of initiating conversations; and (3) acquiring some skills of talking about himself.

Exercise 8.9 gives you practice at helping define problems and goals in behavioural terms. Your summary of what your partner has been saying should clearly be as if in his or her internal frame of reference. Any additional feedback or observations you provide should clearly be from your frame of reference. Your observations should be expressed in such a way that your partner feels under no pressure to agree with what you have said. Your definition of problems and goals should be done as specifically as is feasible. Vagueness is to be avoided.

**Exercise 8.9    Helping define problems and goals in behavioural terms**

This exercise may be performed on your own, in pairs or as part of a training group.

A   *On your own*
   Take a problem or area of concern in your life and write out:
   1.   a description of the problem in everyday terms;
   2.   a definition of the problem in behavioural terms;
   3.   a statement of goals in behavioural terms.

B   *In pairs*
   Your partner discusses a problem for which he/she is having difficulty finding an adequate solution. Your role is to:
   1.   by means of reflective responses and questions help your partner understand and clarify the problem;
   2.   summarise what your partner has been saying;
   3.   provide any additional feedback or observations on the problem that you consider appropriate and check out your partner's reactions to these comments;
   4.   negotiate with your partner a statement of his or her problem in behavioural terms, and
   5.   restate the problem in terms of attaining one or more specific behavioural goals.
   Afterwards reverse roles.

C   *In a training group*
   The trainer demonstrates helping define problems and goals in behavioural terms. The group is then subdivided to perform the pairs exercise above. Afterwards the trainer conducts a plenary sharing and discussion session.

## Evaluating alternative courses of action

Exploring alternatives can form part of the facilitating understanding stage as well as the facilitating action stage. As part of the earlier stage, it can entail exploring alternative ways of looking at and defining the problem. In the action stage, it tends to entail exploring and evaluating alternative courses of action to attain goals.

Exercise 8.10 encourages you to aid another person in generating and assessing the courses of action they might take in attaining their goals. Together you may discover that there are many more possibilities in difficult areas of their lives than they imagine. As well as reflective responding, judicious use of questions may help. For instance, the following are some questions that you might use to aid the other in generating and evaluating alternatives: 'What are the options?', 'Are there any other ways in which you might attain your goals?', 'What might the positive and negative consequences be of _____ course of action?', and 'Is that the behaviour that is going to be of most help to you?'. Though you may suggest some alternatives yourself in a neutral way, this should wait until you have provided your partner with a good chance to generate his or her own alternatives. Here it is important that not only your words but also your intonation leave the decision to the other. Use reflective responding after each time your partner suggests or assesses an alternative before asking any questions. This helps keep the emphasis on others generating and owning their *own* solutions and courses of actions for their problems.

Exercise 8.10 concludes by asking you to help your partner develop a step-by-step plan to attain his or her goals. The idea here is that you help your partner choose the most appropriate course of action. Then you aid him or her in specifying the steps that are necessary to implement the action. It can also be helpful here to anticipate potential difficulties and setbacks and then to include ways of surmounting them in the plan. Remember to make your partner do most of the work when you are aiding their problem-solving and likewise they should make you do most of the work when they aid you. In general the most effective way you can help others is to help them to help themselves.

---

**Exercise 8.10  Aiding the generation and evaluation of alternative courses of action**

This exercise may be done in a number of ways.

A  *On your own*
In Exercise 8.9 you made a statement of goals in behavioural terms for a problem in your life. Write out:
1.  as many different ways of attaining your goals as you can think of in 10 to 15 minutes;
2.  an assessment of the degree to which any of these courses of

action are realistic and useful in helping you attain your goals; and

3. a step-by-step plan, including a time-schedule, for attaining your goals.

B *In pairs*

Either with the statement of goals in behavioural terms made in Exercise 8.9 or with a statement of goals for another problem, facilitate your partner in:

1. thinking of as many different ways of attaining the goals as he or she can in 10 to 15 minutes;
2. assessing the degree to which any of these courses of action are realistic and useful for attaining his/her goals; and
3. developing a step-by-step plan, including a time-schedule, for attaining the goals.

Afterwards reverse roles.

C *In a training group*

The trainer demonstrates aiding the exploration and evaluation of alternative courses of action in relation to a group member's problem. The group is subdivided to perform the pairs exercise above. Afterwards the trainer conducts a plenary sharing and discussion session. Alternatively, the trainer can get the group to suggest alternative courses of action for attaining one or more member's goals. The trainer then helps members evaluate the suggestions and develop step-by-step plans to attain goals.

---

## CONCLUDING INNER SPEECH

Active listening entails me in being able to respond helpfully to others. Reflective responding involves communicating back to them that I have picked up and understood their words and feelings. It requires me to listen and observe and then to formulate a response which illustrates an accurate understanding of their frame of reference. To do this well I need to be sensitive to their vocal and bodily messages as well as to their words. My reflective responses indicate that I am sensitively with the other person as they express and explore their world.

I can also respond helpfully to others if I aid them in their problem-solving. I can help both their understanding of a problem and also their taking action in regard to it. It is important that I do not take over ownership of the problem, but allow others to work towards their own solutions. At first problems may be stated vaguely. Interspersed with reflective responding, I can use questions that help others elaborate, specify, state how they feel about, and clarify their responsibility for sustaining their problems. I can also aid them in defining their problems in tangible behavioural terms and in setting specific goals. Furthermore, I can help them generate and assess alternative courses of action for attaining goals. In general I can be most effective as a helper if I help others to help themselves.

# REFERENCES

1.  Gordon, T. (1970) *Parent Effectiveness Training*. New York: Wyden.
2.  Rogers, C.R. (1975) Empathic: an unappreciated way of being. *The Counseling Psychologist*, **5** (2), pp. 2–10. Reprinted in Rogers, C.R. (1980) *A Way of Being*. Boston: Houghton Mifflin.
3.  Berne, E. (1964) *Games People Play*. New York: Grove Press.
4.  Carkhuff, R.R. (1973) *The Art of Problem Solving*. Amherst: Human Resource Development Press.

# ANSWERS TO EXERCISES

*Exercise 8.1*
1.  (a)  0; External frame of reference, blaming.
    (b)  1; External frame of reference, though showing some understanding.
    (c)  3; A good reflective response.
2.  (a)  4; Very good reflective response. Allows patient to go on talking.
    (b)  3; Misses out her fear of dying, but this could be implicit in the response.
    (c)  0; Patronising, absolutely terrible.
3.  (a)  4; Very good reflective response. Gives permission to explore the problem.
    (b)  1; Slight understanding, external frame of reference.
    (c)  2; Goes beyond what has been said, too strong.
4.  (a)  0; External and defensive.
    (b)  4; Spot on.
    (c)  1; She is asking for consistency rather than reassurance.
The above ratings are the author's and based on an assessment of verbal content only. You might infer different vocal and bodily communication and thus also differ in your ratings.

*Exercise 8.2*
The following paraphrases are intended only as possibilities. There is no single correct response to each statement.
1.  'I would be grateful if you helped more with the household chores. When I get back from a day at work I'm fatigued. You don't appear to appreciate this.'
2.  'You are very attractive. When I should be working I'm not able to pay attention to my studies. See the effect you are having on me.'
3.  'Your spouse was an excellent example. His untimely passing away was a

huge jolt. All of us will feel his loss deeply. You have my most profound
condolences.'
4. 'I'm happy with how you are getting on. When we hired you I had my
reservations. I'm delighted that they've been proved unfounded.'

*Exercise 8.4*
Below are some illustrative voice and body messages. There are many others.

| *Non-verbal cue* | *Anger* | *Friendship* | *Sadness* | *Anxiety* |
|---|---|---|---|---|
| Tone of voice | Harsh | Warm | Soft | Timid Hesitant |
| Voice volume | Loud | Easy to hear | Quiet | Quiet |
| Eye contact | Direct | Good, but unobtrusive | Averted | Averted Very intermittent |
| Facial expression | Clenched teeth | Natural smile | Tearful Mouth turned down | Strained |
| Posture | Rigid | Relaxed | Slouched | Tense |
| Gestures | Fist clenched Finger pointing | Arm round shoulder | Holds head in hands | Finger tapping |

*Exercise 8.5*
There are no single correct responses other than for (a).
1. (a) 'depressing', 'want to get ahead', 'bleak', 'struggle', 'get me down'.
   (b) 'puts me down', 'lowering', 'ambitious', 'want to succeed', 'bad',
       'unpromising', 'fight', 'make an effort', 'depress', 'get to me'.
   (c) 'You feel being unemployed pulls you down. You're young and
       ambitious. At the moment there seems little chance of employment.
       It's a real fight to maintain your morale.'
2. (a) 'keen to be', 'exciting', 'confidence'.
   (b) 'anxious to be', 'want to be', 'thrilling', 'energising', 'faith', 'trust'.
   (c) 'You feel you want to be your own woman. The possibility of success
       thrills you. You're starting to have much more faith in yourself.'
3. (a) 'wish', 'get on better', 'hate', 'unhappy', 'don't like', 'tension'.
   (b) 'would like', 'wait', 'were happier', 'related better', 'dislike',
       'detest', 'miserable', 'low', 'not happy with', 'would prefer not to',
       'stress', 'strain'.

(c) 'You feel you would like your parents to be happier. You detest seeing them ageing and being miserable. Furthermore you're uncomfortable being faced with such a strained atmosphere when you go there.'

4. (a) 'furious', 'Who the hell', 'need', 'go to hell'.

(b) 'hopping mad', 'extremely angry', 'Who on earth', 'Who in God's name', 'require', 'want', 'get stuffed', 'go to blazes'.

(c) 'You feel really mad at his meddling. He's got a nerve telling you what to do. If keeping your paypacket wasn't necessary you would tell him to get stuffed.'

*Exercise 8.6*

Again there is no single correct response.

1. 'You feel mad and isolated because you loathe being teased. Despite your being the same as the others, they take pleasure in joining forces against you.'

2. 'You feel confused and unsure of what to do because, though your neighbour would like her son to play with yours and you would like to please her, you have reservations about his bad behaviour.'

3. 'You feel amazed at the strength of your feelings because you really want to have your baby even though neither of you had planned it. Luckily John shares your feelings.'

4. 'You feel upset because people misunderstand your feelings for Tom. Though you have a deep sympathy for each other, some people read too much into such close male friendships.'

# 9 Managing Anger and Stress

In the earlier part of this book attention was paid both to listening to your feelings and also to expressing them. This chapter focuses on regulating or managing your feelings, in particular anger. Attention is also paid to managing feelings of stress. The chapter mainly looks at how you can help yourself as an individual. The next chapter, on managing conflict, looks at how both people in a relationship can cooperate for mutual benefit. There is substantial overlap between these two chapters.

## Thinking and feeling

The major emphasis here is on the choices you can make in disciplining your thinking so that you can regulate feelings that are negative both for yourself and for others. This, in turn, is likely to help you to act more effectively to reach your goals. It may help to clarify some terms. In everyday conversations people often say 'I think' and 'I feel' interchangeably. For instance, 'I feel she's nice' and 'I think she's nice' virtually mean the same. Here, however, the use of words like 'feelings' and 'I feel' emphasises bodily sensations, for instance, anger and tension. The use of words like 'thinking', 'thoughts' and 'I think' emphasises mental processes and ideas rather than bodily sensations. For example, if Jane says 'I'm angry because Peter has been rude to me', Jane's *feeling* is anger. Her *thoughts* are that Peter has been rude to her.

Having stressed in Chapter 3 that feelings are representations of your animal nature, it may seem strange to talk about regulating something that is 'natural'. However, unlike lower animals, humans have the capacity to think as well as to feel. As should become clear as the chapter progresses, your thoughts can interfere with using your capacity to feel to best effect. Humans have often *acquired* their skills deficits through learning bad habits from others. However, frequently they *perpetuate* them through faulty thinking.

**Personal responsibility and choice**

You are likely to be effective in your relationships to the extent that you assume responsibility for your thoughts, feelings and actions. Assuming responsibility for your feelings entails learning to express them where appropriate and to regulate them where necessary. One set of choices in regard to regulating feelings entails accurately assigning or attributing responsibility for what happens in your life. This is something that needs to be learned. Apart from reflex reactions you always have some choice in how you feel. Even where another in a relationship behaves badly towards you, you still have a choice regarding your thoughts about what is happening. Furthermore, the way you think is likely to influence the way you feel about yourself and another.

Let us take a simple example. Hans treads on Brian's toe. Brian may feel some natural pain concerning which he has relatively little choice. However, Brian may choose to think one of the following thoughts: (a) it was deliberate; (b) it was careless; (c) it was an unfortunate mistake on Hans's part; and (d) my foot was in his way. Each of the above explanations or thoughts is likely to influence differently how Brian feels. However, even if Brian thinks it was deliberate, his feelings are likely to be further regulated by the internal rules he has chosen to espouse. For instance, if he has a rule 'An eye for an eye, a tooth for a tooth', he may feel angry and aggressive. However, if he has a rule that 'Violence only begets violence', he may feel much more calm about the incident.

You can be very skilled at avoiding taking responsibility for acknowledging and managing your feelings. Ways in which you may achieve this include:

- *Denial.* For instance, hating someone and not being prepared to acknowledge this.
- *Projection.* For instance, hating someone yet making out that they hate you.
- *Misattributing responsibility.* An overemphasis on making others responsible for how you feel. Blaming others for your own negative feelings is possibly the prime example.
- *Collusion.* Colluding in situations that are not to your liking through lack of assertion.
- *Enlisting collusion.* Trying to get another to collude in your false definitions of others.

- *Power playing.* Trying to control others' feedback by putting overt and/or subtle emotional pressure on them.
- *Rationalisation.* Deceiving yourself and others by justifying feelings unjustifiably.
- *Avoidance.* Avoiding difficult people or situations.
- *Defences against the good.* Blocking off or diluting both your awareness of and also showing positive qualities such as generosity and concern for others.
- *Distortion.* People create personifications of themselves and of each other. Distortion is used here to incorporate all the ways in which you 'operate' on incoming information so as to maintain your picture of yourself.
- *Misuse of language.* You may use expressions like 'They did it to me', 'It just happened', 'It infuriated me', and 'It's your fault' which contribute to distancing you from owning your feelings. The use of 'I' statements is preferable.

Exercise 9.1 has been designed to help you explore the issue of avoiding or assuming personal responsibility for managing anger and stress. Though the situations involve others, you may see yourself in them. As you think your way through the exercise bear in mind the earlier distinction between thoughts and feelings. In both the vignettes in this exercise the main characters contribute to perpetuating their distressed feelings through their failure to think realistically.

---

**Exercise 9.1   Personal responsibility, choice, and managing anger and stress**

The following exercise may be done on your own, in pairs or in a training group.

A   *On your own*

Below are two situations in which a person is experiencing strong negative feelings. For each situation write out your views concerning:

1.   the degree to which the main character is avoiding or assuming personal responsibility for managing his/her feelings;
2.   what unrealistic thoughts might be contributing to the main character feeling so strongly, and
3.   the choices which the individual might make that would be conducive to managing the feelings more effectively.

*Situation A*

Ron feels deeply resentful about his boss Martha. He disparages Martha to others at every available opportunity. Ron is keen to form alliances with others against what he perceives an inefficient authority figure. Ron is himself perceived by Martha as highly inefficient. Martha similarly disparages Ron to others. Ron's morale is very low and his colleagues have to resist letting him get them down. Ron is underachieving in his job. Though Martha has her share of difficulties with other people in the unit, Ron's resentment towards her is particularly deep and virulent.

*Situation B*

Sally feels in a constant state of tension. She is a high pressure person who expects others to say 'How high?', when she says 'Jump'. Recently Sally has been bad-tempered, sleeping poorly and off her food. Her relations with her family and work mates have been deteriorating. Sally is badly overweight, smokes heavily and takes little exercise. She has a recurrent pain in the left of her chest and quite routinely develops headaches at work by mid-afternoon.

B *In pairs*

*Either* independently work through the above exercise, then discuss.

*Or* together work through the above exercise from the start.

C *In a training group*

The trainer introduces the topic of learning to assume responsibility for managing feelings. The trainer can then work through the above exercise with the whole group. Alternatively, the trainer can divide the group into subgroups to work through the exercise prior to conducting a plenary sharing and discussion session.

---

## MANAGING ANGER

Feeling angry involves ill-will and hostility towards either others, oneself, the environment, or any combination of these. Anger itself may be short-lived. However, in many relationships, anger turns into hatred and resentment which festers and corrodes the relationship to breaking point. However, anger is not always destructive. Positive uses of anger include that: it may be a *signal* for yourself and others that something is wrong; it may be an *energiser* leading to assertion; and the release of angry feelings may *purge* an individual so that they may be more rational and positive. Thus, as a *signal*, an *energiser* and a *purge*, anger can be constructive. However, partners may need to develop an understanding about how and when to express anger in their relationships so that its potentially destructive aspects can be minimised. Using 'I' statements that clearly own the anger, rather than 'You-blame' statements is one way of avoiding negative consequences.

Anger is a complex emotion. For instance, it gets combined with other emotions such as hurt, jealousy, fear, powerlessness, guilt, frustration and depression. Also, there are many variations in the extent to which anger is acknowledged and expressed. For example, angry feelings may be: denied altogether; compensated for by positive behaviour; projected on to others so that they rather than you are perceived as angry; inhibited and not allowed expression; inhibited yet given indirect expression, for instance, through being uncooperative; manifested in aggressive 'put-downs' of others (psychological violence); involving bodily harm to others (physical violence); turned inward on the self contributing to depression; assertively expressed by means of 'I' statements; and worked through in the context of a loving and understanding relationship.

American psychologist Raymond Novaco sees anger as an emotional response to provocation involving thoughts, feelings and behaviour.[1] The thinking aspect covers the appraisals, expectations, attributions and self-statements that occur in the context of the provocation. Novaco considers angry feelings are 'primed and exacerbated by tension, agitation and ill-humor'. Both withdrawal and antagonism are behaviours contributing to anger, 'the former by leaving the instigation unchanged, the latter by escalating the provocation sequence and by providing cues from which the person infers anger'. Chronic anger and proneness to provocation both may have serious implications for relationships.

There is a risk that you bring anger proneness into a relationship. Because of previous rejections your own feelings of self-worth may be low. Consequently you are quick to perceive threats and provocations even where these were unintended. In your past you may have observed models who handled provocations more by getting angry than by problem-solving. Furthermore, you may have been rewarded for getting angry by using it as a power-play to get your way. For a number of reasons some of you live on very short fuses. You appear to have a 'free-floating' store of anger that you allow to be ignited without much provocation. Consequently, some of you may require counselling.

There are many considerations relevant to analysing why and how you get angry, including the following.

- *Nature of the provocation.* What happened or was thought to have happened to trigger the anger.
- *Context of the provocation.* For instance, depending on what else is happening in their relationship, Nancy's request to Chuck to

pick up his socks may be perceived as a simple request or a provocative and nagging statement. Contextual considerations may go beyond the relationship: for instance, the stress of a difficult work situation may have implications in the home.

- *Sense of worth.* The degree of self-confidence that you possess influences the degree to which you perceive events as threatening.
- *Angry feelings.* Your angry feelings have a common element of ill-will. They include: displeasure, rage, hatred and resentment. They may also include other emotions, for example hurt. Depending on how strong these feelings are, they may be hard to control.
- *Anger-related physical reactions.* Your body may experience anger through heightened blood pressure, increased energy, tension, ulcers, insomnia, strained face and blazing eyes.
- *Anger-engendering thoughts.* Thoughts that contribute to anger include unrealistic internal rules and failure to accept personal responsibility.
- *Language and self-talk.* You can express anger with words that distance you from 'owning' your feelings. Additionally, your language may both depersonalise and be unnecessarily provocative to others. Using 'You-blame' language rather than 'I' statements exemplifies both the above points. Furthermore, you may talk to yourself in ways that increase rather than lessen your anger.
- *Defensive thinking.* Denying and distorting the full extent of your anger and its effect on others.
- *Anger-related behaviours.* These behaviours may range from fighting, fleeing to assertion. Anger can be expressed verbally, by rejection, ridicule, disparagement and other forms of negative evaluation. It is also expressed vocally and bodily by shouting, tut-tutting, turning away, finger shaking, physical violence and other negative behaviours.
- *Skills deficits.* Skills deficits contributing to anger include the inability to understand another's position, and poor assertion and problem-solving skills.
- *Reciprocal processes.* People frequently match or reciprocate each other's behaviours. If I talk about a provocation that makes me angry you are more likely to talk about a provocation that makes you angry. If I get angry with you, you are more likely to get angry with me and so on.
- *Consequences of anger.* The positive and negative,consequences of being angry in relation to a perceived provocation are

important to understanding why and how you get angry. However, a seeming paradox of anger is that you may persist in it at your own expense.

Exercise 9.2 encourages you to explore the role of anger in your life. To what extent is anger a problem for you? How do you choose to show it? What are its positive and negative consequences? How do you react when others get angry with you?

---

**Exercise 9.2   Exploring the role of anger in your life**

This exercise may be done on your own, in pairs or as part of a training group.

A   *On your own*
   Write out your answers to the following questions.
   1.   Do you consider yourself to be an angry person?
   2.   To what extent is your anger a problem for you?
   3.   What are the *situations* that are conducive to your feeling angry?
   4.   What *people* are conducive to your feeling angry?
   5.   List the *physical reactions* you experience when angry?
   6.   List the kinds of *thoughts* you have about *other people* when you are angry?
   7.   List the kinds of *thoughts* you have *about yourself* when you are angry?
   8.   How do you actually *behave* when you are angry?
   9.   What, if any, are the *positive consequences* for yourself, others and your relationships stemming from your anger?
   10.   What, if any, are the *negative consequences* for yourself, others and your relationships stemming from your anger?
   11.   How do you *feel, physically react, think* and *behave* when *others* get angry with you?
B   *In pairs*
   *Either* independently work through the above questions, then discuss.
   *Or* Partner A uses his/her helpful responding skills to enable Partner B to work through the above questions, then reverse roles.
C   *In a training group*
   The trainer can introduce the need for people to be aware of the role of anger in their lives. The trainer could take the whole group through the above exercise, question by question. Another option is to divide the group into small groups, let them answer the questions, and then hold a plenary sharing and discussion session.

### Acknowledging and expressing anger

Managing your anger requires you to be aware of when you feel angry. This owning of your angry feelings is both in relation to yourself and to others. You need to develop the capacity to listen to yourself so that you become aware of your angry feelings rather than use the defensive processes mentioned earlier in this chapter. As some of you grew up the consequences for you of expressing your anger directly may have been so negative that it was safer to inhibit not only expressing, but also acknowledging these feelings. Sometimes in counselling there is a cathartic or purging period in which people acknowledge and express their anger from past hurts and humiliations in a way that frees them to look more towards the future. Some of you may need professional help in acknowledging and releasing past resentments which erode your present sense of worth.

An important way of managing anger in a relationship can be to express it assertively. This entails owning your anger by means of 'I' statements rather than automatically shifting the cause of your anger on to another by means of 'You-blame' statements. In Chapter 6 an F.E.R. or feeling, explanation, request format was suggested when you needed to stand up and speak out for yourself (Exercise 6.6). You acknowledge, own and share your angry feelings, explain your reasons for feeling this way and request that the other alter their behaviour. While such an approach can be very valuable, it may be insufficient. Taking responsibility for your angry feelings entails not only acknowledging and expressing them, but being aware of how you may contribute to generating and sustaining your anger. When feeling angry it is very easy only to see others' provocative behaviour as the problem. With closer examination you may see that you have many more choices in how you feel, think and act than you are currently aware. Below we explore how you can change some of the ways in which you may contribute to your anger.

### Developing realistic internal rules

Possessing unrealistic internal rules is one way in which you may contribute to your proneness to anger. Anger, along with other feelings, can be viewed in an A.T.F. framework.

A.   The event (or the provocation)
T.   Your thoughts
F.   Your feelings.

Up until now you may have been aware only of A and F. However, what happens at T can be critical not only for how angry you are because of A but also in regard to how rationally you handle the situation. There is no automatic link between A and F so long as you are reasonably in control of yourself. Therefore you can influence and alter your Fs by learning to think more realistically at T.[2,3]

The realism of your internal rules or standards is very important to the effectiveness of your thinking. In Chapter 5 some illustrations were given of how unrealistic internal rules could contribute to shyness (see Exercise 5.5 and accompanying text). Here the focus is on unrealistic internal rules contributing to anger.

The following unrealistic rules may contribute to *anger with yourself* (anger-in).[4] The feeling may follow from failure to attain your own standards.

> I must always come first.
> I must be rational and consistent all the time.
> I must never make a fool of myself in public.

The following unrealistic rules may contribute to *anger with another* in a relationship (anger-out).

> The other person should always do what I want.
> The other person should never get angry.
> The other person should always appreciate me.
> The other person should not make mistakes.
> Women should always emotionally support men.
> Men should always financially support women.

The anger generated by transgression of the above standards for your own and others' behaviour may be fuelled by thoughts of justification and by feelings of powerlessness. If I or someone breaks one of my internal rules, then I may think I am justified in feeling angry and hence allow myself to do so. Also, I may feel powerless or less confident because my internal rules have been broken. This may add to my feelings of threat and proneness to anger.

The characteristics of *unrealistic* inner rules include that they are based on what Albert Ellis calls 'musturbation'.[5] These overgeneralised 'musts', 'oughts' and 'shoulds' place inflexible and rigid demands on yourself and others. Furthermore, they tend to be unrealistic standards of perfection which may, if broken, then lead to feelings of anger, anxiety and depression.

Some of the main characteristics of *realistic* inner rules include: being based on your own needs and values; a degree of flexibility and, where appropriate, being amenable to change; a functional rating of specific characteristics according to whether they are useful for survival and fulfilment rather than rating yourself as a person; realism about your resources, including acknowledging strengths; having an emphasis on coping with situations to the best of your ability rather than being perfectionist in relation to them; and being conducive to minimising negative emotions and to engendering positive emotions.

When you find yourself experiencing anger, it may help if you do not act impulsively but stop and think whether any of your unrealistic internal rules make a contribution to it. Thus you need to develop the skill of acknowledging not only your feelings, but also your thoughts. Then you need to reformulate unrealistic into more realistic rules. For instance, 'I must always come first' might be reformulated 'That while I like coming first, what is most important for me is to do as well as I can'. Also, 'The other person should always do what I want' might be reformulated 'In my relationships each person should be free to express their thoughts and feelings and then try to resolve, with mutual respect, any areas of conflict'.

Exercise 9.3 helps you to explore your internal rules contributing to harmful rather than to constructive anger. Complete the exercise to the best of your ability.

---

**Exercise 9.3   Coping with anger: developing realistic internal rules**

This exercise may be done on your own, in pairs or as part of a training group.

A   *On your own*
Think of one or more recent situations in your life where you have felt angry. For each write out:
1.   the activating event or provocation;
2.   your thoughts: focus on your unrealistic internal rules;
3.   your feelings;
4.   a reformulation of the unrealistic into realistic internal rules;
5.   any changes in your feelings and actions that may result from your more realistic internal rules.
It may help if you cassette-record your reformulated rules and play them back to yourself at least once a day for the next two weeks.

B   *In pairs*
*Either* complete the above exercise independently, then discuss together before cassette-recording your reformulated internal rules for playing back at home.

*Or* Partner A uses his/her helpful responding skills to enable Partner B to work through the above exercise, then reverse roles.

C  *In a training group*
The trainer illustrates how altering unrealistic internal rules can help people cope better with their anger in relationships. The trainer then takes the whole group through the exercise including, if time is available, making up cassettes of reformulated rules for each trainee's homework. Working with the whole group is probably necessary for this exercise. The trainer will need to both teach and coach trainees in how to develop realistic internal rules.

---

### Using task-oriented inner speech

Those of you with a tendency to be impulsive when you are angry and 'shoot your mouth' might consider using task-oriented inner speech.[6] Basically this consists of two elements. First, you require a task orientation to provocations. You need to think through what your goals are in specific situations and behave accordingly. Anger-evoking situations may be viewed as challenging you to respond in task-oriented rather than in impulsive and self-defeating ways. In fact, in many relationships they are stress situations that are moderately predictable in their occurrence. For instance, you know that your partner has a tendency to keep you waiting. Therefore, this is a task that you can work on coping with better before, during and after its occurrence. If your goal is to be kept waiting less often and long, having a blazing row may only add to rather than lessen your stress.

Second, you may use task-oriented self-instructions to help you achieve your goal of managing a specific provocation better. This entails making choices that increase your sense of mastery and lessen the likelihood of your anger being both unpleasant for yourself and counterproductive in your relationship.

Possible task-oriented inner speech sentences that you might tell yourself *before* a potentially anger-evoking provocation include:

'Keep calm and remember what I want to achieve in this situation.'
'Remember, stick to the issues and avoid put-downs.'
'This could be a difficult situation, but I should be able to handle it if I don't let my pride get in the way.'

Possible task-oriented inner speech sentences that you might tell yourself *during* an anger-evoking provocation include:

'Now calm down. Take your time. I can keep control.'
'Relax. My anger is a signal telling me to keep task-oriented.'
'Take it easy. Calm down and stop being so competitive.'

Possible task-oriented inner speech sentences that you might tell yourself *after* an anger-evoking provocation include:

'I'm learning to cope better without getting aggressive.'
'Even though the situation is unresolved, I'm glad I didn't come on strong.'
'Using my task-oriented inner speech stops me from feeling powerless and overwhelmed.'

As you can see from the above self-instructions, by choosing to use task-oriented inner speech you can help yourself cope better with specific situations. Furthermore, you may wish to control your physical reactions to an anger provocation by breathing slowly and regularly. This may help you to focus on your task. Additionally, sometimes it is highly desirable to choose to defer dealing with a provocation until you have got your feelings more under control. Exercise 9.4 has been designed to give you practice at using task-oriented inner speech to cope with anger.

---

### Exercise 9.4   Coping with anger: using task-oriented inner speech

This exercise may be done on your own, in pairs or as part of a training group.

A   *On your own*
1.  Give at least three examples of the kind of self-talk that contributes to your getting unnecessarily angry in your relationships.
2.  Identify a specific situation in one of your relationships where you feel that your anger is harmful. Write down:
    (a)  your goals in the situation
    (b)  two task-oriented inner speech sentences for each of before, during and after the situation.
3.  Practise your task-oriented inner speech either with a cassette-recorder or in front of a mirror (you may speak aloud) prior to using it in the actual situation.
B   *In pairs*
    *Either* do questions 1 and 2 above independently, then discuss together. Afterwards role-play managing your anger-evoking situations. During this practice use inner as well as outer speech.

*Or* Partner A uses his/her helpful responding skills to enable Partner B to work through questions 1 and 2 above. Then together role-play the situation with Partner B using inner as well as outer speech. Afterwards reverse roles.

C   *In a training group*
   The trainer discusses, and possibly illustrates from his/her own life, how using task-oriented inner speech can help trainees cope with their anger in relationships. The trainer works with the whole group, helping each trainee to:
   (a)   identify a particular anger-evoking situation on which they want to work;
   (b)   set themselves goals;
   (c)   identify their anger-engendering self-talk; and
   (d)   develop realistic task-oriented inner speech for before, during and afterwards.
   The trainer may set up role-plays in the group in which trainees practise their task-oriented inner speech. Additionally, the trainer encourages practice of the skill outside the group.

---

## Being assertive

Feelings of anger tend to be associated with feelings of powerlessness and with having to put up with others' negative behaviours. Consequently, there are many occasions when being more assertive might help you both prevent and handle anger-engendering situations. Below are some examples where people's failure to be assertive contributes to their anger.

● *Not saying what you want.* Jane and Bill usually do what Bill wants to do. Bill is very positive about stating his wants and wishes. Jane is very inhibited about stating hers. Arguably, Bill could be more sensitive to Jane's wishes. However, Jane is colluding in a situation that makes her resentful by not being prepared to state her wants and wishes. Also, Jane needs to learn to stop saying 'yes' when she means 'no'.

● *Not speaking out for yourself.* There may be many occasions when you disapprove of another's behaviour and either bottle up your anger or let it come out indirectly, for instance through cynicism and gossiping. You may neither have tried at all nor have tried hard enough to change the other person's behaviour. Until you have made a genuine effort to do so, you may be colluding in sustaining situations that help you to feel resentful.

● *Not setting limits.* Ken feels like a door-mat because his boss Phyllis is continually asking him to do more work than is specified in his job contract. Ken deeply resents her. He has never made any real effort to state the limits of his contract. Ken wrongly considers that his problems are all Phyllis's doing.

● *Colluding in another's power-plays.* Gary is always telling you what a bastard Dennis is. You quite like Dennis, but Gary's persistent negative comments may contribute to your sharing his anger towards Dennis. You sense that Gary would like you to do his 'dirty work' with Dennis for him by confronting Dennis with Gary's complaints as if they were your own. You need to encourage Gary to handle his unfinished business with Dennis directly rather than by manipulating you. There are many other instances where people need to assert themselves to stop others getting them to define themselves and to act to their own disadvantage.

In Chapter 6 it was stated that there are six possible areas in which you may need to build up your assertion skills. All six are relevant to being assertive to prevent and/or cope with anger-evoking situations.

1. Being aware of when you have the choice of responding in an assertive manner.
2. Overcoming your mental barriers to assertion.
3. Managing your anxiety.
4. Knowing what to say verbally, including use of 'I' statements.
5. Knowing how to say it, including using assertive vocal and bodily communication.
6. Acting appropriately. If necessary, backing up your words with actions.

Before you complete Exercise 9.5, some of you may wish to review Chapter 6 on defining and asserting yourself. Remember that, either intentionally on unintentionally, you may be choosing to sustain situations that cause you anger and unhappiness. Consider whether it is possible to manage your angry feelings by making different and better choices involving being more assertive.

---

**Exercise 9.5   Coping with anger: being assertive**

This exercise may be done on your own, in pairs or as part of a training group.

A   *On your own*
   Think of an important situation in your relationships where your

lack of assertion may be contributing to your angry feelings. Write out

1. the risks and gains from acting more assertively;
2. how you might behave more assertively;
3. how you might cope with any resistances and negative feedback that might result from your assertion. Where appropriate, practise your assertion skills in the real-life situation.

B *In pairs*

*Either* independently write out your answers to the above exercise then discuss.

*Or* Partner A uses his/her helpful responding skills to enable Partner B to work through the above exercise. Then together role-play the situation with Partner B being more assertive. Afterwards reverse roles.

C *In a training group*

The trainer discusses the difference between inhibition, aggression and assertion in coping with angry feelings. He/she helps the group identify situations in their lives where their lack of assertion may contribute to their anger. Group members are asked to role-play these situations. The trainer then helps trainees explore their choices about behaving more assertively. Then he/she uses demonstration, behaviour rehearsal and coaching to develop trainees' assertion skills in these situations. Video-feedback may also be used.

---

### Problem-solving

A further approach towards managing anger assumes that often anger results from a skills deficit in problem-solving. It is sometimes said that difficulties become problems when people's attempted solutions fail. Thus anger remains instead of being defused. American psychologists Moon and Eisler describe a problem-solving approach to treating people, who have problems with their anger, consisting of the following elements.[7]

1. A basic orientation that anger problems are part of life and that effective coping is possible.
2. The need to resist acting impulsively when exposed to an anger-evoking situation.
3. The keeping of a diary of situations evoking anger.
4. Learning to precisely define and formulate anger problems.
5. Brainstorming or generating as many solutions as possible for a particular anger problem.
6. Implementing what you consider the 'best' solution to the anger problem.

The idea is that you may allow yourself to become stuck in unproductive anger-evoking situations because you neither try hard enough nor are sufficiently creative in finding solutions to the problems that frustrate you. As with using task-oriented inner speech, the first step is to define your experiencing angry feelings as a task or challenge to be surmounted. To do this you need to own that you have a problem, at the very least in wanting to rid yourself of the unpleasant sensations of anger. You then need to specify as precisely as possible what it is in the situation and in yourself that may contribute to your anger. For instance, what are the specific behaviours of the other person that you find upsetting? What is your own contribution to your angry feelings? Next you need to generate as many solutions as possible, assess the alternatives, and select the 'best' solution or combination of solutions. These solutions may involve altering the way you think as well as the way you act. Then you may need to develop a plan specifying how to implement your decision. Both your solution and plan may require modification in light of the feedback you obtain when implementing it.

Below is an example of where a problem-solving approach was the best way to deal with an anger provocation.

Ross and Ida were neighbours. Ida used to burn off the rubbish in her garden on sunny days. When she did this she smoked out her neighbour. One fine Sunday this happened again. Ross, who had just been through a very stressful week at work, found himself getting very angry indeed. Ross owned the problem as his rather than Ida's. He defined his goals as: (1) stopping Ida from burning off on Sundays; (2) getting a system organised whereby there were limits to when Ida could burn off during the remainder of the week. Ross resisted his initial impulse to complain angrily to Ida, who was an anxious and easily threatened widow. His other options included: being assertive about expressing the inconvenience she was causing; saying nothing; trying to negotiate an agreement with her; and going to the Council on Monday to find out whether there were any bye-laws regulating bonfires. Ross opted for going to the Council, since at least he would then know his legal position. This proved a happy choice since the Council had bye-laws which met both of his goals. This reduced Ross's anxiety about not being able to handle the situation. Ross let Ida have a copy of the bye-laws which helped her too, since she then knew her rights in the matter. Their neighbourly relationship, while never particularly close, was still intact.

In the preceding vignette, Ross was able to manage his anger and prevent a potential breakdown in communication with Ida by using his problem-solving skills. There are few, if any, for whom managing anger is not a problem in some significant area or areas of their lives.

Saints are rare. Exercise 9.6 encourages you to take a problem-solving approach to your anger. Assertion, developing realistic internal rules and using task-oriented inner speech may each be included among possible solutions to your problem. Hopefully you can generate many other solutions that are highly relevant for the specific anger problem on which you wish to work.

---

**Exercise 9.6   Coping with anger: problem-solving**

This exercise can be done on your own, in pairs or as part of a training group.

A   *On your own*
Think of a situation where, in a relationship, you are experiencing harmful anger. Write out
1.   your view of your *orientation* to seeing anger in problem-solving terms;
2.   as precise a *definition* of the anger problem as you can manage;
3.   as many *alternative solutions* to the anger problem as you can think of (say, in 10 minutes);
4.   your *decision* as to which is the best solution and why;
5.   a *plan* to implement the decision;
6.   how you intend to *evaluate* the effectiveness of following your plan.

B   *In pairs*
*Either* independently write out your answers to the above exercise, then discuss.
*Or* Partner A uses his/her helpful responding skills to enable Partner B to work through the above exercise, then reverse roles.

C   *In a training group*
The trainer discusses the usefulness of taking a problem-solving approach to feelings of anger. He/she helps trainees identify situations in their lives where they have difficulty coping with anger. The trainer, with the assistance of the group, helps individuals develop problem-solving approaches to their areas of difficulty. Alternatively, the trainer can get the group to perform the exercise on an individual or pairs basis followed by a plenary session.

---

**Handling criticism**

Many of you may find other people's criticisms of you to be painful and provocative. Some of you may also find it difficult to handle praise! Here, however, the focus is on coping with negative rather than positive criticism. Sometimes such criticisms are deliberately made to wound. On other occasions they may be tactlessly worded, but without malice aforethought. On still other occasions they may be accurate feedback given in a calm and rational manner. In all the above instances you may feel vulnerable and angry if you consider you are being put-down as a *person* rather than being constructively criticised concerning a specific aspect of your performance or behaviour.

You have a *choice* both in how you perceive and react to criticism. Let's take an example from world-class tennis. Bjorn Borg and John McEnroe might each get a line call with which they disagreed at an important point in a match. Borg would be much more likely to *choose* not to see the line call as highly provocative and thus much less likely to *choose* to engage in aggressively arguing with the linespersons and umpire. McEnroe would be more likely than Borg to make a different set of *choices*.

In everyday life there are numerous skills that you can choose to deploy in coping with negative criticism. These skills, which are not mutually exclusive, include the following.

- *Assessing whether the criticism is worth bothering about.* You can choose not to react to everything. Some criticisms are best ignored.
- *Counting to ten.* Counting to ten means that you avoid an impulsive 'knee-jerk' reaction. Instead you give yourself some time to compose your thoughts and feelings.
- *Regulating your breathing.* Focusing on breathing slowly and regularly may help you control your feelings of anger.
- *Backing off.* You frequently have a choice as to whether to react to a criticism immediately or at some later date. If emotions are running high, you may choose to have a cooling off period. Backing off does not necessarily mean backing down. Rather you husband your resources for when they can be most effective.
- *Reflective responding.* You can reflect the other's criticism partly to ensure that you have received it accurately, but partly also to let the other know you are listening to them.
- *Gathering more information.* You may choose to ask the other person for more information about why he/she feels that way.
- *Clearing up misperceptions and misunderstandings.* The other's criticism of you may be based on a misunderstanding in which case you can set this right.

- *Assertion. Agreeing* with the criticism if you consider it is justified and even thanking the other if they have made a helpful point. *Apologising* if you consider that you have wronged someone. *Disagreeing assertively* if you consider the criticism to be erroneous, unfair and unfounded.
- *Task-oriented inner speech.* Using inner speech to tell yourself to keep calm, decide what your goals are, and not let your pride get in the way of your attaining them.
- *Exploring the rightness of your own position.* You can explore whether your own rules and expectations are realistic in regard to criticism. For instance, if you have a rule: 'I should never make a mistake', this is conducive to your perceiving any negative feedback as threatening. Consequently you may be blocked from seeing when you are wrong.
- *Problem-solving.* You could try to assess what is the real agenda, if any, behind a criticism. For instance, a husband may be nagged by his wife when she goes through a difficult period with her boss at work. He may need overtly to support her with her work difficulties rather than react to her displaced hostility. Problem-solving can entail reappraising a situation so that you see it in a different light.
- *Managing conflict.* Both partners in a relationship may disagree and criticise each other. In Chapter 10 a managing conflict procedure, that you might choose to use, is outlined.

---

**Exercise 9.7   Coping with anger: handling criticism**

The following exercise can be done on your own, in pairs or in a training group.

A   *On your own*
1.   Write down how you see yourself feeling, thinking and acting when you are criticised. Give specific examples.
2.   Which of the following skills might help you to handle criticism more effectively in future?
— assessing whether the criticism is worth bothering about
— counting to ten
— regulating your breathing
— backing off to make your point another time

      – reflective responding
      – gathering more information
      – clearing up misperceptions and misunderstandings
      – assertion (viz. agreeing, apologising, assertively disagreeing)
      – task-oriented inner speech
      – exploring the rightness of your own position
      – problem-solving and reappraising situations
      – managing conflict

B   *In pairs*
*Either* independently do the above exercise, then discuss.
*Or* together work through the above exercise from the start.
In both versions of the pairs exercise finish by practising handling negative criticism assertively by role-playing.

C   *In a training group*
The trainer introduces the concept of *choice* in relation to coping with negative criticism. He/she then reviews skills for dealing with criticism. Trainees then do one of the versions of the pairs exercise, but without the role-plays. The trainer then conducts a plenary session focused on building the trainee's skills of handling criticism effectively. The trainer uses demonstration, behaviour rehearsal and coaching to achieve this end.

---

## MANAGING STRESS

There are a number of possible relationships between anger and stress. For example, if you feel under a considerable amount of stress you may be more irritable and likely to lose your temper. This may contribute to a deterioration in your relationships which becomes an added stress for you. Continuous inability to ventilate anger may also be stressful. Your body may exhibit this tension in many ways, for instance headaches, ulcers.

Stress invariably consists of a transaction between you and one or more stressors. An adjustive demand that may be stressful to Person A may be less stressful to Person B and a positive challenge to Person C. Stress, like beauty, is partly in the eye of the beholder. Each of you has an optimal stress level or a particular level of stimulation at which you feel most comfortable. At this level you may experience what Hans Selye, a noted writer on stress, has termed 'stress without distress'.[8] Beneath this level you may be insufficiently stimulated and bored. Above this level you are likely to experience physiological and psychological distress. Bodily reactions may include hypertension and proneness to heart attacks and ulcers. Feelings of distress may include shock, depression, frustration, anger, disorientation and fears of insanity or nervous breakdown. If the heightened stress is prolonged or perceived as extremely severe, you may feel you are in a state of excessive stress or of crisis.

Below are two examples of relationships that are being adversely affected by stress.

Arthur is a married man in his early thirties with two children, Ian aged 9 and Simon aged 7. Three months ago Arthur was made redundant by the furniture company where he worked. Though his wife Sheila works part-time, Arthur's family are very short of money. His confidence has been affected by his failure to get work, having a lot of time on his hands, and no longer being able to provide for his family as he would like, Arthur has become very irritable and moody. Consequently, Athur and Sheila's marriage and sex life are under a considerable strain.

Hank and Cecily are a happily married couple in their early fifties. Hank is a compulsive worker. He allows himself to get overcommitted by taking on too many projects. He then gets very worried about his ability to maintain his high standards in regard to them. He is overweight and takes little exercise. About a month ago Hank had a mild heart attack and spent some time in the intensive care unit of the local hospital. Hank's doctor advised him to take a couple of weeks off work to recover, but he only took one day off. Hank's wife was very upset over his heart attack and feels very vulnerable. She thinks that Hank is driving himself to an early death and her to an early and unwanted widowhood.

There are numerous situations that contribute to people feeling under stress, though there are wide differences in people's ability to tolerate these various stressors. Additionally, relationships differ in their resilience to stress. Table 9.1 lists some illustrative stressors. Some of these stressors may be perceived as within the relationship. Others, for instance impending examinations, may start outside a relationship and yet have an impact within it.

Stressors can be for good or ill. At their worst they overwhelm the coping capacity of either or both of you in a relationship and may precipitate its disintegration. At best, stressors are challenges stimulating you to develop your resources both as individuals and as partners. Helping each other through periods of stress is an important way in which you develop trust and your relationship is deepened.

**Table 9.1**   *Illustrative stressors*

| | |
|---|---|
| *Relationships* | *Adverse social conditions* |
| Living in a state of continuous conflict | Poverty |
| Having a row with a spouse/parent/ | Poor housing |
| child | Lack of social/community support |
| Marital infidelity | Racial discrimination |
| Interfering in-laws | |
| Problems in sex life | *Intrapersonal* |
| Not being adequately listened to | Loss of meaning in life |
| Unreasonable/angry/dishonest people | Feelings of guilt and worthlessness |
| Pressure to meet others' expectations | Breakdown in self-protective thinking |
| Pressure to collude against others | Severe depression |
| Being financially dependent | Psychotic tendencies |
| Separation or divorce | |
| Death of partner/spouse/child | |
| Birth of a baby | |
| Financial problems | |
| Homosexual tendencies | |
| Moving house | |
| Poor health | |
| Alcoholism and drug abuse | |
| | |
| *Occupational/educational* | |
| Unemployment | |
| Threat of or actual redundancy | |
| Obtaining a job | |
| Changing a job | |
| Reorganisation at work | |
| Poor relations with a boss | |
| Continuous office in-fighting | |
| Overwork | |
| Difficulty in controlling subordinates | |
| Lack of opportunity for mobility/ | |
| promotion | |
| Retirement | |
| Impending examinations | |
| Failing an exam | |
| Public speaking difficulties | |
| Lack of leisure outlets | |

## Self-help interventions

The following are sixteen ways in which you may choose to assume responsibility for managing your stress. Some of these suggestions are ways of preventing stress as well as of coping with it. The list is not intended to be exhaustive. You need to analyse your stress problem and select those interventions that seem most appropriate for you. Invariably more than one intervention is called for. The underlying assumption is that you need to take a problem-solving approach to any significant feelings of distress that you may have. Failure to do so may lessen your happiness and fulfilment in your relationships and, in some instances, may be fatal.

- *Attributing responsibility accurately.* On one level you need to own your distress as a problem to be solved by you. At another level, you need become aware of and change inaccurate attributions in your relationships with others, for instance needlessly blaming them, that are causing you to remain stuck in your distress.
- *Listening to your body.* You may need to learn to become more in touch with your animal self. This includes tuning into your feelings of fatigue, tension and overload rather than denying or minimising them.
- *Talking more about yourself.* Some people bottle up their feelings of stress and tension. These feelings end up being given expression in bodily symptoms such as ulcers or tension headaches. You may both help your own and your partner's understanding of yourself if you share and talk about your feelings of stress. Additionally, by discussing them, you may get your stressors more in perspective.
- *Developing a support network.* On the assumption that 'a trouble shared is a trouble halved', you may wish to develop a support network beyond your relationship with a partner. This is likely to consist of trusted friends, relatives, colleagues and professional people. People without such networks are much more vulnerable to feeling isolated and powerless when things go wrong.
- *Being assertive.* Sometimes people feel under stress because they are insufficiently assertive. For instance, a parent may need to set limits on an over-demanding child's requests for time and attention.
- *Becoming a better listener.* You may contribute to your feelings of stress by failing to pick up messages from others accurately. This may reduce the amount of valid information you have for making decisions in your life. Furthermore, those who feel inadequately listened to by you may in turn become stressors for you, for instance by getting angry.
- *Learning to manage your anger.* Getting angry can release stress, be stressful and generate stress. Much of this chapter has been about learning to regulate your anger.
- *Developing your managing conflict skills.* Conflicts in the home and at work can be very stressful. The next chapter focuses on

the skills of minimising their damage and, if possible, using them creatively to enhance yourself and your relationships.

- *Developing more realistic internal rules.* The more you make unrealistic demands upon yourself, others and the environment the more you are likely to feel under stress when things do not go as you wish. For instance, people who set themselves perfectionist standards for achievement are excellent candidates for feelings of distress.

- *Using task-oriented inner speech.* This is a skill you can develop for managing specific stressors. You need to develop an appropriate set of self-instructions for before, during and after any situation you find particularly stressful, for instance giving a talk in public. Already task-oriented inner speech has been focused on in this book in relation to both shyness and anger.

- *Anticipating the future more realistically.* Past circumstances in people's lives often colour their views of the future, making them more fearful if acting to meet their needs than might reasonably be considered necessary. You may feel more confident, and consequently that life is less stressful, if you learn to be realistic about the gains of taking risks as well as about the possible losses.

- *Learning to break tasks down into smaller steps.* Sometimes you may feel overwhelmed by a task which, if you stood back and took a step-by-step approach to it, might be manageable. Consequently your lack of the skill of breaking a task down into its component parts and developing a plan is contributing to your feelings of stress. If you give yourself the chance of success experiences along the way the likelihood is that your own feelings of stress will lessen.

- *Becoming better at generating alternative solutions.* Your feelings of stress may be due to your inability to see your way through a problem. The better you become at searching for alternative solutions, the less likely you are to remain stuck with stress-engendering problems.

- *Developing adequate recreational outlets.* You may need to explore the extent to which you lead a balanced life based on meeting your own needs rather than others' demands. Specific recreational activities, for example golf or tennis, might be considered and plans developed for participating in them. Knowing when to take recreation can be a most useful way to preventing and managing anger and its related stresses.

- *Learning muscular relaxation.* Progressive muscular relaxation is a popular approach to managing stress.[9] Though there are many self-help books, learning the techniques from a qualified professional is recommended.

● *Participating in your health.* Physical unfitness makes a contribution to many people's feelings of stress. You may be not exercising regularly, smoking, engaging in drug abuse, drinking too much or taking insufficient care over your diet (e.g. eating too much animal fat). If so you need to explore your attitude toward taking more responsibility for your health. Additionally, you should see a doctor if you have physical symptoms attributable to stress, for instance hypertension.

Exercise 9.8 has been designed to help you better understand the role that stress plays in your life and what you can do about it. The exercise directly leads out of the above discussion on the range of self-help interventions for managing your stress. Complete the exercise as best you can.

---

**Exercise 9.8   Managing your stress**

This exercise may be done on your own, in pairs or as part of a training group.

A   *On your own*
   Write out your answers to the following questions.
   1.   To what extent do you consider that you experience 'distress' or excessive stress in your current life?
   2.   What are some of the main stressors in your life?
   3.   Take one of the main stressors you have identified. Which, if any, of the following self-help interventions might aid you in managing the stress? Give reasons for each choice.
      (a)   attributing responsibility accurately;
      (b)   listening to your body;
      (c)   talking more about yourself;
      (d)   developing a support network;
      (e)   being assertive;
      (f)   becoming a better listener;
      (g)   learning to manage your anger;
      (h)   developing your managing conflict skills;
      (i)   developing more realistic internal rules;
      (j)   anticipating the future more realistically;
      (k)   learning to break tasks down into smaller steps;
      (l)   becoming better at generating alternative solutions;
      (m)   developing adequate recreational outlets;
      (n)   learning muscular relaxation;
      (o)   participating in your health.

4. Develop a plan for implementing one or more self-help interventions for managing your stressor.

B *In pairs*
*Either* independently write out your answers to the above exercise, then discuss.
*Or* Partner A uses his/her helpful responding skills to enable Partner B to work through the above exercise, then reverse roles.

C *In a training group*
The trainer introduces the topic of managing stress and indicates the different self-help interventions that are available. The trainer may illustrate managing a stress from his/her own life. The group is then subdivided into pairs and partners are encouraged to take turns at facilitating each other's identification of stressors and development of stress management interventions. Afterwards the trainer conducts a plenary sharing and discussion session.

---

## CONCLUDING INNER SPEECH

The way I think influences how I feel. Just as my ineffective thinking can engender and sustain negative feelings, so my thinking effectively helps me regulate and lessen them. In short, by assuming responsibility for disciplining how I think I can increase the range of choices I have regarding how I feel.

Anger can be a constructive emotion in my relationships. I need to become skilled at understanding when I am angry and at expressing it appropriately. I can also choose to regulate my anger through developing more realistic internal rules, using task-oriented inner speech, being assertive, developing problem-solving skills and handling criticism effectively. If I do not act impulsively, but learn to manage my anger, this will give me a much greater sense of control over my life.

Stress is often related to anger. I need to be able to listen to my body and to be aware of when I am feeling stressed. I then have many options in regard to how I manage my stress. These include disciplining my thinking, improving my relationship skills, and taking better care of my health. The skill with which I manage my feelings of anger and stress is likely to benefit my relationships. Conversely, if I manage my anger and feelings of stress poorly, this may cause immense harm to my relationships.

## REFERENCES

1. Novaco, R.W. (1977) 'Stress inoculation: a cognitive therapy for anger and its application to a case of depression'. *Journal of Consulting and Clinical Psychology*, **45**, 600–608.

2. Ellis, A. (1980) 'Overview of the clinical theory of rational-emotive therapy'. In R. Grieger & J. Boyd (eds.) *Rational-emotive Therapy: a Skills-based Approach*, pp. 1–31. New York: Van Nostrand Reinhold.
3. Beck, A.T. (1976) *Cognitive Therapy and the Emotional Disorders*. New York: New American Library.
4. Tavris, C. (1982) Anger defused. *Psychology Today*, November issue, pp. 25–35.
5. Ellis, A. (1980) 'Overview of the clinical theory of rational-emotive therapy'. *Op. cit.*
6. Meichenbaum, D. (1983) *Coping with Stress*. London: Century Publishing.
7. Moon, J.R. & Eisler, R.M. (1983) 'Anger control: an experimental comparison of three behavioral treatments'. *Behavior Therapy*, **14**, 493–505.
8. Selye, H. (1974) *Stress Without Distress*. Sevenoaks: Hodder and Stoughton.
9. Bernstein, D.A. & Borkovec, T.D. (1973) *Progressive Relaxation Training: A Manual for the Helping Professions*. Champaign, Illinois: Research Press.

# 10 Managing Conflict

Managing conflict involves both sender and receiver skills. As such it encompasses many of the skills mentioned throughout the book. For instance if you possess good skills at clearly expressing your wants and wishes, listening well, responding helpfully and managing your anger there is less risk of your participating in unnecessary conflicts. Furthermore, if you do find yourself in conflict with others, the above skills can help you manage it effectively.

## DEFINING CONFLICT

The word conflict comes from the Latin roots *com-*, together and *fligere*, to strike. Dictionary definitions of conflict emphasise words like 'fight', 'struggle', 'antagonism', 'incompatibility' and 'sharp disagreement, as of interests or ideas'.[1,2] These dictionary definitions have three elements: first, a difference or disagreement; second, the disagreement is severe; and third, there is ill-will. In this chapter conflict is viewed differently. The essence of a conflict remains that there are conflicting ideas, interests, wishes and needs. However, though frequently otherwise, differences and disagreements need neither be the cause of severe conflict nor of ill-will.

A further issue in defining a conflict entails the relationship between perception and reality. Real conflicts exist objectively and are perceived accurately. However, frequently conflicts start and get sustained because of misperceptions and misunderstandings. Furthermore, the manifest conflict may mask one or more underlying conflicts which get expressed indirectly. These 'hidden agendas' may often be more serious or less 'safe' than the surface agendas. Additionally, sometimes conflict with someone else can be displaced into conflict with a third party who has another's problems 'taken out on' them.

Below is an example of the manifest content of a conflict being different from the underlying content.

> Marie and Vic were both in their early twenties and had been seeing each other for over a year. The moment they became engaged their

previously happy relationship became full of conflict. Whereas before they had made decisions easily, now they argued over practically everything: which restaurants to go to, which films to see, and so on. This went on for six months until it gradually dawned on Marie that getting engaged had symbolised to her the loss of her autonomy and independence, which caused her to panic. Once she was able to work through with Vic her underlying fears, the relationship steadily improved. Marie and Vic are now happily married with two children.

Perhaps it is obvious that conflicts are inevitable in relationships. American psychologist Morton Deutsch says that there are usually five basic types of issues in conflicts: control over resources; preferences and nuisances; values; beliefs; and the nature of the relationship between the parties.[3] Michael Argyle writes: 'It is necessary to have a correct *understanding* of the basic properties of relationships. For example a high level of conflict is normal in marriage, and is perfectly compatible with a high level of satisfaction. . . .'[4] People differ in their backgrounds, tastes and interests, beliefs and values, expectancies about each other, stimuli to which they are exposed, and rates of and capacity for personal change, to mention but some considerations. Add to this that many people are deficient in their relationship skills, including those of managing conflict, and the inevitability of conflict becomes even more obvious.

### Productive and destructive conflict

The negative effects of conflict scarcely need cataloguing. Conflicts can cause immense psychological pain. Relationships which offer promising opportunities for both parties can founder because conflicts have not been managed effectively. Families can become distressed, marriages broken and children's psychological well-being damaged. On a more subtle level conflicts can fester in a relationship and contribute to distance where previously there was happiness and closeness.

Work environments are also frequently characterised by destructive conflicts. Not only can these cause great stress and unhappiness, but they can also lower output; the extreme case being a strike. A degree of conflict is inevitable in work relationships just as in personal relationships. There may be scarce resources, your personal styles may grate, values and beliefs may differ, and you may have different expectations of each other and of the work-place. Additionally, you do not leave your relationship skills deficits at home. You take them to work. This increases the likelihood of the conflict taking a destructive course both for individual participants and also for attainment of group goals.

Conflict can be for good as well as ill. Conflict itself may be desirable. The course of conflict may be productive rather than destructive. The outcomes of conflict may be more positive than negative. It is very easy to state the negative aspects of conflict. To redress the balance four positive aspects of conflict in relationships are stated here.

● *Greater trust.* Conflicts can build trust. People who can relate despite differences, as well as work through differences together, may feel that their relationship is much less fragile than those who have not had such experiences.
● *Increased intimacy.* An important aspect of intimacy is the ability to give and receive honest feedback. A fuller sharing of self can occur where partners can reveal and work through their differences rather than just inhibit their disagreements.
● *Increased self-esteem.* Partners who manage their conflicts effectively may gain in self-esteem for a number of reasons. They know that their relationship is strong enough to withstand conflict. Each may feel better for being able to say what they think and feel. Problems may be identified, aired and solved rather than allowed to fester. Each may gain a firmer sense of their identity as well as greater knowledge of the other. Both may gain valuable practice in managing conflicts effectively.
● *Creative solutions.* The course of productive conflict can be viewed as a process of mutual problem-solving. Creative solutions which meet both parties' needs, sometimes called 'Win–Win' solutions, may be the outcome of this process. The opposite of a 'Win–Win' solution is a 'Lose–Lose' one where neither party gets their needs met. In a 'Win–Lose' solution only one party gets their needs met.

Exercise 10.1 encourages you to look at your thoughts and assumptions about managing conflict. Do the exercise as best as you can. Some answers are suggested at the end of the chapter.

---

**Exercise 10.1   Exploring your thoughts on managing conflict**

This exercise can be done in a number of ways.

A   *On your own*
B and C   *In pairs or in a training group*

One option is to complete the whole questionnaire independently and then together discuss your answers to each item. Another option is to go through the questionnaire independently answering single items, each of which is discussed together before moving on to answering and discussing the next item.

*Exercise*

For each statement write down whether you consider it to be true (T) or false (F). Answer every item.

*T or F*

_____   1. Conflicts are best approached in a climate of mutual respect and concern.

_____   2. People who carry round much pain and unfinished business from their relationships with their parents are less inclined to engage in destructive conflicts than those who do not.

_____   3. It pays to act impulsively in conflicts.

_____   4. Effective management of conflicts requires people to be able to discipline their thinking.

_____   5. It is generally better to avoid than to face up to differences within a relationship.

_____   6. Managing differences effectively entails getting a clear picture of what the differences really are.

_____   7. People can be ruled by their fears when in conflict.

_____   8. The way to win in a conflict is always to compete as hard as you can.

_____   9. More often than not people who try to handle conflicts cooperatively are likely to be taken advantage of.

_____  10. Conflicts never have positive outcomes.

_____  11. Managing conflicts in a relationship is best viewed as an exercise in joint problem-solving for mutual benefit.

_____  12. Tit for tat is fair play.

_____  13. No one individual holds a monopoly on the truth.

_____  14. In conflicts the strength of people's emotions may narrow the scope of their vision.

_____  15. Effective management of conflict requires you to have a repertoire of relevant skills.

_____  16. If a conflict persists, despite your best efforts to resolve it, you should feel guilty.

_____  17. Heavy stresses in other areas of people's lives can make them prone to engage in destructive conflicts in their relationships.

_____  18. Sometimes conflicts result from misunderstandings rather than from genuine differences of interest.

_____  19. Searching for mutually acceptable solutions is a useful skill in handling conflicts.

_____ 20. The less aggressive people are during conflicts the more likely they are to achieve satisfactory outcomes.

_____ 21. A good way of managing a conflict is to talk about it with third parties rather than with the person directly involved.

_____ 22. In conflicts it is often helpful to blame the other.

_____ 23. Never admit your own contribution to sustaining a conflict.

_____ 24. It is never helpful to express anger when in conflict with another.

_____ 25. People are always rational in conflict.

_____ 26. Listening to and understanding the other's viewpoint is a useful skill in managing conflicts.

_____ 27. Partners who truly care about and really know one another should always be able to sense each other's needs and preferences without being told.

_____ 28. Basically men and women are psychologically as well as physically different.

_____ 29. People who feel others must be perfect sexual partners place unrealistic expectations on them.

_____ 30. Intimate partners can be capable of changing both themselves and the quality of their relationship.

## BARRIERS TO MANAGING CONFLICT EFFECTIVELY

Just as in all other aspects of your relationships, the way you manage conflict involves making either good or bad choices. Good choices increase and bad choices decrease the chances of your own and others' happiness and well-being. Making good choices in conflicts can be particularly difficult. You can be under considerable pressure to make poor choices because of the differences that exist and the intense emotions they may arouse. Additionally, each party to a conflict, in trying to sustain their own view of themselves, may challenge the other's self-concept. This process may be very threatening.

The emotional context in which conflicts takes place often has a long history. Conflicts are more likely to be destructive when people come into them harbouring past resentments rather than mindful of each other's previous pleasing behaviours. Much of the skill of avoiding destructive conflicts concerns using good relationship skills on a day-to-day basis to create and maintain good-will. Below are some of the more important skills deficits in managing conflicts effectively once they occur.

● *Combative rather than collaborative attitude.* Earlier the distinction was made between 'Win–Win' and 'Lose–Lose' or 'Win–Lose' solutions to conflicts. Where you adequately take responsibility for your own happiness and fulfilment in a relationship, if possible you seek collaborative 'Win–Win' rather than competitive solutions. Collaborating or cooperating with another shows that you value meeting their needs as well as your own. Additionally, you acknowledge that they may have a positive contribution to make. Furthermore, that conflicts are likely to remain inadequately resolved if only one of you has contributed to and is happy with the solution.

● *Poor orientation to conflict.* If you possess a realistic orientation to conflicts you acknowledge that they are a part of life. You see conflicts as problems which can be handled constructively or destructively. You do not act impulsively, but are prepared to work your way through the problems posed. If you have a poor orientation to problems you are deficient in the above attitudes.

● *Poor confrontation skills.* Poor confrontation skills include: avoiding acknowledging and owning your differences with another person; inability to raise issues at all, sometimes coupled with the expectation that the other should mindread you; and raising issues in an aggressive way that creates defensiveness.

● *Bad timing.* In managing conflict effectively you need to be sensitive to issues of timing for yourself, for the other person and for both of you. You may create difficulties if you try to confront and work through conflicts when you do not feel ready, for instance if you are still too emotionally upset. Also, the other person may be in unfavourable circumstances, an obvious example is after a bereavement, in which case it may be best to keep quiet. Furthermore, it may be in both parties' interests to attempt to work through conflicts when you can both set aside sufficient time and emotional energy to do so properly.

● *Poor listening skills.* Already poor listening skills have been discussed at some length. With regard to conflict they include: inability to handle another's expression of feelings; unwillingness to hear the other's viewpoint; talking too much; needing to see the other in negative terms; and being too ready to criticise.

● *Poor use of language.* Major skills deficits here include the use of 'You-blame' rather than 'I' statements and inability to state clearly what you think and feel. Also, emotive words, like 'You fool', are 'put-downs'. They trigger another's anger and should be avoided. Repetition can also be counter-productive. It may seem that you want just to dominate with your own viewpoint rather than collaborate to resolve the conflict.

● *Threatening bodily communication.* Threatening bodily communication includes pointing fingers, shaking fists and glaring eyes. By using such signals of ill-will, you raise the emotional temperature and risk lowering the other person's willingness to be rational. Instead they may match your behaviour by using similar negative signals.

● *Threatening vocal communication.* You can use your voice in ways that set out to cause pain to others. You can dominate with a loud voice, frighten with a shrill voice, and chill with a cold voice. You may, however, remain unaware both of how you behave and also of the costs to others, to yourself and to your relationships.

● *Lack of openness.* There are many ways in which lack of openness may be destructive. First, you may avoid stating the real reasons for the conflict. Second, you may lie. Third, you may suppress information, especially if unfavourable to your case. This may be either intentional or the result of defensive thinking processes of which you are not fully aware. Fourth, you may fail to admit any positive feelings you have for the other. This can create a very negative emotional climate: 'You always tell me when things go wrong, but never express appreciation.' Fifth, you may fail to give honest feedback to each other, thus possibly colluding in sustaining your conflict.

● *Playing the defining game.* Stemming from a competitive and combative attitude, when in conflict you may try to define yourself positively and the other party negatively. For instance, you may never acknowledge your own contribution to a conflict. You may act provocatively and then play the hurt victim, thus making out that the other person is the aggressor. You may engage in 'tit-for-tatting' in which you both match each other's negative definitions of each other. You may seek allies for your position by disparaging the other in your conflict to third parties. All of the above create a contest or combat situation based on a 'Win–Lose' model, which risks ending up with a 'Lose–Lose' outcome.

● *Poor problem-solving skills.* All the deficits mentioned in this list of barriers to managing conflict effectively are barriers to effective problem solving. Some specific problem-solving deficits are: not acknowledging common ground; not defining problems clearly and specifically; either altogether missing out searching for or inadequately searching for alternative solutions; making decisions based on insufficient evaluation of options; and resisting a rational consideration of solutions – for instance, by continually creating difficulties by saying 'Yes, but . . .' to proposed solutions.[5]

● *Poor managing anger skills.* In conflicts you often need the ability to manage other people's as well as your own anger and stress. Managing other people's anger may involve helping them to express and cope with it. Furthermore, you many need to cope with your own feelings in regard to being the target of their anger. The managing anger skills mentioned in the previous chapter are relevant to not letting yourself be overwhelmed by others' as well as by your own anger.

● *Poor contracting skills.* A contract is another term for an agreement. Your agreements may be stated insufficiently clearly and consequently misunderstood by either or both of you. You may sustain an existing or create a new conflict by breaking your agreements. If you wish to change your agreements it is generally best to try to renegotiate them.

● *Poor follow-up skills.* You may: continue to bear resentment even though you have agreed to a solution; remain in a combative rather than a collaborative frame of mind; fail to implement your agreement in the spirit in which it was made; adhere to a policy of combat rather than conciliation; and fail to acknowledge the value of a problem-solving orientation to future areas of difference in your relationship. All the above indicate that the overall course of your future relationship may be more destructive than constructive.

Exercise 10.2 is based on the preceding discussion. It is designed to help you locate your areas of difficulty in managing conflict effectively.

---

**Exercise 10.2   Assessing your skills deficits in managing conflict**

This exercise can be done on your own, in pairs or in a training group.

A   *On your own*
    1.   Write out a brief assessment of the extent to which you possess each of the following barriers to managing conflict effectively.
        (a)   Combative rather than collaborative attitude
        (b)   Poor orientation to conflict
        (c)   Poor confrontation skills

(d)    Bad timing

(e)    Poor listening skills

(f)    Poor use of language

(g)    Threatening bodily communication

(h)    Threatening vocal communication

(i)    Lack of openness

(j)    Playing the defining game

(k)    Poor problem-solving skills

(l)    Poor managing anger skills

(m)    Poor contracting skills

(n)    Poor follow-up skills

2.  List in rank order the managing conflict areas in which you most need to change.

B  *In pairs*

*Either* independently write out your answers to the above questions, then discuss.

*Or*, using your talking about yourself and helpful responding skills, work through the above questions from the start.

C  *In a training group*

The trainer introduces each barrier to managing conflict, gets the group to assess themselves on it either verbally or in writing, before moving on to repeating the procedure with the next item. Trainees are then asked to list in rank order the areas in which they most need to change. Alternatively the trainer can describe all the barriers prior to dividing the group into pairs or subgroups in which members assess themselves. This is followed by a plenary sharing and discussion session.

---

## PERSONAL RESPONSIBILITY AND CONFLICT

When in conflict you may find it difficult to perceive yourself and others accurately. For instance, by choosing to attribute blame to others, you may also be choosing to absolve yourself of any responsibility to make your life more fulfilled. Exercise 10.3 provides some case studies of people making poor choices in conflicts. As such the conflicts are being sustained, if not worsened. Work through Exercise 10.3. Try and identify the poor choices being made by the main characters in each of the case studies. Each of the skills deficits mentioned in the previous exercise represents poor choosing. If you accurately identify the poor choices of the main characters, you are in a strong position to state what might be better choices for helping them meet their needs. Each main character in the exercise needs to take more effective responsibility for managing conflict in their lives.

**Exercise 10.3   Exploring personal responsibility for managing conflict – some case studies**

This exercise may be done on your own, in pairs or as part of a training group.

A   *On your own*
   For each of the following excerpts write down:
   1.   the specific ways in which the main character or characters behave ineffectively, and
   2.   what specific relationship skills they require to behave more effectively;
   3.   how each of them might act differently to attain their goals.
   *Excerpts*
   1.   Steve is an 18 year old who enjoys his girlfriend's company, but has frequent rows with her. During the rows he tends to make comments like: 'You women are all the same. You just can't make the effort to understand the male viewpoint.'
   2.   Mary and Eddie are 17 year old twins who share the use of the second car in the family. Each is extremely touchy and jealous over the other's use of the car. Each believes that the other is taking advantage of their weakness. They get very emotional and argue a lot. Their parents are getting fed up with their arguments and are threatening to stop both of them from having the use of the car.
   3.   Nancy is a 50 year old widow who lives with her 18 year old son, Eric, and 16 year old daughter, Kate. Nancy is constantly nagging the children to help her more with the house work and to be less messy. She makes remarks like: 'You are selfish children' and 'If your father were alive he would not let you behave this way'. Eric's reaction to Nancy's remarks is to get angry and sulky. Kate says that since Eric is not pulling his weight why should she.
   4.   Andy and Russ are junior executives both with very fixed ideas about how their unit should be run. They appear to be in a constant power struggle. When in meetings with their boss, both are trying to argue the strength of their case with him. Each presents his own point of view as though it were the only way and gets defensive when challenged by the other. Each is anxious for the approval of their boss and sees their meetings in 'Win–Lose' terms. Their boss regards both of them as rather immature and not yet ready for promotion.
   5.   Cherryl and Pete have been married ten years and feel they are drifting apart. They rarely go out together and each increasingly

resents the other. They argue about how to bring up the children, how much to see their in-laws, what friends each other should have, how they should spend their money and so on. Pete's way of getting what he wants is to become emotional and angry. Often Cherryl gives in, but carries around a residue of resentment which shows up in snide remarks, deliberately not doing things which would please Pete, and telling Pete how difficult other people, like her friends and her mother, view him. Every now and then Cherryl explodes and they have a blazing row. During these rows they catalogue each other's deficiencies. Each has lost the desire to give real happiness to the other. The emotional atmosphere in their home is tense and bitter. Their children welcome the opportunity to play in their friends' homes.

B  *In pairs*
For each of the above excerpts identify and discuss
1.  the specific ways in which the main character or characters behave ineffectively, and
2.  what specific relationship skills they require to behave more effectively;
3.  how each of them might act differently to attain their goals.

C  *In a training group*
The trainer discusses the concept of personal responsibility in relation to the choices that people make in managing conflicts. The trainer divides the group into pairs or other subgroups and gets them to answer the questions about each case study. Afterwards the trainer conducts a plenary sharing and discussion session. During this session some trainees may wish to share and analyse the skills deficits involved in their own current conflicts. Also, how they might act differently to attain their goals.

---

### Role-playing managing conflicts

Exercises 10.2 and 10.3 were designed to develop your skills at discriminating various skills deficits in managing conflict. Exercise 10.4 below encourages you to look at a sample of your own managing conflict behaviour and to evaluate your managing conflict skills resources and deficits. Furthermore, the exercise allows for the provision of much feedback. The exercise may also be conducted with two partners who are in a distressed relationship so that they can identify and be helped to identify communications which are helpful and harmful to working through their conflict.[6]

---

**Exercise 10.4   Role-playing how you manage conflicts**

This exercise may be conducted in pairs or in a training group.

A   *In pairs*
1. Each partner thinks of either a current or a recent conflict in their lives.
2. Partner A sets the scene for the role-play by describing the conflict and how each party behaves in it.
3. Both partners role-play the conflict, with Partner A trying to act as close to how he/she behaves in conflicts as possible. Preferably this role-play is video-taped, failing that audio-taped.
4. The video-tape or audio-tape is played back and both partners discuss which behaviours were helpful and which harmful for managing the conflict.
5. If necessary, Partner A sets himself or herself goals for acting more effectively in this or other conflicts.
6. Reverse roles and repeat the cycle working on Partner B's conflict.

B   *In a training group*
The trainer discusses how role-play can be used to increase people's awareness of their managing conflict skills resources and deficits. The trainer may choose to have individual members role-play their conflicts in front of the group. These should be video-taped or audio-taped. As well as the participants in each role-play assessing their managing conflict skills, feedback gets provided by the trainer and by other group members. This can be highlighted with reference to the video-tape or audio-tape. Trainees are encouraged to set themselves goals for acting more effectively in conflicts outside the group.
   Some variations on the above exercise include that trainees can:
(a) role-play the case studies in Exercise 10.3;
(b) make up their video-tapes or audio-tapes outside the formal session, thus enabling much more of the session time to be devoted to self-assessment and feedback, and
(c) work in threes, with the third person's duties being those of observing, assessing and providing feedback.

---

## CUDSA: A FIVE STEP FRAMEWORK FOR MANAGING CONFLICT

### Why a framework?

CUDSA is a systematic approach to managing conflicts. Its five steps are:

Step one:    *Confront* the conflict
Step two:    *Understand* each other's position
Step three:  *Define* the problem(s)
Step four:   *Search* for and evaluate alternative solutions
Step five:   *Agree* upon and implement the best solution(s).

The five steps of this *confront – understand – define – search – agree* framework frequently overlap.

CUDSA provides an easily comprehensible and memorised framework for you and your partner to use in managing your conflicts. At risk of oversimplification, the five steps provide a structure to which you can attempt to adhere, even during the most heated of conflicts. Sometimes conflicts can be handled in a more informal way. However, on other occasions, a conflict may need to be worked on in a systematic fashion. In such instances, ideally both of you should agree to adhere to the CUDSA framework. Even where only one of you is prepared to adhere to the framework, it can help that person make the conflict management process as constructive as possible. However, unfortunately some people are so prone to defensive thinking in conflicts that there are limitations to the applicability of a framework which assumes some capacity to be rational in both of you.

The CUDSA framework espouses a collaborative approach to managing conflicts. It encourages both of you to make the choices that increase the chances of the course of conflict being constructive rather than destructive. The framework helps avoid escalating false conflicts through misunderstanding. Furthermore, if a real conflict exists, the framework challenges both of you to cooperate so that neither feels resentful and violated by either the process or outcome of managing your conflict. Now let us look at each step in turn.

*Step one: confront the conflict*

The first set of choices that parties to a conflict have to make is whether or not to confront it openly. There are many decisions involved here including whether the conflict is important enough to either or both of you to merit bringing it out into the open.

Confronting a conflict in a relationship can involve at least three stages. First, self-awareness or being prepared to 'own' the existence of a conflict in your relationship. There may be numerous reasons why, either consciously or unconsciously, you may wish to avoid owning the conflict. For instance, you may believe that: conflict is bad, you are too powerless to influence the course of the conflict, and you will end up the loser anyway. Furthermore, your partner may be skilled at defining you to your disadvantage. An outcome of this may be that a legitimate claim feels like an unreasonable request.

The second stage is that of confronting your partner with the existence of a conflict. You can not expect them to mindread your thoughts and feelings all the time. In Chapter 6 it was stated that there are inhibited, aggressive and assertive ways of coping with negative behaviour. However, conflicts do not necessarily involve negative behaviour. For instance, there can be genuine differences in regard to preferences or to how resources should be spent. Here neither of you may be seeking to harm or diminish the other. Nevertheless, there are still inhibited, aggressive and assertive ways of confronting the other person with the existence of a conflict. Furthermore, the double standard in regard to gender may mean that some conflicts are still easier to confront for women, for instance in the area of child-rearing, and others easier to confront for men, for instance in the area of love-making.

Confronting a conflict may entail assertion in being able to state positively your wants, wishes and preferences. Additionally, it may entail letting the other person know that you wish their behaviour to be altered. Furthermore, if the other person resists owning that there is a conflict in your relationship, it involves asserting yourself to the point where they recognise that the fact that the conflict is a problem for you means that it is also a problem for them. Chapter 6 focused in some detail on assertion and on avoiding the twin dangers of inhibition and aggression. Consequently, this aspect of confronting a conflict is not elaborated here, apart from mentioning that sensitivity needs to be exercised in relation to the *what*, *when* and *how* of the confrontation.

Some conflicts may be resolved amicably and quickly on the basis of just being aired and discussed. However, if this is not the case, the third stage in confronting the conflict may be necessary. This is the stage of trying to enlist the other person's cooperation in taking a collaborative problem-solving approach to the conflict. In short you are saying that: 'We have a problem in our relationship and let's see if we can collaborate together to solve it for our mutual benefit.'

Even given goodwill on the part of the other person, it is possible to go round in circles in trying to solve a conflict. It is here that the CUDSA framework may provide a simple and neutral approach within which both of you can work. This approach involves inviting the other person to give the conflict enough priority so that you both set aside sufficient time and energy for dealing with it. A quiet and comfortable location, free from interruptions and other distractions, is conducive to such mutual problem-solving.

Exercise 10.5 is designed to give you practice at confronting conflicts assertively. To emphasise that conflicts involve at least two people the terms *collusive, combative* and *collaborative* have been substituted for inhibited, aggressive and assertive. The exercise encourages you to 'look before you leap' by making you think of your personal goals in the conflict before confronting the other person. If you develop the skills of confronting others with tact and firmness concerning the existence of a conflict, you have taken the extremely important first step towards steering the course of the conflict to a productive rather than to a destructive outcome.

---

**Exercise 10.5  CUDSA – step one: confront the conflict**

This exercise may be done on your own, in pairs or in a training group.

A  *On your own*
   If possible think of one or two situations in your previous or current relationships where you either tacitly or openly were or are in conflict with someone. For each conflict write out
   (a)  your goals
   (b)  a collusive, combative and collaborative way of confronting or failing to confront the other person with your view that there is a problem between you that needs solving
   (c)  if necessary, a request for time and space to work on the conflict.

B  *In pairs*
   *Either* independently write out your responses to the above questions, then discuss.
   *Or* each of you identify a conflict where it would be beneficial to use good skills in confronting the other person with your view that there is a problem between you that needs solving. Help each other decide on appropriate goals in managing these conflicts. Then, for each of your conflicts, role-play a collusive, combative and collaborative way of confronting or failing to confront the other person with the problem and requesting that you work on it together.

C  *In a training group*
   The trainer discusses the difference between collusion, combativeness and collaboration in confronting or failing to confront problems or areas of difference with others. He/she then helps the trainees identify conflicts where they experience difficulty confronting other people appropriately. Individual members are asked to define their goals and then to role-play acting more effectively. The

trainer uses demonstration, behaviour rehearsal and coaching to help trainees confront problems with others assertively. Video-feedback may also be used. Trainees are encouraged to act more effectively outside the group.

---

*Step two: understand each other's position*

There are a number of reasons why taking the time and trouble to understand each other's position is critical to managing conflict effectively. First, you may become much clearer whether you have a real conflict rather than just a series of misunderstandings and misconceptions. Second, it indicates that each of you has a commitment to a collaborative process of managing conflicts. Third, it shows respect for each other. Fourth, it may take some of the emotional steam out of the conflict in that each person's feelings may be ventilated. For some this may be a necessary pre-requisite to being able to think rationally about the conflict. Additionally, being able to state the facts of one's position may be calming. Fifth, it enables both of you to start identifying the real rather than the imaginary issues in the conflict.

Understanding each other's position involves both sender and receiver skills. Each of you can help the other in two ways: you can state your own position as clearly and specifically as possible and also help the other person to do likewise. In both instances the distinction between being collusive, combative and collaborative is relevant. For instance, as a talker you may: collusively fail to state your thoughts and feelings adequately through suppressing information you think is too sensitive; engage in a combative series of 'You-blame' statements; or constructively and collaboratively state your position in a genuine spirit of mutual problem-solving. As a listener and responder you may be very inhibited and thus make it awkward for the other person to reveal their position, listen in a combative fashion continually responding from your frame of reference, or facilitate their sharing of thoughts and feelings as part of a collaborative conflict management process.

Three of the main dangers of coping with this stage of conflict management effectively are: lack of a clear and specific statement of your respective positions; being too involved in your own to be able to listen to the other's agendas; and allowing yourself to be overwhelmed by the strength of your own and each other's anger. Where possible state your own position and help the other person state theirs so that the relevant thoughts and feelings are communicated clearly and specifically. It greatly helps you as a sender and the other person as a receiver if you use 'I' statements rather than 'You-blame' language. Also, avoid negative trigger words and threatening vocal and bodily communication. It is one thing to state your position. It is another to have it listened to as well. The choices you make as a sender of information are crucial to whether you talk *with* or talk *at* or *past* another.

Agreeing that each of you has an allocated time to state your position may be one way of preventing yourself getting too involved in your own agendas. You know your turn as a speaker is guaranteed. Another way is to discipline yourself to use reflective responding after each point the other makes prior to making your own points. Just interspersing some reflective responses should lessen the chances of your failing to listen adequately.

Dealing with another person's anger can be difficult. It is a help if the other person owns their anger by using 'I' statements rather than aggressively blaming you. As mentioned in Chapter 9, as a signal, an energiser and a release, anger can be constructive. Thus if you use your reflective responding skills to help the other express their anger the consequences may be positive rather than negative. However, you may have to stand up for yourself if the other person is clearly being destructive. Some of you may be so threatened by being the target of anger that you overreact. You may be too quick to attribute destructive intentions rather than waiting to see whether the anger is a passing phase. Though sometimes slanging matches clarify positions, they risk rigidifying them. Thus they block the process of effective conflict management.

In conflicts many of you may be better at stating your own than at really listening to and understanding another's position. Thus, Exercise 10.6 below focuses on building up your skills of 'stepping into another's shoes'. With slight modification the exercise can be used with partners who are in real conflicts.

---

**Exercise 10.6   CUDSA – step two: understand each other's position**

This exercise may be done on your own, in pairs or in a training group.

A   *On your own*
   If possible think of one or two situations in your previous or current relationships where you either tacitly or openly were or are in conflict. For each situation write out your perception of how the other person

   (a)   feels about the conflict;
   (b)   thinks about the conflict;
   (c)   perceives your feelings and thoughts in the conflict.

B  *In pairs*
  *Either* independently write out your responses to the above exercise, then discuss.
  *Or* each of you identify a conflict of yours. Partner A uses his/her helpful responding skills to get Partner B to say in relation to his/her conflict
   (a)   how he/she feels;
   (b)   what he/she thinks;
   (c)   how the other person feels;
   (d)   what the other person thinks;
   (e)   how the other person perceives Partner B's feelings and thoughts.

  Partner A then listens as Partner B describes the other person's position in the first person. For instance: 'I am Lisa. I don't like the way Hugh treats me. My feelings are . . . My thoughts are . . . I think Hugh's feelings are . . . I think Hugh's thoughts are . . .'
  Afterwards reverse roles.

C  *In a training group*
  The trainer discusses the importance in managing conflicts of accurately understanding each other's feelings and thoughts. He/she demonstrates the pairs exercise above that involves using helpful responding skills and then having someone talk as though they were the other person in a conflict. One option is for the group to then perform the exercise in pairs prior to a plenary sharing and discussion session. Another option is for the trainer to continue working with individuals in front of the group. The trainer discusses with the group how the skills of helpful responding and understanding another's position can be integrated into their everyday lives.

---

*Step three: define the problem(s)*
In step two each of you may have been offering your own definitions of the problem. The task of stage three is to try and arrive at a mutually acceptable definition of the problem. For reasons already mentioned, such as emotional release and clarifying real agendas, stage two should have provided a good basis for this process.

  The course of conflict can get very destructive if either or both of you persist in a combative approach to defining problems. Basically you are still in an 'I win – You lose' frame of mind with its attendant risks of an 'I lose – You lose too' outcome. Defining problems can become a power struggle in which each endeavours to label oneself positively and the other negatively. Both of you may repetitively state our position and get increasingly frustrated and resentful. Furthermore, you may use numerous unfair fighting tactics.[7] These include:

Mindreading and ascribing negative motives.
Unnecessarily attacking psychologically vulnerable spots.
Engaging in overkill and coming on far too strong.
Using 'You-blame' language.
Tit-for-tatting.
Engaging in character assassination.
Using threats that engender insecurity.
Using threatening bodily communication, including physical abuse.
Using threatening vocal communication, such as shouting, yelling and screaming.
Using lies, omissions and half-truths.
Engaging in conversational intimidation to inhibit the other.
Monologuing and dominating the conversation.
Unnecessarily dragging in third parties' opinions to support your own.
Using passive-aggressive tactics, such as attacking under the guise of being the victim.
Using tears to engender guilt.
Sulking and emotional withdrawal.
Hitting and running, for instance making a point and then either storming out of the room or slamming down the 'phone.
Playing games, such as feigning collaboration yet always frustrating reaching a collaborative outcome.

American psychologist Claude Steiner has developed the concept of power-plays.[8] A power-play is an attempt to control, exploit and manipulate another against their will. He writes: 'Power plays are the tools of Control and competition. When they are introduced into a loving, co-operative relationship they affect it profoundly.' All the above unfair fighting tactics could be seen as power-plays designed to control other people's definitions of you, themselves and the problem areas between you.

A collaborative approach to defining problems assumes both of you are genuine in wanting to solve them. Additionally, both of you have sufficient respect and concern for each other that you wish to avoid power-plays. Furthermore, both of you need to be able to accept responsibility for your feelings, thoughts and behaviour. You

need to be able to acknowledge your strengths and vulnerabilities
listen to feedback, and be prepared to change if necessary.

Constructive definition of problems entails focusing on issue
rather than labelling persons. As a result of stage two, you shoul
have an idea of how much common ground exists between you. It ca
avoid further polarising the conflict if this common ground
identified and acknowledged.

During the understanding each other's position stage you wer
asked to be relatively passive when the other was talking. During th
defining problems stage you are able to react to the feedback yo
have received and are still receiving. A risk here is getting defensiv
rather than being prepared to acknowledge any contribution you ma
be making to sustaining the conflict. Somebody has to make the firs
move in being able to own their part in the conflict. If you are able t
do this you may find others prepared to match your honesty an
openness. Acknowledging your contribution to a conflict does nc
mean that you do not stand firm where you consider it necessary.

Trying to identify and deal with real rather than surface agenda
can be an important aspect of defining conflicts. Both of you need t
be honest with yourselves and with each other. For instance, if
spouse suspects his or her partner is having an affair, picking on tha
person on a whole range of other issues is not the best way of trying t
define and solve the problem. Ideally both of you should be able t
communicate your needs, including those that are unmet, simply an
clearly. Being allowed to say 'I want' and 'I need' withou
recrimination can contribute to identifying the real agendas in
conflict.

Clarity and specificity are important in defining problems. Some
times the problems in a conflict require little definition and can b
simply stated from the start. On other occasions partners may need t
work on identifying issues in the conflict and stating them clearly
Exercise 10.7 below is designed to help you improve your skills in thi
regard.

---

**Exercise 10.7   CUDSA – step three: define the problem(s)**

This exercise may be done on your own, in pairs or in a training group.

A   *On your own*
   If possible think of one or two situations in your previous or curren
   relationships where you either tacitly or openly were or are i

conflict. These may be conflicts that you worked on in Exercises 10.5 and 10.6. For each conflict write out

(a) whether there are any hidden agendas and, if so, what are they;
(b) what needs of each person require meeting;
(c) what common ground exists in the area of conflict;
(d) as specific a definition as possible of the remaining problem or problems;
(e) your perception of your own contribution, if any, in sustaining the problem.

B *In pairs*
*Either* independently write out your answer to the above questions, then discuss.
*Or* Partner A uses his/her helpful responding skills to enable Partner B to answer the above questions, then reverse roles.
*Or* Partner A and Partner B each identify a conflict. Together they then role-play in regard to each of their conflicts

(a) confronting the problem;
(b) understanding each other's position;
(c) defining the problem as specifically as possible in a spirit of collaboration.

C *In a training group*
The trainer discusses the importance of collaborating to define problems accurately. He/she illustrates concepts like hidden agendas, unmet needs, identifying common ground and cooperating rather than competing to define problems as accurately and specifically as possible. One option is for the trainer to work with individual members in front of the group in defining specifically and accurately the problems underlying their conflicts.

Another option, which could follow the preceding option, is for group members to do one of the pairs exercises before coming together for a plenary sharing and discussion session.

---

*Step four: search for and evaluate alternative solutions*
Step four involves the collaborative search for mutually acceptable solutions. In general it is preferable to deal with one problem at a time. It can also be useful to try and solve the most manageable problem first before moving on to more difficult ones.

Searching for alternative solutions involves generating and evaluating solutions. Often it is best to have two distinct stages: first, *generation*, and second, *evaluation*. The reason for this is that generating solutions is a creative process that may be inhibited by too much premature evaluation of the emerging solutions. Also too much time might be spent on evaluating a mediocre solution when, given more time, better solutions might have surfaced. In the previous chapter you were encouraged to brainstorm or think of as many solutions as possible to an anger problem in 10 minutes (Exercise 9.6). Here there is a difference in that the problems are mutually owned. Thus you have the opportunity of working together rather than alone. This can involve communicating your suggestions clearly and specifically, helping others articulate their suggestions, and jointly developing one or more solutions. Hopefully the old adage that 'Two heads are better than one' may apply in the search for solutions. A final point is that if one person considers themselves weaker in a relationship than the other, for instance a child in relation to a parent, it may help this person's confidence if they are encouraged to share their ideas first.[9]

When the time comes to evaluate solutions both of you try to answer the question 'Which of these solutions looks best?' In combative conflict management, you look to your own advantage. In collaborative conflict management, you look for solutions that meet the needs of both. Thus each of you evaluates any reasonable looking solution both from your own vantage point and according to how well it seems to meet the other's needs. The best solution is that which maximises the fulfilment or happiness of both whilst leaving neither feeling violated nor taken advantage of. During this process each needs to check out what the other person actually thinks and feels rather than to assume accurate understanding. Exercise 10.8 below gives you practice at searching for and evaluating alternative solutions to a conflict.

---

**Exercise 10.8   CUDSA – step four: search for and evaluate alternative solutions**

This exercise may be done on your own, in pairs or in a training group.

A  *On your own*
   In Exercise 10.7 you defined the problem(s) underlying a conflict in one of your relationships. Write out
   1.  as many possible solutions to the problem that you can think of in 10 minutes without evaluating their merits;
   2.  an evaluation of the advantages and disadvantages of your two most appealing solutions;
   3.  whether the solutions you prefer are based on a combative 'I win – You lose' or a collaborative 'I win – You win too' approach to the problem(s).

B  *In pairs*
   *Either* independently write out your responses to the above exercise, then discuss.
   *Or* for each of the problems you defined in Exercise 10.7, together:
   1.  generate as many possible solutions as you can;
   2.  evaluate the advantages and disadvantages of the two most appealing solutions;
   3.  assess whether the solutions you prefer are based on a combative 'I win – You lose' or a collaborative 'I win – You win too' approach to the problem(s).

C  *In a training group*
   The trainer discusses the importance in managing conflicts of the collaborative search for alternative solutions to problems. Group members are asked to share their definitions of their problem(s). The trainer may help individuals define their problem(s) more specifically and accurately. The definition of each individual's problem(s) is followed by a brainstorming period in which the whole group is encouraged to generate solutions. The trainer then helps the individual to evaluate the most appealing of the proposed solutions, including the extent to which they are based on a 'Win – Lose' or a 'Win – Win' approach.

---

*Step five: agree upon and implement the best solution(s)*

Having evaluated the better of your possible solutions in terms of which works best for both of you, you then come to an agreement. Agreements can be viewed as contracts in which each party's rights and obligations need to be clear. If agreements are unclear they are more likely to be broken, if only through misunderstanding. This risks rekindling your conflict. Obviously agreements vary according to the nature of the conflict. For instance, if your conflict has been about household chores, the contract will concern *who* is to do *what* and *when*. You may also agree to *what consequences* will follow if the contract is broken. Sometimes it is desirable to put agreements in writing to avoid a conflict over what were the terms of an agreement that was meant to have resolved the conflict.

Not keeping agreements may be a problem in some relationships. If you cannot, for whatever reason, live within an agreement, it is generally much preferable to try to renegotiate it than unilaterally to break it. Unilaterally breaking a contract may well be regarded as a breach of trust and as such harm your relationship. Furthermore, if one of you breaks an agreement the other may consider that this gives them similar rights. This may further damage the relationship.

Some agreements involve planning. For instance, Katrina and Andrew have been in considerable conflict how to spend their vacation. Having finally agreed to spend two weeks motoring around a specific foreign country, they now need to plan how best to go about this. Possibly their agreement should indicate who plans which aspects of the vacation by when.

Despite being the result of the CUDSA process, some solutions may turn out deficient on implementation. Frequently this entails only relatively minor modifications to the initial agreement. However, on other occasions, either or both of you may discover that the 'best' solution has major deficiencies. Here, assuming you still accept your original definition of the problem, you need to agree upon a new solution. Possibly you have another reasonable solution from your earlier search for alternatives. Otherwise you need to generate and evaluate further solutions.

A further point is that partners in a conflict may also wish to evaluate the success of their managing conflict procedures and to modify them if necessary. The *confront – understand – define – search – agree* framework advocated here is not meant to be a straightjacket. Partners may need to adjust it to suit personal styles. If you find that the CUDSA framework has been helpful, this is likely to motivate you to use it in future conflicts.

Exercise 10.9 is designed to develop your skills at contracting or making agreements. The more each of you owns the agreement, the less likely is it to be broken. Making agreements involves clear and unambiguous communication.

---

**Exercise 10.9  CUDSA – step five: agree upon and implement the best solution(s)**

This exercise may be done in pairs or in a training group.

A  *In pairs*

Partner A and Partner B each have a conflict whose problem(s) they have both defined and also to which they have searched for and evaluated alternative solutions. Taking the problem(s) in Partner A's conflict first, together the partners

(a)  discuss and agree upon the most acceptable solution(s);

(b)  if necessary, develop a plan for implementing the proposed solution(s);

(c)  discuss how they are going to evaluate how well the solution(s) turned out;

(d)  discuss how they are going to handle any breaches of their agreement.

The above process is then repeated in respect of Partner B's conflict.

B  *In a training group*
The trainer discusses the importance in managing conflicts of making clear agreements and, if necessary, clear plans for implementation of the agreements. He/she demonstrates the above exercise with one of the group members in respect of his/her proposed solutions. Trainees are then asked to do the exercise in pairs prior to reconvening for a plenary sharing and discussion session.

---

### CUDSA: putting it all together

Exercises 10.5 to 10.9 cover each of the five steps of the CUDSA framework. The exercises have focused on specific aspects of the approach. Exercise 10.10 below gives you the opportunity to work through the five steps of the framework in relation to a specific conflict in your life. As with all the exercises in this section, you may perform it with someone with whom you are in real conflict and not just by role-playing with a partner.

---

### Exercise 10.10  CUDSA: putting the five steps together

This exercise can be done on your own, in pairs or in a training group.

A  *On your own*
Pick a conflict that is currently worrying you. Failing that use a recent conflict. Write out as specifically as possible how you would handle each of the following subskills in managing this conflict effectively.

Step one:    C,  confronting the conflict
Step two:    U,  understanding each other's position
Step three:  D,  defining the problem(s)
Step four:   S,  searching for and evaluating alternative solutions
Step five:   A,  agreeing upon and implementing your solution(s).

B  *In pairs*
*Either* Partner A uses his/her helpful responding skills to enable Partner B to work through a conflict, then reverse roles;
*Or* Partner A role-plays the other person in Partner B's conflict and

together they use the CUDSA approach to managing the conflict.
Afterwards, they reverse roles.

C   *In a training group*
The trainer breaks the group down into pairs or threes (with one
person as observer) for the role-play exercise above. Afterwards
there is a plenary sharing and discussion session. The group
discusses implementing the CUDSA approach to managing conflicts in their everyday lives.

---

## WHEN CONFLICTS PERSIST

The CUDSA framework for managing conflict is not a magic cure-all.
Being in conflict with another can test your relationship skills under
the most difficult circumstances. The CUDSA framework may need
discipline and effort on both sides if it is to succeed. To take
responsibility for your own choices in a conflict may stretch you to
your limits. Indeed you may make some wrong choices in the heat of
the conflict which need to be retrieved.

There are a number of considerations if a conflict persists.
Ultimately you are only responsible for your own choices in a
relationship. If you have genuinely worked hard on making the
correct choices and continue doing so, you have done and are doing
all you can under the circumstances. When conflicts persist there is a
danger that you undermine your own confidence through unrealistic
self-blame. It helps for you to be clear as to the limits of your
responsibility. Furthermore, if the conflict is not in a major area, you
may simply agree to differ.

The persistence of conflicts does not necessarily mean that they are
intractable. There are a number of choices that either or both of you
can make. First, you may agree to defer further consideration of the
conflict until a later and possibly better time. This may act as a
cooling off period which gives both parties time for reflection.
Additionally, the passage of time may provide a different perspective
on the conflict. Second, you can both review your own behaviour in
the conflict. This requires a further close examination of the ways you
think, feel and act which contribute to sustaining the conflict. Third,
you may wish to review the adequacy with which you have used the
CUDSA framework for managing the conflict. Have you genuinely
tried to approach the conflict in a collaborative rather than a
combative or collusive way? How hard has each of you worked to
solve the problems entailed in the conflict? Fourth, you may wish to

use the conciliation services of a trusted third party; for example, a professional marriage guidance counsellor. Hopefully such a person is impartial and helps you to develop your own skills of managing this and subsequent conflicts. Whichever option you choose, you can show your commitment to each other by avoiding unnecessarily provocative behaviour. Furthermore, the more you can use your relationship skills in other areas of your life together, the more chance there is of a fertile emotional climate for resolving your conflict.

Sometimes the existence of a persistent conflict may raise issues about continuing a relationship. The impact of discontinuing a relationship varies greatly according to such factors as: its centrality in the lives of the partners, their expectations about it, its longevity, dependent children, financial commitments etc. Even when a relationship is in the early stages of development, it can be a great shame to discontinue it just for lack of the requisite managing conflict skills. However, on other occasions, a persistent conflict may indicate to either or both of you that you would be better developing an intimate relationship elsewhere. Thus the conflict may be learning experience for both, the outcome of which is to free you to seek happiness and fulfilment with others.

Many of the skills mentioned throughout this book are relevant to ending relationships. Exercise 6.8 focused on ending relationships assertively. Where conflicts have persisted, both managing anger and minimising the destructive course of conflict skills are relevant to ending relationships. If at all possible relationships, especially those of some length, should be ended collaboratively rather than combatively. Regrettably by this stage partners are often in such pain that they get tunnel vision and cause themselves, each other, and any children involved further pain. After a relationship has ended, partners need to learn from their mistakes. Additionally, they need to work through rather than harbour any residual feelings of hurt and resentment.

## CONCLUDING INNER SPEECH

Below is a sample of inner speech that summarises some of the main points in this chapter.

> Conflicts are inevitable in my close relationships. They may help as well as harm them. What is important is that I develop the skills of

managing conflict as effectively as possible. It is best that I adopt a collaborative rather than either a combative or a collusive approach to working on them.

When in conflict, it may help if I and, if possible, the other person adhere to a simple five step conflict management framework called CUDSA: first, if important, *confront* the conflict; second, make the effort to communicate clearly and to *understand* each other's position accurately; third, identify and *define* the problem(s); fourth, work together to *search* for and evaluate alternative solutions; and fifth, *agree* on the 'best' solution, implement it, evaluate how we find it, and if necessary modify or discard it.

I may have to work hard and not give up easily when using my relationship skills in managing conflicts. However, ultimately I can only be responsible for the adequacy of my behaviour. If a conflict persists my choices include a cooling off period, re-examining my behaviour, reviewing how well we used the CUDSA framework, and availing ourselves of the conciliation services of a third party. A further choice is that of ending the relationship. Here I may save myself and the other person further pain if I can help us to do this collaboratively rather than combatively.

## REFERENCES

1. Fowler, H.W. & Fowler, F.G. (eds.) (1964) *The Concise Oxford Dictionary*. Oxford: Clarendon Press.
2. Guralink, D.B. (ed.) (1958) *Webster's New World Dictionary*. New York: Popular Library Inc.
3. Deutsch, M. (1973) *The Resolution of Conflict*. New Haven: Yale University Press.
4. Argyle, M. (1984) 'Some new developments in social skills training'. *Bulletin of the British Psychological Society*, **37**, 405–410.
5. Berne, E. (1964) *Games People Play*. New York: Grove Press.
6. Margolin, G. & Weiss, R.L. (1978) 'Communication training and assessment: a case of behavioral and marital enrichment'. *Behavior Therapy*, **9**, 508–520.
7. Lieberman, M. & Hardie, M. (1981) *Resolving Family and Other Conflicts*. Santa Cruz, California: Unity Press.
8. Steiner, C.M. (1981) *The Other Side of Power*. New York: Grove Press.
9. Gordon, T. (1970) *Parent Effectiveness Training*. New York: Wyden.

## *ANSWERS TO EXERCISE*

*Exercise 10.1*

| | | | | | | |
|---|---|---|---|---|---|---|
| 1. T | 2. F | 3. F | 4. T | 5. F | 6. T | 7. T |
| 8. F | 9. F | 10. F | 11. T | 12. F | 13. T | 14. T |
| 15. T | 16. F | 17. T | 18. T | 19. T | 20. T | 21. F |
| 22. F | 23. F | 24. F | 25. F | 26. T | 27. F | 28. F |
| 29. T | 30. T. | | | | | |

# 11 Maintaining and Developing Your Relationship Skills

This chapter focuses on ways in which you can maintain and develop your relationship skills. Throughout this book the view taken of relationship skills is that they are series of choices. Skills resources entail making good choices. Skills deficits entail making poor choices. For the remainder of your life you are faced with the possibility of making good or poor choices: choices that work for you and achieve your goals or choices that work against you and end you in trouble. Thus you need to maintain your relationship skills on a daily basis. Additionally, you have the responsibility of trying to develop them for the sake of your own and of others' happiness and fulfilment.

## REASSESSING YOUR RELATIONSHIP SKILLS

In Chapter 1 you were asked to give an initial assessment of your relationship skills (Exercise 1.1). There are a number of requirements for you to keep maintaining and developing these skills. First, possessing an attitude of personal responsibility whereby you acknowledge the necessity throughout your life of striving to make the choices that are conducive to maximising your happiness and fulfilment. Second, having an adequate way of conceptualising relationships. Here four key elements are: viewing how you relate in skills terms; acknowledging that each skill represents a series of choices; knowing which are the important skills to develop; and understanding that relationships are processes that can be affected for good or ill by the level of skills employed by each participant. Third, being able to assess and monitor your resources and deficits in each skills area. Fourth, having the capacity to set yourself goals and implement strategies for maintaining and developing your skills.

In Exercise 11.1 you are asked to reassess your relationship skills in light of reading this book. Also, hopefully, you have performed some, if not all, of the exercises either on your own, in a pair or as part of a training group. Additionally, you will probably have tried to develop many of the skills by practising them in your daily life. Take your time over the exercise. Accurate assessment is vital in pinpointing deficits. Once deficits are clearly identified you have made considerable progress towards doing something about them.

**Exercise 11.1 Reassessing your relationship skills resources and deficits**

This exercise is best done individually at first, though it can be incorporated into pairs or a training group format.

A *On your own*
1. Write down an assessment of your relationship skills in each of the following areas. Identify specific deficits on which you need to work.
    (a) Possessing an attitude of personal responsibility for how you relate.
    (b) Having a good knowledge of concepts and terms with which to understand how you and others relate.
    (c) Being in touch with and able to express your feelings.
    (d) Being able to start relationships.
    (e) Being able to develop relationships through the way in which you talk about yourself.
    (f) Being able accurately to listen to and understand others.
    (g) Being able to respond helpfully to others so that they can talk to you and, if necessary, clarify their own problems.
    (h) Being able to manage your feelings of anger.
    (i) Being able to manage conflicts.
2. Make a list of the skills deficits on which you most need to work.
B *In pairs*
Write out your answers to the above questions, then discuss with a partner.
C *In a training group*
The trainer discusses the importance of trainees assessing their relationship skills. He/she asks them to assess their deficits and resources, either in class or as a homework assignment. This is followed by a plenary sharing and discussion session.

## MAINTAINING YOUR RELATIONSHIP SKILLS

Part of the challenge of relationship skills is the requirement to continue making correct choices after acquiring the skills in the first place. Often approaches to relationship skills are strong on acquiring the skills initially but less strong on helping you acquire the motivation to sustain them. This is why it is important to impart an attitude of personal responsibility along with training in specific skills. The following quotation from Goethe's *Faust* is relevant to all wishing to maintain their relationship skills:

> Yes! to this thought I hold with firm persistence
> The last result of wisdom stamps it true;
> He only earns his freedom and existence;
> Who daily conquers them anew.[1]

There are numerous reasons why you may fail to maintain your relationship skills. Some of these pressures come from within. For instance, there may be the pull to revert to long-established deficits where skills resources have only recently been learned. This may be especially so when the support of peers and a trainer gets withdrawn at the end of a training course. Also, if you feel insecure, you may fail not only to perceive accurately how you behave, but also to receive loud and clear others' messages about your behaviour.

Unrealistic and ineffective thinking may also block maintaining your skills. Some of you may give up too easily because you have insufficiently learned that maintaining relationship skills, for instance in times of conflict, can be a struggle. You expect to be able to wave your relationship skills magic wand rather than realise the inner strength and toughness required to sustain the skills. Some may play the comparison game whereby, because somebody else fails to use good skills, this legitimises you in relinquishing them too. Virtually everyone is prone to defensive thinking at times and thus more able to acknowledge others' deficits rather than their own. Also, once you allow yourself to be sucked into competitive power struggles you are well on the way to relinquishing, temporarily at least, some of your relationship skills.

Though ultimately each of you is responsible for maintaining your relationship skills, nevertheless pressures to relinquish them may come from others. For instance relatives, friends and colleagues may exert pressure on you to be careful about saying what you really think and feel. Additionally, they may express themselves in ways that make it difficult for you to want to listen to them. In many of your relationships others may need you to be the sort of person that corresponds with their picture of themselves which may not coincide with what is best for you. As the nineteenth century British prime minister Benjamin Disraeli is reported to have said: 'My definition of an agreeable person is one who agrees with me.' Every day you will be exposed to situations in which people in the home or at work model or demonstrate poor relationship skills, often without acknowledging this. Furthermore, sometimes they get rewarded for their poor skills. Additionally, the rewards for using good skills can never be guaranteed. For instance, you may try and develop a relationship by being more open, only to find your disclosures either not reciprocated or shunned. Thus it is important to be realistic both about other people's rights to their own choices and also about their vulnerabilities rather than to let them get you down.

Some of the pressures not to maintain your relationship skills may come from the broader environment. For instance, the notion of people working hard on their relationship skills is not that common. Though all people learn some maths and history at school, few are required to take courses in relationship skills.[2] However, a welcome start is being made in this area. Furthermore, the notion of personal excellence is not widespread. Consequently, people may feel that there is less support than they would like for working to develop their own and others' full humanity. Additionally, the media are constantly bombarding people with messages conducive to superficial rather than to genuine relationships.

Exercise 11.2 encourages you to explore the pressures within and on you to lose your skills. Many of these pressures may be very individual to you. Try to identify the pressures. Then try to develop and to implement strategies for combating them.

---

### Exercise 11.2    Maintaining your relationship skills

This exercise can be done on your own, in pairs or as part of a training group.

A    *On your own*
1. Write down as many pressures that you can think of in each of the following categories that might hinder you from maintaining your relationship skills
   - pressures from within you
   - pressures from others
   - pressures from your broader environment.
2. Make a list of those pressures that you consider potentially most harmful.
3. Develop strategies for combating these harmful pressures.

B    *In pairs*
*Either* individually do the above exercise, then discuss together.
*Or* work through the above exercise together from the start.

C    *In a training group*
The trainer discusses the importance of trainees working to maintain their relationship skills. Also, how there may be numerous pressures not to maintain them. The trainer divides the group into syndicates who do the exercise. Then there is a plenary session in which a representative from each syndicate reports to the group

followed by a discussion. Alternatively the trainer may ask the group to perform the exercise either individually or in pairs prior to holding a plenary sharing and discussion session.

---

## DEVELOPING YOUR RELATIONSHIP SKILLS

There are numerous ways in which you can not only maintain, but develop your relationship skills. Below are some suggestions.

- *Inner empathy.* Inner empathy means awareness of your own feelings and thoughts. Developing the skill of sensitively listening to yourself is important in two ways. First, you become more aware of when you are experiencing unpleasant feelings. Second, you become more able to monitor your thinking and identify thoughts which may contribute to your distress. In both instances inner empathy, if necessary, can act as the stimulus for improving your relationship skills.

- *Practising your skills.* The old saying 'Practice makes perfect' needs to be honoured in spirit rather than in the letter of the law. Perfection in relationship skills is probably both unattainable and undesirable. However, by practising your skills conscientiously and by being aware of their consequences for yourself and others, you are likely to improve them. Two reasons contributing to this are that you may be more confident in using them and hence also achieve greater flexibility in applying them to specific situations. There can be a very important gap between learning a skill and putting it into practice. Psychologists call overcoming this gap 'transfer of training'. However transfer of training can go beyond maintaining a skill to improving it with continued practice.

- *Co-counselling.* In co-counselling you meet with another person on a regular basis. Person A attempts to make it easy for Person B to examine his/her relationship concerns and skills. This may last for 10 or 15 minutes, longer if necessary. Afterwards you reverse roles. This may be followed by a sharing and discussion session. You may choose to co-counsel with someone other than someone with whom you live. This has risks if your partner disapproves of sensitive material being discussed with a third party. Co-counselling with a spouse or partner has much to recommend it. Not only might this contribute to maintaining communication between you, but also you could work together to improve your own and each other's relationship skills.

● *Relationship skills contracting.* Commitment and motivation are crucial to maintaining and improving relationship skills. Relationship skills contracts can be created to suit the needs of either individuals, couples, families or work groups. A relationship skills contract establishes a written commitment amongst those of you participating to use, maintain, develop and to help each other use, maintain and develop your relationship skills. Table 11.1 contains an example of an individual contract. This can be amended where others are involved. Also you can create your own contract. This should be expressed in simple language.

**Table 11.1**   *An individual relationship skills contract*

---

*The Contract*

1. I am ultimately responsible for my feelings, thoughts and actions in my relationships.
2. I commit myself to using, maintaining and developing my relationship skills.
3. Where appropriate, I commit myself to helping others to whom I relate use, maintain and develop their relationship skills.
4. The relationship skills that I commit myself to using, maintaining and developing include:
   - being in touch with my feelings
   - starting relationships, where appropriate
   - being prepared to develop relationships through openness and honesty
   - listening to and helping others to feel understood
   - responding helpfully to others
   - managing my feelings of anger constructively
   - managing conflict constructively.
5. Though I may make mistakes and have shortcomings, I commit myself to persisting in trying to honour this contract.

Signed _____

Date _____

This contract should be posted in an obvious place as a reminder.

---

● *Peer support groups.* You may choose to meet on a regular basis with a group of other people to work on your relationship skills. Being in a group setting has the advantage of your being able to practise the skills with others as well as to obtain feedback from them. Peer support groups can be specifically focused on discussing relationships and helping each other with relationship skills. Alternatively, within the context of another focus, for instance a women's or men's group or a bereavement group, you can work on the relationship skills pertinent to the group's main task.

● *Workshops and training courses.* There are no hard and fast distinctions between training courses and workshops. However, if anything, training courses are spread out over a longer period, say two months or more, whereas workshops are relatively intense experiences lasting a day, a weekend, a week or possibly two weeks. Means of finding out about relationship skills workshops and training courses include: contact with a counselling service or personnel office; getting in touch with professional associations in psychology, counselling and social work; and keeping an eye on relevant journals and newsletters. In all instances look before you leap. Furthermore, by now you are aware that acquiring good relationship skills requires much work and practice. Consequently, courses and workshops offering miracle cures should be avoided. Table 11.2 below provides a checklist for assessing training courses and workshops.

**Table 11.2** *Checklist for assessing relationship skills training courses and workshops*

1. What are the goals?
2. What are the methods that may be employed during its life?
3. What is the pertinent training and experience of the trainer or trainers?
4. What is the size of the course or workshop and is there a screening process prior to entry?
5. When does the course or workshop start? How long is each session? Over what period will the course or workshop continue? Where will it be held? Are the facilities adequate?
6. What, if any, is the fee for the course or workshop and are there any additional expenses that may be incurred?

● *Professional counselling.* Some of you may consider that you need the services of a professional counsellor to help you improve your skills. Such a counsellor may provide you with psychological space, detachment, knowledge and skill. On a training course or workshop there may be little chance for the trainer to work extensively with individuals' problems. Furthermore, there may be insufficient time. Additionally, some people may be so anxious that they require the safe environment provided by one-to-one counselling. Couples and families may also seek the services of a professional counsellor.

Group counselling may be desirable for some of you instead of, concurrently with, or after individual counselling. Counselling groups tend to be composed of a leader and around six to ten members. They provide a more sheltered environment for working on emotional and relationship issues than that found in many training groups and workshops. All the items on the checklist in Table 11.2 are relevant to assessing counselling groups prior to entry.

You may not be immediately aware of a counsellor you could go to. You may find the name of someone appropriate by asking any helping service professional whom you know: for instance, a psychologist, social worker, doctor or clergyman. You could look up the phone book to find if there is a relevant counselling agency nearby: for example, a marriage guidance service. You could also contact a citizen's advice bureau. Additionally, you could make enquiries to a relevant professional association. Table 11.3 provides a listing of some such associations in a number of countries.

**Table 11.3**   *Names and addresses of national professional associations for counselling and psychology in Australia, Britain, Canada and the United States*

*Australia*
Counselling:   No national counselling association at time of writing.
Psychology:   The Australian Psychological Society, National Science Centre, 191 Royal Parade, Parkville, Victoria 3052.

*Britain*
Counselling:   British Association for Counselling, 37A Sheep Street, Rugby, Warwickshire, CV21 3BX.
Psychology:   The British Psychological Society, St. Andrew's House, 48 Princess Road East, Leicester LE1 7DR.

*Canada*
Counselling:   Canadian Guidance and Counselling Association/Société Canadienne D'Orientation et de Consultation, Faculty of Education, University of Ottawa, Ontario, K1H 6K9.
Psychology:   Canadian Psychological Association/Société Canadienne de Psychologie, 588 King Edward Avenue, Ottawa, Ontario, K1N 7N8.

*United States*
Counselling:   American Personnel and Guidance Association, 2 Skyline Place, Suite 400, 5203 Leesburg Pike, Falls Church, Virginia 22041.
Psychology:   American Psychological Association, 1200 Seventeenth Street, N.W., Washington, D.C. 20036.

● *Relationship skills reading.* Though needing supplementation by practice, relevant reading is a further way to develop your relationship skills. Other books which cover a number of different skills include: Johnson's *Reaching Out*,[3] Egan's *You and Me*,[4] Bolton's *People Skills*,[5] and Gordon's *Parent Effectiveness Training*.[6] Some more focused references are to be found at the end of the different chapters in this book. Books like Johnson's *Reaching Out* and Egan's *You and Me* contain many exercises. Consequently you may wish to read them and, at the same time, work through the exercises in pairs or in a training group. A further suggestion is to re-read this book and, possibly, redo some of the exercises. One approach is to go through the whole book every now and then as a refresher. Another approach is to focus on specific chapters when and where you feel you need to make further effort to maintain or to develop a skill. Again, if possible, it may help to work in conjunction with others.

● *Miscellaneous.* There are a number of indirect ways in which you can influence, if not develop, your relationship skills. For instance, you can choose your friends so that at least some of them model and reward the skills you wish to maintain and develop. You can engage in leisure pursuits that both give you the opportunity to do things with others and also act as an emotional safety valve. You can participate in your health by keeping reasonably fit and well. Additionally, you can help others in a voluntary or paid capacity and, through helping them, help yourself too.

Exercise 11.3 has been designed to get you thinking about how *you* might develop and improve *your* relationship skills. Above a number of different ways have been mentioned of developing your skills. You may be able to think of other ways that will work for you. Additionally, there may be a number of different ways in which you could develop a single skill. It is an exercise that you may wish to do, informally or formally, again and again in future.

---

**Exercise 11.3   Developing your relationship skills**

This exercise can be done on your own, in pairs or as part of a training group.

A   *On your own*
In Exercise 11.1 you listed those relationship skills on which you most need to work. There are many different ways to develop your skills including: developing inner empathy; practising in your daily

life; co-counselling; creating and working hard to adhere to a relationship skills contract; attending a peer support group; going on relevant workshops and training courses; working with a professional counsellor; pertinent reading; and a number of indirect approaches, for example, choice of friends. Design a plan for developing at least one of your relationship skills. Write down as specifically as possible:
1. your goal(s)
2. the methods that you intend to use to achieve each goal,
3. a realistic step-by-step plan, including a time-schedule, to achieve each goal, and
4. how you intend to monitor and evaluate your progress.

B  *In pairs*
*Either* individually do the above exercise, then discuss.
*Or* work through the above exercise together from the start.

C  *In a training group*
The trainer discusses the importance of people continuing to maintain and develop their relationship skills. He/she describes ways in which trainees can do this. Trainees are asked to perform the above exercise either individually or in pairs. The trainer then conducts a plenary sharing and discussion session.

---

## CONCLUDING INNER SPEECH

I am responsible not only for acquiring relationship skills initially, but also for maintaining and developing them. Thus I am constantly being challenged to make good choices in my relationships. Pressures not to maintain my skills may come from me, others and from my broader environment. I need to identify these pressures and to develop strategies to combat them.

There are many ways in which I can both maintain and develop my relationship skills. I need to continue developing the capacity to listen to my own feelings and thoughts. Other ways in which I can develop my relationship skills include: practising them conscientiously, co-counselling, committing myself to a relationship skills contract, joining a peer support group, attending workshops and training courses, using a professional counsellor, relevant reading, and a number of more indirect ways such as choosing my friends carefully.

Ultimately I am responsible for my own happiness and fulfilment. A major part of this is derived from my relationships. Though I can relate more effectively, I also have the potential to relate less effectively. Consequently, using, maintaining and developing my relationship skills is a lifelong challenge for me. I CAN AND WILL RELATE MORE EFFECTIVELY.

# REFERENCES

1. Goethe, J.W. (1951) *Faust*. London: Faber.
2. Nelson-Jones, R. (1985) Research in progress with Australian college and secondary school students on variables pertinent to human relationship skills training.
3. Johnson, D.W. (1981) *Reaching Out* (2nd ed.). Englewood Cliffs, NJ: Prentice-Hall.
4. Egan, G. (1977) *You and Me: the Skills of Communicating and Relating to Others*. Monterey, California: Brooks/Cole.
5. Bolton, R.W. (1979) *People Skills*. Englewood Cliffs, NJ: Prentice-Hall.
6. Gordon, T. (1970) *Parent Effectiveness Training*. New York: Wyden.

# Glossary

**Acceptance**   Unconditional approval of or by another. Absence of rejection.

**Advice**   Telling another how they should think, feel or act rather than letting them come to their own conclusions.

**Affection**   Experiencing and being able to show fond and tender feelings toward another.

**Agape**   A Greek word for unselfish love.

**Aggression**   Hostile or attacking behaviour which is an over-reaction to a perceived provocation and involves 'putting-down' another.

**Alternatives**   Alternative ways of viewing yourself or others. Alternative approaches to solving a problem or taking a course of action.

**Ambivalence**   Simultaneously holding both positive and negative feelings about another, yourself or a situation. Loving and hating the same person.

**Anger**   Possessing, and possibly showing, feelings of ill-will or hostility towards either others, yourself or your environment, or any combination of these. Anger is usually combined with other emotions such as hurt, frustration and depression.

**Anger management**   Being able to cope with your feelings of anger in ways which are constructive rather than destructive.

**Anticipating risk and gain**   Assessing the positive and negative consequences of future behaviour and events.

**Anxiety**   Feelings of fear and apprehension which may be either general or associated with specific people and situations, for example, being shy with someone.

**Anxiety management**   Being able to acknowledge your feelings of anxiety and then, if necessary, adopt appropriate strategies for coping with them.

**Assertion**   Stating positive and oppositional thoughts and feelings in an appropriate way that is neither aggressive nor inhibited. Defining yourself and not letting others manipulate you or define you on their terms.

**Assessment**   Being able accurately to monitor and to evaluate your relationship skills resources and deficits.

**Attributing responsibility**   Assigning responsibility for your own or other people's feelings, thoughts and actions. See *Misattributing responsibility*.

**Avoidance**   Thinking and acting in ways that avoid dealing directly with the realities of life, for example by withdrawing from a person rather than discussing difficulties with them.

**Awareness**   Consciousness of and sensitivity to yourself, others and environment.

**Behaviour rehearsal**   Rehearsing behaviour, usually by role-play, prior to enacting it. Behaviour may also be rehearsed in the imagination. In a training group it often involves demonstration followed by practice and coaching.

**Bisexuality**    Being sexually interested in one's own as well as in the opposite sex.

**Blaming**    Finding fault with and assigning responsibility, frequently inaccurately, to another. Self-blame is also a possibility. See *Scapegoating*.

**Bodily communication**    Sending messages with your body about thoughts and feelings in ways that either do not accompany words or frame the use of words (e.g. facial expression).

**Catharsis**    Release and discharge of emotional tension by talking about and expressing it.

**Challenging**    'Challenging' is another term for 'confrontation'. See *Confrontation*.

**Closed family system**    In a closed family system people feel threatened and inhibited about communicating to each other their thoughts and feelings about themselves, each other and what they see going on in the family. See *Open family system*.

**Collaboration**    Working together with another to obtain mutual benefit, for example, in working through a conflict.

**Collusion**    Either consciously or unconsciously allowing another to maintain their picture of themselves and/or of you, even though inaccurate. Intentionally or unintentionally avoiding asserting yourself.

**Competitiveness**    Being in a power struggle with another frequently based on an 'I-win – You-lose' assumption.

**Conditioning**    Shaping behaviour usually by means of reward.

**Confidentiality**    Keeping trust with others by not divulging personal information about them unless granted permission.

**Conformity**    Thinking, feeling and acting how others either behave or want you to behave rather than being true to yourself.

**Conflict**    Differences or disagreements regarding ideas, interests, wishes or needs.

**Confrontation**    Challenging another person's view of themselves, of you, or of a situation. Focusing on discrepancies in people's thoughts, feelings and actions.

**Congruence**    Genuineness or lack of façade. Having and being seen to have your thoughts, feelings, words and actions match each other.

**Continuation responses**    Brief responses designed to give another person the message 'I am with you. Please continue.'

**Contracting**    Making agreements with others which may be either implicit, or verbal, or written and countersigned.

**Counselling**    Counselling aims to help clients, who are mainly seen outside medical settings, to help themselves by assuming more personal responsibility and making better choices. The counsellor's repertoire of psychological skills includes both those of forming an understanding relationship with clients and also skills focused on helping them to change specific aspects of their feeling, thinking and behaviour.

**Co-counselling**    Taking turns with another person in counselling each other.

**Couples counselling**    Counselling two partners in a relationship either jointly or with a mixture of counselling them separately and jointly.

**Courage**    Being able to affirm and define your existence despite obstacles.

**Crises**    Situations of excessive stress in which people feel that their coping resources are severely stretched or inadequate to meet the adjustive demands being made upon them.

**Defensive thinking** The processes by which people deny and distort information that varies with their picture of themselves when this information threatens their feelings of adequacy and worth.

**Defining game** Defining others in ways that sustain false elements of your own self-picture, then trying to control the way they see themselves by putting overt and/or subtle emotional pressure on them.

**Defining yourself** Making the choices that create your existence and, where appropriate, communicating them to others.

**Delusions** Strongly held false ideas: for example, delusions of being persecuted.

**Demonstration** Either intentionally or unintentionally showing someone how to think or behave by doing it yourself. See *Modelling*.

**Denial** Denial is a defensive process by which people protect themselves from threatening aspects either of themselves or of external reality by refusing to recognise them.

**Dependency** Relying on support from another or others rather than on self-support.

**Depression** Feelings of sadness and of loss. Symptoms may include apathy, withdrawal, disturbed sleep, lack of appetite and lowered sexual interest.

**Developing relationships** Getting to know and trust each other through a process of spending time together, talking about yourselves, listening, understanding, supporting each other, working through conflicts and engaging in shared activities.

**Directiveness** Behaving in ways that give direction to another whether or not they wish it.

**Distracting** Distracting another's attention, possibly to avoid either negative feedback or handling a difficult area directly.

**Distortion** Distortion is a defensive process involving 'working on' aspects of reality in order to make them less threatening and more consistent with existing self-pictures. Positive as well as negative feedback may be distorted.

**Double standards** Different standards for behaviour depending on such considerations as gender, age and who is more powerful in a relationship.

**Ego** Literally means 'I'. Other meanings include confidence, e.g. 'good for my ego' and arrogance, e.g. 'he/she has a big ego'.

**Egotism** Placing your own needs above those of others. Self-centredness.

**Empathy** The capacity to understand another's world accurately and to respond so that they feel understood.

**Encounter groups** An intensive method of group counselling emphasising expression of feelings and group interaction.

**Evaluative comments** Remarks that pass positive and negative judgement. Such remarks may create an unsafe emotional climate for others.

**Existential awareness** Being aware of your human finitude and of other parameters of your existence, for instance fate and suffering.

**Expressing feelings** The capacity to acknowledge and to share your experiencing of your feelings. Spotaneity rather than inhibition.

**Family counselling** Family counselling involves working with members of a family, in varying combinations, and focuses on improving communication between them.

**Family rules**  Implicit and explicit rules that establish the nature and limits of permissible behaviour in a family.

**Feedback**  Receiving messages about yourself and sending messages to others about themselves.

**Feelings**  Emotions, affective states of varying degrees of positiveness and negativeness.

**Feelings words**  Words used to label, describe, and express feelings.

**Forgiveness**  Letting bygones be bygones, thus avoiding letting them get in the way of the future.

**Friendship**  Having a relationship with another, that may be independent either of sexual attraction or of family ties, yet entail an emotional bond and shared interests and activities.

**Games**  Not communicating openly and directly with another. Two people may collude in playing a game such as: 'Why don't you . . .?' . . . 'Yes, but . . .'

**Gay**  A colloquial word for homosexual. People of varying degrees of bisexuality are much more common than exclusively homosexual people: for evidence of this, see the Kinsey reports.

**Gender conditioning**  Rewarding people for exhibiting the characteristics popularly associated with their gender.

**Gender role**  Expectations of how people should behave according to their gender.

**Gender script**  The directives you internalised concerning feelings, thoughts and actions appropriate for your gender.

**Genuineness**  Absence of façade and insincerity. See *Congruence.*

**Gossiping**  Indirect release of aggression by sharing negative thoughts and feelings about someone with a third party.

**Group counselling**  The relationships, activities and skills involved in counselling two or more people at the same time.

**Guilt**  Feelings of distress, involving self-devaluation and anxiety, resulting from having transgressed a code of behaviour to which you subscribe.

**Habit**  A learned tendency to respond in a consistent way to a person or situation.

**Helpful responding**  Responding in ways that help others listen to themselves, feel understood, and clarify problem areas.

**Homosexuality**  Sexual interest in people of the same sex. See *Bisexuality, Gay.*

**Honesty**  Being sincere and saying what you think and feel without deception.

**Hostility**  Thoughts, feelings and actions aimed at attacking, destroying or damaging a perceived source of frustration or threat. See *Anger.*

**Humorous**  Being amusing, comic, telling jokes, creating laughter. Humour may be used as a defensive process to dilute feedback or prevent intimacy.

**Hurt**  Feelings of psychological injury and pain.

**'I' statements**  Owning and directly stating what you think and feel starting with the words 'I think . . .' or 'I feel . . .' etc.

**Identity**  A sense of continuity and sameness and of defining yourself on your own terms.

**Illusion**  False perception or belief.

**Imaginal rehearsal**  Role-playing desired thoughts and behaviours in imagination prior to enacting them. See *Behaviour rehearsal.*

**Immediacy**  Comments that focus on the 'here and now' of a relationship, perhaps by focusing on what has previously been left unsaid. Sometimes expressed as 'you–me' talk.

**Infatuation**  Unreasoning passion and attraction. See *Love.*

**Inhibition**  Inadequately acknowledging and/or restraining yourself from expressing or acting on a feeling.

**Initiating**  Being active in getting something started, e.g. either a relationship or the deepening of a relationship.

**Inner empathy**  The capacity to listen accurately to your own feelings and thoughts.

**Inner speech**  Self-talk. Often takes the form of an internal dialogue. See *Self-instruction.*

**Integrity**  Honesty, soundness, trustworthiness. Having the courage of your own convictions.

**Intellectualising**  Using thoughts to avoid dealing with feelings.

**Internal frame of reference**  The subjective world of a person rather than an external viewpoint. Understanding how another person thinks and feels 'as if' you were them.

**Internal rules**  Self-standards, beliefs. Possessing an inner rule-book about appropriate behaviour for yourself and others.

**Interpretation**  Explanations from another's frame of reference of a person's feelings, thoughts, words, dreams and actions.

**Intimacy**  Sharing and being attuned to each other's thoughts and feelings, including those likely to be too threatening to reveal in other contexts. May include physical intimacy.

**Introjection**  Taking something from another person or other people and treating it as part of oneself. See *Projection.*

**Language**  Having a realistic set of concepts with which to describe and understand relationships. The vocabulary with which you relate to others.

**Lesbianism**  Female sexual interest in people of the same sex. See *Bisexuality, Gay.*

**Life skills**  The skills required for effective living, for example relationship skills.

**Listening**  Not just hearing but understanding another.

**Listening, sources of interference**  Everything that gets in the way of messages being received accurately. Sources of interference may be in the receiver, the sender or in the environment.

**Loneliness**  A state of not having your needs for companionship, friendship and/or intimacy met.

**Love**  Strong affection, liking or caring for someone. Not to be confused with infatuation.

**Managing anger**  See *Anger management.*

**Managing anxiety**  See *Anxiety management.*

**Managing conflict**  See *Conflict management.*

**Managing stress**  See *Stress management.*

**Manipulation of feedback**  A defensive process whereby individuals place open or subtle pressure on others to provide feedback that is consistent with their conceptions of themselves.

**Marital counselling**   Counselling, preferably with both partners, in relation to marital difficulties. Can include counselling partners before they marry.

**Matching**   Reciprocating or matching the intimacy level of another's disclosures. Matching may include reciprocating each other's positive and negative behaviours.

**Misattributing responsibility**   Inaccurately assigning responsibility; for example, either defensively blaming another for your own misbehaviour or engaging in unnecessary self-blame.

**Modelling**   Demonstrating before another feelings, thoughts and actions. Much modelling is unintentional.

**Monitoring**   Observing and keeping a check on your own or others' feelings, thoughts and behaviour. Keeping a record of behaviour.

**Muscle**   A colloquial term for the degree of force or strength you use in asserting yourself. Aggression involves inappropriate use of muscle.

**Negative feelings and thoughts**   Not feeling good about yourself and putting yourself down. Not feeling good about others and, possibly, putting them down.

**Nervous breakdown**   A reaction to excessive stress involving marked physiological and psychological debilitation as well as a drastic lessening of ability to cope with life.

**Non-verbal communication**   See *Bodily communication*.

**Open family system**   In open family systems people can communicate to each other their thoughts and feelings about themselves, each other and what they see going on in the family. See *Closed family system*.

**Openers**   Remarks which indicate both attention and interest and also permission and psychological space to talk.

**Ownership**   Acknowledging to yourself and/or others your feelings, thoughts and actions as your own. See *'I' statements*.

**Partial disclosure**   Engaging in information control and not telling the whole story. 'Economising on the truth'. Concealing as well as revealing.

**Peer self-help groups**   Groups of people with similar characteristics or with similar problems who meet regularly for mutual help.

**Permissions to talk**   See *Openers*.

**Personal responsibility**   The process of making the choices that maximise your happiness and fulfilment.

**Personification**   The picture that you have 'made' of yourself or of another. This does not necessarily correspond with reality.

**Plan**   A step-by-step outline, verbal or written, of the specific actions necessary to obtain your goals.

**Positive thoughts and feelings**   Feeling good about yourself and building your confidence. Feeling good about others and, where appropriate, showing it.

**Possessiveness**   Wishing to control another for your own ends rather than to help them develop as a unique individual.

**Power plays**   Open and subtle ways of pressurising people to do things against their will. Means of controlling people.

**Problem-clarification**   The process of clarifying and defining a problem area.

**Problem-solving**   The process of finding effective solutions to problems, conflicts and feelings of anger and of stress.

**Projection**   Taking something from oneself and treating it as part of another person or other people. See *Introjection*.

**Psychiatry**   The branch of medicine dealing with understanding, treating and preventing mental disorders.

**Psychological damage**   Negative psychological outcomes resulting from your own or others' behaviour.

**Psychological pain**   Mental as contrasted with physical pain.

**Psychological space**   Being allowed the time, safety and freedom to experience and talk about yourself.

**Psychology**   The science and study of human behaviour.

**Psychotherapy**   Often used as another term for counselling. May have connotations of moderately to severely disturbed clients seen in medical settings, but not necessarily so. More accurate to speak of the psychotherapies, since there are many theoretical and practical approaches to psychotherapy.

**Put-down**   A colloquial term for thoughts and behaviours that disparage either yourself or others. Engaging in either self-oppression or oppression of others.

**Reaching out**   Taking risks to show another person that you like and care for them.

**Realistic standards**   Standards or internal rules for behaviour and self-evaluation which are functional in helping you cope with life and meet your needs.

**Realistic thinking**   The process of accurately perceiving and thinking about yourself, others and the environment in ways that maximise your chances of happiness and fulfilment.

**Reciprocity**   Matching another person's feelings, thoughts and/or behaviour, for example reciprocating the intimacy level of their disclosures. See *Matching*.

**Reconciliation**   Getting together again either psychologically and/or physically. Settling a quarrel.

**Reflective responding**   Responses that mirror the verbal and/or emotional content of another's communications.

**Regulating thinking**   Working on your thinking both to make it more effective and also to lessen or eliminate negative feelings.

**Rejection**   Either not accepting or not being accepted by another person in whole or in part.

**Relationship**   Being connected in some way with another. Often used to describe a close connection with another.

**Relationship skills**   The skills of relating to others effectively. See *Skills*.

**Relaxation**   There are numerous approaches to relaxation, for example tensing and relaxing various muscle groupings, imagining restful scenes etc.

**Repression**   A defensive process by means of which anxiety-evoking material and memories are kept out of awareness or consciousness.

**Resentment**   Persistent negative feelings towards another. See *Anger*.

**Resistances**   All processes in yourself or in others that interfere with your progress towards self-awareness and psychological well-being.

**Responsibility avoidances**   All the ways in which people avoid assuming personal responsibility for their lives.

**Retrieving mistakes**   The capacity to acknowledge your own contribution to negative events in your relationships and to alter your behaviour accordingly.

**Reward**   Something that increases the probability of a behaviour being repeated.

**Rewardingness**   Behaviours that reward other people for relating to you.

**Role-playing**   Learning by enacting behaviours in simulated settings. See *Behaviour rehearsal.*

**Scapegoating**   Taking your troubles out on somebody else. Displacing your aggression and blaming someone erroneously.

**Self-acceptance**   Accepting yourself as a person while remaining aware of your strengths and limitations.

**Self-awareness**   Being aware of your significant thoughts, feelings and actions and of the impact that you make on others.

**Self-concept**   The way in which people see themselves and to which they attach terms like 'I' or 'me'.

**Self-definition**   Making the choices that define you both to yourself and to others.

**Self-disclosure**   Revealing personal information and expressing thoughts and feelings.

**Self-esteem**   Sense of adequacy, positive and negative evaluation of yourself as a person. Sense of your own worth.

**Self-evaluation**   The process of placing positive and negative values on your personal characteristics.

**Self-instruction**   The process of talking to yourself with coping statements that reduce anxiety and facilitate the performance of tasks. See *Inner speech.*

**Self-protective thinking**   See *Defensive thinking.*

**Self-standards**   The standards or internal rules by which you lead your life and which form the basis of your positive and negative evaluations of yourself. See *Internal rules.*

**Sex-role**   See *Gender-role.*

**Sexual behaviour**   Thoughts, feelings, fantasies and actions related to physical attraction and reproduction.

**Sexual problems**   Persistent manifestations of difficulty in having sexual intercourse.

**Shyness**   Anxiety in social situations.

**Skills**   Areas in which you can make and implement an effective sequence of choices so as to achieve a desired objective.

**Skills deficit**   A predisposition to make poor choices in a skills area.

**Skills resource**   A predisposition to make good choices in a skills area.

**Social rules**   The implicit and explicit rules of conduct which vary according to the social contexts in which relationships take place.

**Specificity**   Being concrete, clear and specific. Avoiding vague generalisations.

**Strengths**   Those aspects of yourself that you value and that help you attain your goals.

**Stress**   Perceived demands on your energy and coping abilities.

**Stress management** Coping with stress constructively by understanding it and then developing and implementing appropriate strategies to deal with it.

**Stressor** An individual item that causes stress.

**Summarising** Making statements which clarify what you and/or another has been saying over a period of time. Summaries may include feedback from you.

**Support** Giving strength and encouragement to another.

**Support networks** Networks of people available to support you or each other, especially when in difficulty.

**Task-oriented inner speech** Using self-talk in ways that calm anxiety and enhance attainment of goals.

**Terminating relationships** Ending a relationship. This may be done either constructively or destructively.

**Thinking errors** Faulty habits of thinking that contribute to negative feelings and poor relationships.

**Threat** Perception of real or imagined danger.

**Timing** The 'when' of making statements and taking initiatives in relationships.

**Tit-for-tatting** In an argument, matching each negative comment directed at you with a similar one directed at the sender.

**Touch** Physical contact with another. This may or may not be sexual.

**Transference** The process by which people transfer feelings and thoughts from previous to present relationships.

**Transition** Changes which people undergo during the course of their lives, for example the birth of a first child or retirement.

**Trust** Faith and confidence in the honesty and reliability of another.

**Trustworthy** Being honest and reliable.

**Tunnel vision** A narrowing of perception under threat so that the individual focuses only on certain factors in a situation and excludes others which may be important.

**Unconscious** Beneath the level of conscious awareness.

**Unrealistic standards** Standards or internal rules for behaviour and self-evaluation which are dysfunctional in helping you cope with life and meet your needs.

**Uptight** A colloquial word for someone who exudes tension and anxiety.

**Values** Deeply held internal rules or beliefs.

**Verbal communication** Sending messages by means of words.

**Vocal communication** Sending messages, often about your feelings, by means of your voice in ways that frame your words. However, sometimes vocal communication, for instance a sigh, can be independent of verbal communication.

**Vulnerability** Being psychologically at risk, especially when faced with negative occurrences and feedback. A tendency to contribute to, if not cause, your own difficulties.

**'You' statements** Statements starting with the word 'you' by which people label or blame others. See *'I' statements*.

# Name Index

# Subject Index